THE
SECOND
AMENDMENT
PRIMER

THE
SECOND
AMENDMENT
PRIMER

**A CITIZEN'S GUIDEBOOK TO THE
HISTORY, SOURCES, AND
AUTHORITIES FOR THE
CONSTITUTIONAL GUARANTEE OF
THE RIGHT
TO KEEP AND BEAR ARMS**

LES ADAMS

Skyhorse Publishing

Skyhorse Publishing books may be purchased in bulk at special
discounts for sales promotion, corporate gifts, fund-raising, or
educational purposes. Special editions can also be created to
specifications. For details, contact the Special Sales Department,
Skyhorse Publishing, 307 West 36th Street, 11th Floor, New York, NY
10018 or info@skyhorsepublishing.com.

Skyhorse® and Skyhorse Publishing® are registered trademarks of
Skyhorse Publishing, Inc.®, a Delaware corporation.

Visit our website at www.skyhorsepublishing.com.

10 9 8 7 6 5 4 3 2 1

Library of Congress Cataloging-in-Publication Data is available on file.
ISBN: 978-1-62087-627-5

Printed in the United States of America

The great ideals of liberty and equality are preserved against the assaults of opportunism, the expediency of the passing hour, the erosion of small encroachments, the scorn and derision of those who have no patience with general principles, by enshrining them in constitutions, and consecrating to the task of their protection a body of defenders.

> Justice Benjamin Cardozo
> *The Nature of the Judicial Process*
> (New Haven, 1921)

THE BILL OF RIGHTS
TO THE CONSTITUTION
OF THE UNITED STATES

*(The first ten Amendments,
ratified on December 15, 1791)*

★★★★★★★★★★★★★★★★★★★★★★★

AMENDMENT 1

Congress shall make no law respecting an establishment of religion, or prohibiting the free exercise thereof; or abridging the freedom of speech, or of the press, or the right of the people peaceably to assemble, and to petition the Government for a redress of grievances.

AMENDMENT 2

A well regulated militia being necessary to the security of a free state, the right of the people to keep and bear arms shall not be infringed.

AMENDMENT 3

No Soldier shall, in time of peace be quartered in any house, without the consent of the Owner, nor in time of war, but in a manner to be prescribed by law.

AMENDMENT 4

The right of the people to be secure in their persons, houses, papers, and effects, against unreasonable searches and seizures, shall not be violated, and no Warrants shall issue, but upon probable cause, supported by Oath or affirmation, and particularly describing the place to be searched, and the persons or things to be seized.

AMENDMENT 5

No person shall be held to answer for a capital, or otherwise infamous crime, unless on a presentment or indictment of a Grand Jury, except in cases arising in the land or naval forces, or in the Militia, when in actual service in time of War or public danger; nor shall any person be subject for the same offence to be twice put in jeopardy of life or limb; nor shall be compelled in any criminal case to be a witness against himself, nor be deprived of life, liberty, or property, without due process of law; nor shall private property be taken for public use, without just compensation.

★★★★★★★★★★★★★★★★★★★★★★★

AMENDMENT 6

In all criminal prosecutions, the accused shall enjoy the right to a speedy and public trial, by an impartial jury of the State and district wherein the crime shall have been committed, which district shall have been previously ascertained by law, and to be informed of the nature and cause of the accusation; to be confronted with the witnesses against him; to have compulsory process for obtaining witnesses in his favor, and to have the Assistance of Counsel for his defence.

AMENDMENT 7

In Suits at common law, where the value in controversy shall exceed twenty dollars, the right of trial by jury shall be preserved, and no fact tried by a jury, shall be otherwise re-examined in any Court of the United States, than according to the rules of the common law.

AMENDMENT 8

Excessive bail shall not be required, nor excessive fines imposed, nor cruel and unusual punishments inflicted.

AMENDMENT 9

The enumeration in the Constitution, of certain rights, shall not be construed to deny or disparage others retained by the people.

AMENDMENT 10

The powers not delegated to the United States by the Constitution, nor prohibited by it to the States, are reserved to the States respectively, or to the people.

★★★★★★★★★★★★★★★★★★★★★★★★

CONTENTS

CONTENTS

THE
SECOND
AMENDMENT
PRIMER

A well regulated militia being necessary to the security of a free state, the right of the people to keep and bear arms shall not be infringed.

U.S. Constitution, amend. 2

FOREWORD

*"This Right Most Valued by Free Men"**

ORRIN G. HATCH

When the Subcommittee on the Constitution, which I chaired, originally released this report in February 1982, few could have foreseen the wholesale political attacks on the right of law-abiding citizens to keep and bear arms which have occurred in the years since. During this time we have witnessed the imposition of a federal waiting period and background check on firearms purchasers, outright bans on whole classes of firearms and ammunition, and the systematic abuse of power by governmental agencies directed toward those who would exercise this right. We have also seen legislative efforts which would limit the access of law-abiding sportsmen to hunt or shoot upon the nation's public lands and, through calls for imposition of exorbitant excise taxes on firearms and ammunition, measures which would simply price the right to keep and bear arms beyond the financial means of many Americans.

A decade of attack on the right to keep and bear arms

*SUBCOMMITTEE ON THE CONSTITUTION OF THE COMMITTEE ON THE JUDICIARY, 97th Cong., 2d. Sess., S. Doc. 2807 (1982) (from the foreword to a new edition by Orrin G. Hatch, Chairman, Senate Committee on the Judiciary, April 2, 1995).

The picture is not completely bleak, however. In 1986 the country saw the passage of the McClure-Volkmer Firearms Owners' Protection Act which, even if only briefly, lessened the burdens on America's law-abiding gun owners. We have also seen a renewed interest among scholars in the Second Amendment, and we are beginning to see among the nation's federal courts a recognition that there are, indeed, limits upon the powers of Congress to legislate in this area.

So as we prepare to enter a new millennium it is perhaps time to pause and reflect upon the pillars on which this great nation was founded and which have allowed our country to grow and prosper over the past two centuries. Just as scholars have rediscovered the Second Amendment, so too is it time for those of us in the Congress to become reacquainted with the meaning of this basic right which has served for so long as a means to guarantee our liberty. As I assume the chairmanship of the Senate Judiciary Committee, I restate my pledge that the Committee will concern itself with a proper recognition of, and respect for, this right most valued by free men. . . .

Time to become reacquainted with this basic right

INTRODUCTION

I confess that for most of my adult life, I really never thought much about the Second Amendment to the Bill of Rights and the controversial issue of gun control. As a boy I plinked at birds with a .22; as a young man I hunted deer, quail, and turkey; and as time passed, even though I gave up hunting for other pursuits, I continued to possess a small collection of firearms. Today in my home I still have two shotguns in the closet and a small handgun in my bedside table.

Since I did not intend to acquire additional guns, laws to control or prohibit gun purchases held no particular interest for me. Nor did I contemplate that Congress might ever seriously consider, much less enact, legislation to regulate, control, or confiscate the firearms already in my lawful possession. After all, we still have a Fourth Amendment.

At that time, since I did not hunt or engage in target shooting and had no particularly strong convictions about the gun control issue one way or the other, I did not see the need to become a member of the National Rifle Association. In fact, whenever my attention was drawn to the issue of gun control, my vague and unfocused thought was that the NRA's position on Second Amendment rights was probably erroneous. I recalled that Congress had passed a law in the 1930s outlawing machine guns

Initially I thought the NRA was wrong

and that it probably had the constitutional authority to enact further gun control legislation beyond
the bounds of the laws that were already on the
statute books.

Even though I am a lawyer and had studied
constitutional law in law school, I more or less
accepted the view that when the Founding Fathers
drafted the controversial modifying clause of the
Second Amendment, "A well regulated militia being necessary to the security of a free state," they
did not mean to endorse the proposition that the
people had the individual right to keep and bear
arms; but only that the states had the right to create
their own militias. And what's more, I had assumed
that, with the establishment of the National Guard
in the late nineteenth century, the Second Amendment had probably become null and void, or at the
least obsolete.

In other words, I generally had supported what
has become known as (and as I will be discussing
in more detail later on) the "collective" interpretation of the Second Amendment (as opposed to the
"individual" interpretation advocated by the NRA
and other Second Amendment rights activists).

**But
doubts
began to
arise**

But from time to time, doubts would arise. I
recall in particular being troubled when I read that
former United States Chief Justice Warren Burger
had said in a televised interview that "the Second
Amendment has been the subject of one of the
greatest pieces of fraud, I repeat the word 'fraud,'
on the American public by special interest groups

that I have ever seen in my lifetime. . . . They [the NRA] have misled the American people."

Whenever Warren Burger begins making pronouncements, I become uneasy. I've read a number of Burger's legal opinions. But I've read my Oliver Wendell Holmes, too, and Warren Burger is no Oliver Wendell Holmes. Considering the ignorance he demonstrated in that television interview, for the correct interpretation of the Second Amendment I'd just as soon have the opinion of Donald Duck as that of Warren Burger.

Also, I was aware that in 1990, a chief justice whose opinions I do respect, William Rehnquist, had reviewed the phrase "the people" as used by the framers of the Constitution and had concluded with the concurrence of four other Supreme Court justices:

> While this textual exegesis [explanation] is by no means conclusive, it suggests that "the people" protected by the Fourth Amendment, and by the First and *Second* Amendments, and to whom the rights and powers are reserved in the Ninth and Tenth Amendments, refers to a class of persons who are part of a national community or who have otherwise developed sufficient connection with this country to be considered part of that community.[1] [Emphasis added.]

Chief Justice Rehnquist defines "the people"

Now, William Rehnquist has a first-rate legal mind, and he writes his opinions with care and precision, so his quite deliberate inclusion of the

Second Amendment in the paragraph above began to raise substantial questions in my mind.

A personal journey of discovery

Then, in late 1994, I was presented with an opportunity to publish a series of historical firearms books for the National Rifle Association. Before undertaking that task, I decided that I could not work for the NRA, in good conscience, without being able wholeheartedly to support its position on the issue of Second Amendment rights. So I set myself about the task of either confirming or allaying my doubts about the issue by learning everything I could in order to reach a final personal decision, one way or the other. What facts I found on my personal journey of discovery, and what conclusions I drew from those facts, are what led me to the preparation of this little book.

What I discovered, first, was that the literature on the Second Amendment to the Constitution is substantial — not as large, perhaps, as that of the First, Fourth, and Fifth Amendments — but still an intimidating amount of information to absorb. Aside from the voluminous English and American historical literature, there also exists a substantial body of contemporary commentary on the Second Amendment — scores of books, innumerable articles in journals and newspapers, and more than one hundred law review articles and comments.

But if one has the motivation and interest and time, as I did, to read all that has been written concerning this subject, there is a big surprise in store very early in the game. And that surprise is that a controversy over the meaning of the Second Amendment *even exists*. The evidence is overwhelmingly in favor of the interpretation that the drafters of the Second Amendment deliberately intended, with the specific words they chose to use and with the specific way they chose to organize those words into one long sentence, to recognize the existence of both a "collective" and an "individual" right of the American citizen to keep and bear arms.

A collective and an individual right

For all these years, I came to realize, the NRA had been taking considerable heat in the popular press for its unyielding defense of the right of the individual citizen to keep and bear arms, whereas all along, in steadfastly denying that the right existed, the proponents of banning guns were — and continue to be — *wrong*.

For, from reading and analyzing this material over the last year, and applying a ration of simple common sense, I am now convinced, unequivocally and unquestionably, that *the Second Amendment to the U.S. Constitution ratifies and preserves for every citizen the right to keep and bear arms;* and, moreover, that *Congress or any other instrumentality of the federal government is constitutionally barred from infringing that right.*

It doesn't take a lawyer to figure this out. But don't take my word for it. Simply examine what I will be presenting in this book — a selection of original documents and speeches together with some informed interpretative commentary — and

I believe you should and will reach the same conclusion.

There are two problems associated with studying the literature of the Second Amendment, however.

On the one hand, the writings of law professors on the subject have been published in law reviews, academic journals, and books of limited and special circulation, all deliberately aimed at a professional audience of other scholars, law professors, attorneys, and judges. Commonly, these scholarly writings make reference, without further explanation, to legal cases and historical precedents that are familiar only to their elite and learned readers. What's more, more often than not, their pages are heavily footnoted and are exceedingly difficult to read, much less comprehend — all and all, pretty forbidding stuff for most laymen to tackle.

On the other hand, there exist a number of books intended for consumption by the popular market. These books may be relatively easy to read, but most suffer from a lack of thoroughness or intellectual honesty or are simply inadequate to satisfy the thirst for knowledge of the serious lay reader.

The need for a Second Amendment Primer

Despite the inadequacies — insofar as the general reader is concerned — of either category of this literature, with all that has been written about this controversial subject, what then is the need for yet another book — this one?

The need, I think, is this. The need is to present a book that is fully informative, accurate, and yet easily accessible to all the public.

That is what this book will attempt to do. I call it a "primer" because it is elementary. But that does not mean it is superficial. On the contrary, you will find it contains a wealth of information. And that information is deliberately organized for easy access and understanding by the lay reader. Also, to the greatest extent possible, it will present the original statements and documents of our Anglo-American heritage that have clearly recognized and brought forward through hundreds of years of democratic thought the concept that a free people in a democratic society have the duty and right to keep and bear arms lawfully.

Doesn't it make sense to study original statements if they are available? In law, the "best evidence" rule states that if an original document or any other original item of proof is available, it is to be accorded a higher degree of credibility in the courtroom than a copy or other secondhand proof. Fortunately, we can apply this rule when studying the Second Amendment because the original documents do exist. And you'll find they are quite easy to read. The statesmen and philosophers you'll be meeting in these pages had a clear vision of what they wanted to say, and for the most part they said it clearly and well.

A study of the original statements

But of course, any field of study needs some background facts and analysis too. So I will be injecting short commentaries into the text to link historical events and aid comprehension. And I am also including as an Appendix to this book three recent interpretative essays that originally appeared in intellectual journals of limited circulation. Of all the writings that I have read on the gun control issue — and that's literally hundreds of pages of analysis and interpretation on both sides of the argument — I thought these three essays were particularly distinguished and deserved a much wider audience than they may thus far have enjoyed. If you don't read anything else in this book, I hope you will spend a half hour or so with the thoughts of these three writers. I guarantee that you will receive rich rewards in exchange for your time.

Three thoughtful essays

The first essay is Professor William Van Alstyne's "The Second Amendment and the Personal Right to Arms," which originally appeared in the *Duke Law Journal*. This is a short but masterful presentation by one of our leading constitutional law professors and scholars.

The second is from another of our most esteemed constitutional law professors and scholars, Professor Sanford Levinson. I found his essay, "The Embarrassing Second Amendment," which originally appeared in the *Yale Law Journal,* to be one of the most balanced and thoughtful in the literature on this issue.

The third is Jeffrey R. Snyder's "A Nation of Cowards," which originally appeared in *The Public Interest*. Snyder, an attorney in private practice in Washington, D.C., presents a novel and highly persuasive argument in support of the right to keep and bear arms. It's an essay I think you'll enjoy reading.

There are several other features of the book that I hope you will find helpful:

- Especially important paragraphs are summarized in short notes at the side of the text.

- To present an uncluttered page that's easy to read, all reference and quotation sources are placed at the end of the book.

- Synonyms are provided (only when necessary) for the fancy lawyerly words that scholars sometimes use and for obsolete or archaic words that no longer mean today what was intended by their writers at the time the words were first published.

  A "user-friendly" Citizen's Guidebook

- At the back of the book are three reference sections: 1) a subject index, 2) biographical profiles of all authorities quoted in the primer, and 3) a twentieth-century bibliography of articles and books on the Second Amendment.

- It is designed in a pocket-size format for easy reference.

What I hope this book accomplishes, then, is to provide you with a small and handy compilation of sources for contemplation, review, and quotation, in a readable and "user-friendly" format. You

might say it is a citizen's guidebook to the Second
Amendment.

***

**An
individual
right to
equal all
others**

This book endorses the proposition that in addition to providing for the formation of general militias by the states, the right to keep and bear arms
enunciated by the drafters of the Amendment was
understood by them to be an *individual* right, as
individual and as personal as our rights of free
speech and a free press, our freedoms to worship
and assemble as we wish, our rights to a trial by
jury and against self-incrimination, our rights to
due process of law, and all the other constitutional
guarantees that we routinely take for granted.

**To the
advocates
of gun
control**

To the people who believe that we need more
gun control laws in this country, who have constructed their philosophical position on the "collective right" reading of the Second Amendment, I
say, please read on. For I believe that — despite
all the heat with very little light that has been and
continues to be generated by this controversy in the
popular press — those of you who are possessed of
intellectual honesty and are willing to examine
anew the evidence presented in this book may be
persuaded to change your position . . . to come to a
new understanding, in other words, of why the right
to keep and bear arms is indeed "this right most
valued by free men."

And for those of you who already share my
conviction that Americans do have a right to keep

and bear arms, I hope that this little book comes to be a valuable tool, providing you with a powerful armamentarium of historical facts and references to combat even the most strident arguments of gun control advocates.

***

For at least the last three decades, a controversy has raged in this country over what, if any, additional controls the federal government should levy upon our right to keep and bear arms. And a good deal of that controversy has arisen because the people on either side of the controversy have disagreed about the meaning of the words of the Second Amendment.

But isn't it time for those who believe that firearms should be controlled by the government no longer to be able to rely upon their faulty interpretation of the Second Amendment?

Isn't it time for those of us who believe that the Second Amendment guarantees the right to keep and bear arms no longer to have to defend an interpretation that is clearly correct in light of an enormous body of documentary evidence?

Isn't it time we recognize that the meaning of the Second Amendment is a settled issue and lay this argument to rest, once and for all?

Time to lay the Second Amendment to rest

If this little primer makes only a small contribution to the hastening of that event, it will have been well worth the time I have spent in preparing it for you. Thank you for reading it.

***

As I began my study, one of the scholarly works that I found most helpful and illuminating was *To Keep and Bear Arms: The Origins of an Anglo-American Right* by Professor Joyce Lee Malcolm. To close these introductory remarks, I can think of no better way than to share with you the marvelously constructed set of thoughts with which she ends her book:

Professor Malcolm's thoughts

Should the Second Amendment to the American Constitution be permitted to go the way of the English right to be armed, as a dangerous relic of another era? In fact, it cannot be legislated out of existence in the same way. The American Congress is not sovereign, our Constitution is. The Constitution has a clear procedure for altering its contents — amendment. If the government and people in their wisdom come to the conclusion that no need for the right of the people to be armed exists, or that such a right does more harm than good, then amendment is the course that should be followed. While it is unconstitutional to legislate a right out of existence, this particular right is threatened with misinterpretation to the point of meaninglessness. Granted, this is a far easier method of elimination than amendment, being much quicker and not requiring the same rigid consensus or forthright discussion of its constitutional relevancy. But it is also the way of danger. For to ignore all evidence of the meaning and intent of one of those rights included in the Bill of Rights is to create the most dangerous sort of precedent, one whose consequences could flow far beyond this one issue and endanger the fabric of liberty.

Should the Second Amendment be altered or eliminated through amendment? Before that is considered it is imperative to grant the founders of the American Constitution, whose wisdom in so much else has borne the test of time, the courtesy of considering why they included this right. Their original intent is of not only academic but immediate interest. What does the right actually mean, and why did they consider it essential? Are standing armies still a threat to a twentieth-century world? Do the people need a right and a means to revolution? Will other rights suffice? Are individuals still in need of personal weapons . . . for protection "in case of extremity"? I am not an advocate but a historian and ask merely for a decent respect for the past. We are not forced into lockstep with our forefathers. But we owe them our considered attention before we disregard a right they felt it imperative to bestow upon us.[2]

The intent of the Founders

I

EARLY EXPRESSIONS
OF THE RIGHT
IN ANCIENT TIMES

ᕙ❨❖❩ᕗ

A s one begins an examination of the history of
the Second Amendment, it is essential to
keep in mind that the Founding Fathers of the new
American republic, the framers and ratifiers of its
new Constitution and Bill of Rights — among them
Tom Paine, Sam Adams, Patrick Henry, George
Washington, Thomas Jefferson, John Adams, Alexander Hamilton, Richard Henry Lee, George
Mason, and James Madison — had been rigor-
ously educated in the *classical European tradition*.

As children, in their homes they surely would
have been exposed to family dialogues steeped in
European thought, custom, and values. European
traditions would have been passed down to them
quite naturally by their parents and grandparents,
many of whom had been born, reared, and educated in England. Of these forebears, these original
colonists, and of what influences we could reasonably expect they would have passed along to their
soon-to-be-famous sons, Tocqueville commented:

> Born in a country [England] which had been
> agitated for centuries by the struggles of faction,

**Founding
Fathers
had been
educated
in the
classical
European
tradition**

and in which all parties had been obliged in their turn to place themselves under the protection of the laws, their political education had been perfected in this rude school, and they were more conversant with the notions of right, and the principles of true freedom, than the greater part of their European contemporaries.[1]

They had been thoroughly schooled in the history of England and Europe

In their formal educations, the Founding Fathers had been thoroughly schooled in the history of England and Europe — the Age of Enlightenment, the Reformation, the Thirty Years' War, the Renaissance, the Crusades, Charlemagne and the rise of the Franks, the Middle Ages, the Byzantine Empire, the classical civilizations of Rome and Greece, the Pyrrhic and Punic Wars. And it is in those ancient classical civilizations that we find the earliest expressions of man's inalienable right to keep and bear arms.

As we go back into ancient history to locate the origins of that right, we are more or less embarking on an archaeological exploration, in the sense that, like archaeologists, we will be able to uncover only bones and skeletons, fragments and shards. But we will find proof enough, as you will see, that the philosophical concept first enunciated over two thousand years ago — that the people have a right, collectively as a nation and individually as persons, to bear arms in their defense — has survived and has continued to influence legal thought up through the present day.

You will find that the reasons ancient societies valued so highly the right to keep and bear arms were, in fact, identical to the reasons that the right was valued by the framers of the Bill of Rights (the first ten amendments to the Constitution) in 1789 and remains highly valued by thoughtful Americans today.

This really makes understanding the Second Amendment quite simple, just as its framers intended it should be. They were well-educated statesmen intimately familiar with classical philosophy, European history, and the English common law. Moreover, these men knew how to say things in plain eighteenth-century English, *and they meant what they said*.

The Second Amendment is quite simple to understand

In drafting the Second Amendment, what did they say? They said that the American people have a collective right to protect themselves against the evil of standing armies by forming a general militia composed of all the people:

A well-regulated militia being necessary to the security of a free state . . .

And they said that American citizens have an individual and inviolable right to arm themselves to protect their lives and property:

. . . the right of the people to keep and bear arms shall not be infringed.

The two categorical imperatives of the Second Amendment

Stephen Halbrook, one of our leading contemporary Second Amendment scholars, expresses it this way: "The two categorical imperatives of the Second Amendment — that a militia of the body of the people is necessary to guarantee a free state and that all of the people all of the time (not just when called for organized militia duty) have a right to keep arms — derive from the classical philosophical texts concerning the experiences of ancient Greece and Rome and seventeenth-century England. Aristotle, Cicero, Machiavelli, and the English Whigs provided an armed populace with the philosophical vindication to counter oppression, which found expression in the Declaration of Independence and the Bill of Rights. In this sense, the people's right to have their own arms was based on the philosophical and political writings of the greatest intellectuals of the past two thousand years."[2]

Although it is correctly understood that the cradle of philosophical thought regarding the right of a free people to bear arms was the classical Mediterranean civilizations of Greece and Rome, a very early and rare expression was unearthed in ancient China:

> Your subject has heard that when the ancients made the five kinds of weapons, it was not for the purpose of killing each other, but to prevent tyranny and to punish evil. When people lived in peace, these weapons were to be prepared against emergencies and to kill the fierce animals. If there

were military affairs, then the weapons were used
to set up defenses and form battle arrays.[3]

Moving to ancient Greece, we find first, in the
words of the philosopher Aristotle, this analysis of
an authoritarian form of government that had been
advocated by Plato:

> The whole constitutional set-up is intended to be
> neither democracy nor oligarchy but mid-way be-
> tween the two — what is sometimes called "pol-
> ity," *the members of which are those who bear
> arms.*[4] [Emphasis added.]

And in criticizing the monopolization of arms
bearing in the hands of one class that was being
advocated by his colleague Hippodamos, Aristotle
commented:

**Aristotle
criticizes
the
restriction
of arms**

> Hippodamos planned a city with a population of
> ten thousand, divided into three parts, one of
> skilled workers, one of agriculturists, and a third
> to bear arms and secure defense.[5] [But the legal
> restriction of arms bearing to a given class would
> mean that] the farmers have no arms, the workers
> have neither land nor arms; this makes them
> virtually the servants of those who do possess
> arms. In these circumstances, the equal sharing of
> offices and honours becomes an impossibility.[6]
> [And since] those who possess arms must be su-
> perior in power to both the other sections [the con-
> stitution proposed by Hippodamos would breed
> inequality and discontent.][7]

Aristotle was the first influential commentator in the history of Western civilization to recognize the dangers of a standing army. In describing the difference between a constitutional kingship and a tyranny (which was founded upon the existence of a standing army), he pointed out that

> a king's bodyguard is composed of citizens carrying arms; a tyrant's of foreign mercenaries. . . .[8]
>
> . . . Arms are included [among the things needed by every city] because members of the constitution must carry them even among themselves, both for internal government and in the event of civil disobedience and to repel external aggression. . . .[9] For those who possess and can wield arms are in a position to decide whether the constitution is to continue or not.[10]

The right to bear arms derives from the human form

The right of the individual to bear arms for his own defense was thought by Aristotle to derive from the nature of the human form:

> Now it must be wrong to say, as some do, that the structure of man is not good, in fact, that it is worse than that of any other animal. Their grounds are: that man is barefoot, unclothed, and void of any weapon of force. Against this we say that all the other animals have just one method of defence and cannot change it for another: they are forced to sleep and perform all their actions with their shoes on the whole time, as one might say; they can never take off this defensive equipment of theirs, nor can they change their weapon, whatever it may be. For man, on the other hand, many means of defence are available, and he can change them

at any time, and above all he can choose what weapon he will have and where. Take the hand: this is as good as a talon, or a claw, or a horn, or again, a spear or a sword, or any other weapon or tool; it can be all of these, because it can seize and hold them all. And Nature has admirably contrived the actual shape of the hand so as to fit with this arrangement.[11]

The other central figure from antiquity whose influence extended far beyond his time was Marcus Tullius Cicero, who served in the tumultuous final years of the Roman Republic. You can search all of literature and you'll likely not better this description of man's right to defend himself:

There exists a law, not written down anywhere, but inborn in our hearts; a law which comes to us not by training or custom or reading but by derivation and absorption and adoption from nature itself; a law which has come to us not from theory but from practice, not by instruction but by natural intuition. I refer to the law which lays it down that, if our lives are endangered by plots or violence or armed robbers or enemies, any and every method of protecting ourselves is morally right. When weapons reduce them to silence, the laws no longer expect one to await their pronouncements. For people who decide to wait for these will have to wait for justice, too — and meanwhile they must suffer injustice first. Indeed, even the wisdom of the law itself, by a sort of tacit implication, permits self-defence, because it does not actually forbid men to kill; what it does, instead, is to forbid the

Cicero defends man's right to protect himself

bearing of a weapon with the intention to kill.
When, therefore, an inquiry passes beyond the
mere question of the weapon and starts to consider
the motive, a man who has used arms in self-
defence is not regarded as having carried them
with a homicidal aim.[12]

And this:

Civilized people are taught by logic, barbarians by
necessity, communities by tradition; and the lesson is inculcated even in wild beasts by nature
itself. They learn that they have to defend their
own bodies and persons and lives from violence of
any and every kind by all the means within their
power.[13]

And from the celebrated Roman historian Livy,
whose 142-volume *History of Rome* was one of the
most widely read and admired books throughout
Europe even until the Renaissance period:

**Livy
recognizes
that the
common
man had
to provide
himself
with arms**

Formerly [under the reign of Servius Tullius (the
sixth Roman king, 578–535 BC)] the right to bear
arms had belonged solely to the patricians. Now
plebeians were given a place in the army, which
was to be reclassified according to every man's
property, i.e., his ability to *provide himself* a more
or less complete equipment for the field. . . .[14] [All
the citizens] capable of bearing arms were required to provide [their own swords, spears, and
other armor.][15] [Emphasis in original.]

From the Roman poet Horace, who had fought
at Brutus' side at the battle of Philippi:

But my pen will never jab without a provocation
at anyone on earth, for it protects me like a sword
kept in the sheath. Why should I ever pull it out if
no criminal attacks me? Jupiter, Father and King,
may my weapon stay unused and perish from rust,
and no one injure me.[16]

And from the Roman poet Ovid:

The laws allow arms to be taken against an armed
foe.[17]

Anyone who doubts the influence of these classical writers upon succeeding generations of legal
thinkers in Europe (and America) should be aware
that the short quote from Ovid was repeated, almost word for word, as Halbrook points out, by the
English jurist Sir Edward Coke in *Institutes of the
Laws of England* sixteen hundred years later.[18]

**Classical
writers'
influence
to be felt
1600 years
later in
England**

For as we shall see, philosophical inquiry into the
right to keep and bear arms was to reach its peak
in continental Europe and England during the
sixteenth to eighteenth centuries. The next chapter
will briefly examine the important writings of that
period from continental Europe. That will be followed by a more exhaustive treatment of the English commentary that was to exert a powerful
influence upon constitutional thought in the American Colonies.

II
EXPRESSIONS OF THE RIGHT IN SIXTEENTH- TO EIGHTEENTH-CENTURY CONTINENTAL EUROPE

I f you were to ask an informed American what he knew about two historic Italian cities, Florence and Milan, he would probably respond that Florence was the site of Michelangelo's *David* and paintings by Raphael, Titian, and Fra Angelico, a city rich in Renaissance architecture and sculpture, and the home of the Medici family. As for Milan, he perhaps would recall it was the site of its great Duomo, or cathedral, La Scala opera house, and Leonardo da Vinci's famous painting *The Last Supper.*

But for the student of the right to keep and bear arms, Florence and Milan have an even greater significance. Because these cities were the homes of two men whose writings were to have a profound, even extraordinary, influence over the evolution of the political theories that were to culminate in the words of the Second Amendment to the U.S. Con-

The significance of Florence and Milan

stitution. I am referring of course to Florence's Niccolò Machiavelli and Milan's Cesare Beccaria. In studying their writings, I have become so intimately familiar with these two fellows that I like to call them the "Two Gentlemen of Verona." Now, I know that's not exactly right; Verona is 125 miles north of Florence and 90 miles east of Milan. But that's close enough for government work, and that's what we're up to, isn't it?

But European expressions on the right to keep and bear arms were not confined to Italy. We will also be examining the thoughts of three other political philosophers of the period: Hugo Grotius of Holland and Montesquieu and Jean-Jacques Rousseau of France.

NICCOLÒ MACHIAVELLI

Niccolò Machiavelli, the Florentine political philosopher, published five books between 1520 and 1532. Today he is best known for his last work, *The Prince,* which describes how a political leader — a prince — can acquire and maintain political power. This study, which has often been regarded as a defense of the despotism and tyranny of such rulers as Cesare Borgia, was based on Machiavelli's belief that a ruler cannot be bound by traditional ethical standards. In his view, a prince should be concerned only with power and be bound only by rules that would lead to political success. Taken to the extreme, this means a ruler is free to use any methods at all to maintain power, for "the end justifies the means," a maxim that has led, in turn, to the addition to our language of a new term for gross political opportunism: *Machiavellianism*.

But as a keen student of political philosophy, Machiavelli did not limit himself to a single theory, as revealed by his two other major works: *Discourses on the First Ten Books of Titus Livius,* a commentary on *History of Rome* by the Roman historian Livy; and *On the Art of War.* In these books, Machiavelli describes the advantages of conscripted soldiers over mercenary troops and begins to develop his theories regarding the relationship between arms and politics, particularly the virtues of an "armed citizenry."

Machia-velli the first to recognize virtue of an armed citizenry

Stephen Halbrook writes, "In expressing his clear preference [in *Discourses*] for republics over principalities, Machiavelli draws on the Roman experience to show that an armed populace has *virtù* [civic virtue or valor], while a disarmed people is subject to the whims of *fortuna* [fortune]. . . . According to Machiavelli, Caesar had destroyed the liberty of the Roman republic by engaging in conquests and developing a standing army of professionals. No longer could the populace check the empire's power by refusing to enlist for the wars, and the slavery imposed abroad prompted slavery at home. The demise of the armed citizen meant the end of civic virtue and with it the end of the people's control over their destiny."[1]

In Machiavelli's words:

> If a city be armed and disciplined as Rome was,
> and all its citizens, alike in their private and official
> capacity, have a chance to put alike their virtue
> and power of fortune to the test of experience, it
> will be found that always and in all circumstances
> they will be of the same mind and will maintain
> their dignity in the same way. But, when they are
> not familiar with arms and merely trust to the
> whim of fortune, not to their own virtue, they will
> change with the changes of fortune.[2]

And, continues Halbrook, in *On the Art of War,*
"[which Machiavelli was particularly qualified to
examine] . . . [because] he had successfully organized and led a citizen militia in the early sixteenth
century, [Machiavelli praised] the Roman republic
example of part-time common soldiers, who 'entered voluntarily into the service,' while working in
other occupations, [lauding] 'the important privilege accorded Roman citizens of not being forced
into the army against their will.' [But] the demise
of the republic was also the demise of the armed
populace. 'For Augustus, and after him Tiberius,
more interested in establishing and increasing their
own power than in promoting the public good,
began to disarm the Roman people (in order to
make them more passive under their tyranny)
and to keep the armies continually on foot within
the confines of the Empire.' Similarly, according
to Machiavelli, the Venetians employed foreign
troops 'to prevent any of their own citizens from

**Demise of
the Roman
republic
was also
the demise
of its
armed
population**

staging a coup' while the French king 'disarmed all his subjects in order to rule them more easily.' "[3]

Here are a few selected passages from the three works of Machiavelli discussed above:

> For either I have my country well equipped with arms, as the Romans had and the Swiss have; or I have a country ill equipped with arms, as the Carthaginians had, and as have the king of France and the Italians today. In the latter case the enemy should be kept at a distance.[4]

> But when states are strongly armed, as Rome was and the Swiss are, the more difficult it is to overcome them the nearer they are to their homes: for such bodies can bring more forces together to resist attack than they can to attack others. . . . In attacking a foreign country, [the Romans] never sent out armies of more than fifty thousand men; but for home defense they put under arms against the Gauls after the first Punic war eighteen hundred thousand.[5]

> [I]t is certain that no subjects or citizens, when legally armed and kept in due order by their masters, ever did the least mischief to any state. . . . Rome remained free for four hundred years and Sparta eight hundred, although their citizens were armed all that time; *but many other states that have been disarmed have lost their liberties in less than forty years.*[6] [Emphasis added.]

Disarmed states have lost their liberties in less than 40 years

> [A]n armed republic submits less easily to the rule of one of its citizens than a republic armed by foreign states.[7]

Among evils caused by being disarmed, it renders you contemptible. . . . [I]t is not reasonable to suppose that one who is armed will obey willingly one who is unarmed; or that any unarmed man will remain safe among armed servants.[8]

A prince, therefore, who would reign in security, ought to select only such men for his infantry as will cheerfully serve him in war when it is necessary, and be as glad to return home when it is over. This will always be the case with those who have other occupations and employments by which to live.[9]

[Such a prince, he explained, would found his state upon] good laws and good arms. And as there cannot be good laws where there are not good arms, and where there are good arms there must be good laws, I will not now discuss the laws, but will speak of the arms.[10]

Machia-velli's influence over later political writers

These theories, as we shall see, were later to influence the writings of a number of European commentators, including Grotius, Thomas Hobbes, James Harrington, Algernon Sidney, John Locke, John Trenchard, Montesquieu, Thomas Gordon, Rousseau, James Burgh, and Adam Smith. (David Hardy reports that quotations from *On the Art of War* began appearing in English diplomatic dispatches as early as 1537 and an English translation of the book had gone through no fewer than three printings by 1588.)[11] And from these succeeding generations of European commentators came additional writings that were to become the standard

educational fare and a major influence in the lives
and thought of our Founding Fathers.

CESARE BECCARIA

More than two and a quarter centuries after
Machiavelli's death, Beccaria, a Milanese jurist,
economist, and criminologist, published his principal work, *On Crimes and Punishments* (1764). In
the book, an argument is advanced against abuses
in the criminal law, especially torture and capital
punishment. Beccaria also included a criticism of
legal sanctions against the mere possession and
carrying of firearms that was to become a corner-
stone of Second Amendment thought in the American Colonies. John Adams thought so highly of this
writing that he began his opening argument in the
Boston Massacre trial in 1770 with a quote from
this text; and, just months before drafting the Declaration of Independence, Thomas Jefferson copied
into his *Commonplace Book* (a journal in which he
recorded his favorite passages by philosophers) the
entire paragraph in its original Italian. (Jefferson
also was influenced by Beccaria's theories on legal
reform, which were later to manifest themselves in
the language of the Eighth Amendment's prohibition against cruel and unusual punishment.) Here
is what Beccaria wrote about gun control laws:

**Important
statement
by
Beccaria**

> False is the idea of utility that sacrifices a thousand
> real advantages for one imaginary or trifling incon-
> venience; that would take fire from men because

Should we forbid water because one can drown in it?

it burns, and water because one may drown in it; that has no remedy for evils, except destruction. The laws that forbid the carrying of arms are laws of such a nature. They disarm those only who are neither inclined nor determined to commit crimes. Can it be supposed that those who have the courage to violate the most sacred laws of humanity, the most important of the code, will respect the less important and arbitrary ones, which can be violated with ease and impunity, and which, if strictly obeyed, would put an end to personal liberty — so dear to men, so dear to the enlightened legislator — and subject innocent persons to all the vexations that the guilty alone ought to suffer? Such laws make things worse for the assaulted and better for the assailants; they serve rather to encourage than to prevent homicides, for an unarmed man may be attacked with greater confidence than an armed man. They ought to be designated as laws not preventive but fearful of crimes, produced by the tumultuous impression of a few isolated facts, and not by thoughtful consideration of the inconveniences and advantages of a universal decree.[12]

HUGO GROTIUS

In 1625, approximately one century after Machiavelli's works were published, the Dutch humanist and statesman Hugo Grotius, who is recognized today as having laid the foundation for modern international law, was weighing in with his thoughts on the rights of individuals in his landmark book *On the Law of War and Peace*. Halbrook writes that Grotius "justified armed force, whether carried out solely for defense by persons or by states. Relying extensively on the republican classics, Grotius upholds, early in this work, the natural character of using weapons to preserve life and limb."[13] Halbrook then goes on to quote from the book:

> [F]or all animals are provided by nature with means for the very purpose of self-defence. See Xenophon, Ovid, Horace, Lucretius. Galen observes that man is an animal born for peace and war, not born with weapons, but with hands by which weapons can be acquired. And we see infants, without teaching, use their hands for weapons.[14]

Halbrook further observes that "Grotius relies on Aristotle for the proposition that 'every one ought to use arms for himself, if he has received an injury, or to help relatives, benefactors, allies who are injured.' Also cited as authoritative are Cicero's orations for Milo, 'in which he appeals to the testimony of nature for the right of self defense. . . . If the right of inflicting capital punishments, and of defending the citizens by arms against robbers and plunderers, was taken away, then would follow a vast license of crime and a deluge of evils.' "[15]

CHARLES LOUIS DE SECONDAT MONTESQUIEU

Another century later, in 1748, mankind was delivered of one of the most important works in the history of philosophy, Montesquieu's *The Spirit of Laws*. In this celebrated masterpiece, Montesquieu distinguishes the three principal types of government — republic, monarchy, and despotism — and introduces the proposition that a relationship exists between an area's climate, geography, and general circumstances and its form of government. Montesquieu advocated the separation and balance of powers within government as a means of guaranteeing the freedom of the individual, a doctrine that was later to form the philosophical basis of the U.S. Constitution. Here is a representative sampling of his thoughts on the right of self-defense:

Montes-quieu on self-defense

Who does not see that self-defence is a duty superior to every precept [of personal freedom]?[16]

[T]he life of governments is like that of man. The latter has a right to kill in case of natural defence: the former have a right to wage war for their own preservation.[17]

If a slave, says Plato, defends himself, and kills a freeman, he ought to be treated as a parricide. This is a civil law which punishes self-defence, though dictated by nature.[18]

It is unreasonable . . . to oblige a man not to attempt the defence of his own life.[19]

[T]he laws of an Italian republic [Venice], where bearing fire-arms is punished as a capital crime and where it is not more fatal to make an ill use of them than to carry them, is not agreeable to the nature of things.[20]

JEAN-JACQUES ROUSSEAU

Machiavelli's warning against use of mercenary soldiers is echoed in this passage from Rousseau, the famous French philosopher whose writings became one of the principal influences behind the French Revolution:

Rousseau warns against the use of mercenary soldiers

> [A]ll the victories of the early Romans, like those of Alexander, had been won by brave citizens, who were ready, at need, to give their blood in the service of their country, but would never sell it. Only at the reign of Veii did the practice of paying Roman infantry begin. . . . [The mercenaries'] swords were always at the throats of their fellow-citizens, and they were prepared for general butchery at the first sign. It would not be difficult to show that this was one of the principal causes of the ruin of the Roman Empire.[21]

As our tour of continental Europe comes to a close and we prepare to cross the English Channel to continue our investigation of the sources and authorities on the right to keep and bear arms, let us review what we have discovered so far. We have found that just as political commentators in Greece and Rome more than a thousand years before them had done, continental Europeans, as exemplified in the words of Machiavelli and Rousseau, recognized the right and duty of nation-states to form armed groups for collective protection rather than relying upon mercenaries. And coupled with that right, as set forth in the words of Beccaria, Grotius, and Montesquieu, was the right of the individual to protect himself with arms.

The blossoming of republican ideals

These twin themes of collective and individual armed protection that blossomed into concrete republican ideals in continental Europe were to meet with strong interest among Whig thinkers in England, as outlined in the next chapter.

III

THE DEVELOPMENT
AND DECLARATION
OF THE RIGHT IN
ENGLAND

I n her book *To Keep and Bear Arms: The Origins of an Anglo-American Right,* historian Joyce Lee Malcolm points out that "a belief in the virtues of an armed citizenry had a profound influence upon the development of the English, and, in consequence, the American system of government."[1] (Incidentally, in the balance of this review of the history of the right to keep and bear arms in England, I am borrowing heavily from Professor Malcolm's book. It is the definitive study on this aspect of English constitutional history and I highly recommend it to you.)

In preparing this chapter, I found it helpful to divide English history into the two periods before and after the date of passage by Parliament of the English Declaration of Rights — certainly the most important date as far as the right to bear arms is concerned — February 12, 1689.

It is helpful to divide English history into two periods

Prior to 1689, that is, throughout the entire early and medieval periods of English history and as far back as 500 AD, there was never any doubt about the legality of keeping and bearing arms. During this time, England was subjected to periodic invasions by Germanic tribes (principally Saxons, but also Jutes and Angles). In these primitive and violent times, the ancient kings demanded of their subjects that they be armed for combat. Later, the Laws of Alfred (871–899)[2] and the Laws of Cnut (1020–1023),[3] among others, considered armed defense, particularly against robbers and burglars, a right and duty, levying fines upon those who failed to answer a call to arms.

In ancient England people had a duty and a right to bear arms

"Under the Saxon laws," according to the English historian Francis Grose, "every freeman of an age capable of bearing arms, and not incapacitated by any bodily infirmity, was in case of a foreign invasion, internal insurrection, or other emergency, obliged to join the army. . . . Every landowner was obliged to keep armor and weapons according to his rank and possessions; these he might neither sell, lend, nor pledge, nor even alienate [transfer of ownership] from his heirs. In order to instruct them in the use of arms, they had their stated times for performing their military exercise; and once in a year, generally in the spring, there was a general review of arms, throughout each county."[4]

During the reign of Henry II there was issued one of the earliest statutory pronouncements of these rights and duties, the Assize of Arms of 1181:

THE ASSIZE OF ARMS (1181)

Whoever holds one knight's fee shall have a coat of **A legal** mail, a helmet, a shield and a lance. . . . Every free **require-** layman having in chattels [movable property] or **ment to** rent [lands] to the value of 15 marks, shall keep a **keep armor** coat of mail, a helmet and shield and lance. . . . **and weapons** Every free layman who shall have in chattels or rent 10 marks, shall have a habergeon [sleeveless armored coat], a chaplet [skullcap] of iron and a lance. Also all burgesses and the whole community of freemen shall have a wambais [inexpensive leather body armor], a chaplet of iron, and a lance. . . . Every one of these shall swear that he will have these arms before the Feast of St. Hillary . . . and no man having these arms shall sell, pledge, nor lend them, nor alienate [transfer ownership of] them in any manner; nor shall the Lord take them from his vassal by forfeiture, gift, pledge, or other manner.[5]

A century later, Edward I proclaimed the following law:

THE STATUTE OF WINCHESTER (1285)

And further, it is commanded that every man have in his house Harness [armor] for to keep the peace after the antient Assize; that is to say, Every man between fifteen years of age and sixty years of age shall be assessed and sworn to armor according to the quality of their Lands and Goods; that is, to wit, from Fifteen Pounds Lands and Goods Forty

Marks, an Hauberke [tunic of chain mail] of iron, a sword, a knife and a horse . . . and he that hath less than Forty Shillings yearly, shall be sworn to keep Gisarms [poleaxes], knives and other less weapons . . . and all others that may, shall have Bowes and Arrows.[6]

These statutes reflect the classical world view, as Don Kates has observed, that "arms possession for protection of self, family and polity was both the hallmark of the individual's freedom and one of the two primary factors in his developing the independent, self-reliant, responsible character which classical political philosophers deemed necessary to the citizenry of a free state. The symbolic significance of arms as epitomizing the status of the free citizen represented ancient law.[7]

"From Anglo-Saxon times, as A. V. B. Norman reports in his book *The Medieval Soldier,* 'the ceremony of freeing a slave included the placing in his hands of arms as a symbol of his new rank. Anglo-Saxon law forbade anyone to disarm a free man, and Henry I's laws applied this even to the man's own lord.' "[8]

The three-tiered defense system of medieval times

By medieval times, the nations of Europe, including England, had developed a defense system that divided their armed forces into three components:

1. The standing army, termed "housecarls" in England, consisted primarily of knights mounted on horses and bowmen and lancers on foot. These

soldiers, commonly referred to as "freebooters" or "soldiers of fortune," were professionals and, more often than not, mercenaries.

2. The next group, referred to as "the select fyrd," was similar to the "trained bands" that were to develop later in Stuart England. The fyrd — roughly comparable to today's National Guard in the United States — was composed of semiprofessional soldiers who frequently practiced other professions. It was divided along class lines, and selection of armor and weapons was done by class.

3. The third group, called the "great fyrd" or "arriereban," consisted of untrained citizens, generally all able-bodied men in a certain age bracket. These untrained men were usually required to keep certain weapons in their homes, such as a bow and arrows, a sword, or a pike. Failure to maintain such arms could result in stiff fines or imprisonment. The Statute of Winchester reproduced above was an important codification of this duty to be armed. Citizens were expected to have suitable weapons at hand and were assessed according to their wealth for a contribution of arms to the militia.

This system prevailed for hundreds of years, so that until late in the seventeenth century, England had no standing army. It was everyone's business to maintain order, with the exception of persons of the Catholic faith. After the Reformation — in the mid-sixteenth century — Catholics were a notable exception to the tolerant attitude toward the individual ownership of weapons, as they were looked

Everyone's business to maintain order

upon as subversives. It is well to keep in mind, however, that no more than two percent of the English population at that time was Catholic. Moreover, they were allowed to keep arms for self-defense, even though they were prohibited from storing large amounts of arms.

The social problem of violent crime

Too, the political turmoil that existed in the corridors of power in London during much of this period of English history was accompanied across the countryside by an unsettling social problem — violent crime. As Kates reports, "Until the early nineteenth century, the nations of Europe, including England, were enormously violent areas overrun with cutthroats, cutpurses, burglars, and highwaymen, and in which rioting over social and political matters was endemic. But no less a menace to the general population were pillaging soldiers, loosed upon society because of the King's inability to pay and thus control them. Often the soldier was a common criminal inducted directly out of jail and unleashed upon the King's enemies. In England, the perpetration of such outrages upon his critics by Charles I engendered the Petition of Right in 1628 and hastened his eventual dethroning and execution by the English people."[9]

In an effort to combat such violence, particularly the depredations of highwaymen, limited weapon and gun control measures were enacted. A 1541 statute, for example, limited ownership of crossbows and handguns (weapons that could be concealed beneath a cloak) to persons with an annual income exceeding 100 pounds. However, the same statute specified that the general population could keep certain handguns. It reads in part as follows:

ACT OF HENRY VIII

. . . [lords, knights, esquires, gentlemen, and the inhabitants of every city, borough, and market-town] to have and keep in every of their houses any such hand-gun or hand-guns, of the length of one whole yard . . . to the intent to use and shoot the same, at a butt or bank of earth only . . . whereby they and every one of them, by the exercise thereof . . . May The Better Aid And Assist To The Defence of This Realm, When Need Shall Require.[10]

Meanwhile, as the Middle Ages were coming to a close and nation-states were being created throughout Europe, their monarchs and statesmen were becoming well aware, as Machiavelli had predicted in 1521 in his classic treatise *On the Art of War,* of the greater security that could be provided them by an army conscripted from the local population — an armed citizenry — rather than by hired mercenaries.

However, there was one European monarch, Charles II, who apparently had not read his Machiavelli. His concerns about the strength of his monarchy, coupled with his uneasiness about the quantity of arms in the country, led him to create

Charles II had not read his Machiavelli

a select militia of unprecedented size and effectiveness. At the same time, he began to issue royal
proclamations to limit the use of arms and to require gunsmiths to record and report to the Crown
all weapons they had manufactured and to whom
those weapons had been sold. Parliament cooper-
ated with Charles and in 1661 and 1662 passed a
series of Militia Acts that, among other things,
authorized the seizing of arms in the possession of
"any person whom they judged dangerous to the
Peace of the Kingdom."[11]

**The
Militia
and Game
Acts**

Next, a series of Game Acts was enacted, culmi-
nating with the most famous of such legislation, the
Game Act of 1671,[12] which for the first time in
history deprived the vast majority of Englishmen
of their legal right to keep weapons. While these
Game Acts were ostensibly designed to protect the
wild game owned by royalty and to preserve the
privilege of hunting game only for the wealthy,
arguably the underlying motive was Charles II's
goal of disarming the entire population.

Since the vast majority of the population lived in
poverty, 95 percent of the population was affected
by this law, which stated that "[A]ll and every
person or persons, not having Lands and Tene-
ments of the clear yearly value of One hundred
pounds . . . are not allowed to have or keep for
themselves, or any other person or persons, any
Guns, Bowes . . . or other Engines."[13] Now it was
no longer necessary for the Crown to prove illegal

intent; mere possession of a proscribed firearm was illegal.

This state of affairs ended in mid-February 1689. A few months earlier, James II (who had ascended to the throne upon the death of Charles II in 1685) had been forced to vacate the throne and flee to France. Parliament subsequently declared Prince William of Orange and his wife Mary as the new king and queen of England after they had agreed to accept a Declaration of Rights as a condition of their ascension to the throne.

English Declaration of Rights

William convened the parliamentary convention that passed the English Declaration of Rights on February 12, 1689. It was signed by William and Mary upon their ascension to the throne on February 13, 1689. The Declaration set forth thirteen basic rights that the new parliament believed in need of reaffirmation, the seventh of which proclaimed that it was the right of all Protestants to "have Arms for their Defence, suitable to their Conditions, and as allowed by Law."[14] This Declaration, viewed as the "new magna charta," was thereafter enacted as a statute known as the English Bill of Rights.[15]

Also, it was at this parliamentary convention that the controversy about whether the right to keep and bear arms was collective or individual first appeared in the parliamentary debates. It is instructive for us at this time to see how the convention resolved that controversy.

The first draft of the Declaration included these words:

> It is necessary for the publick Safety, that the subjects which are Protestants, should provide and keep Arms for their common Defence. And that the Arms which have been seized, and taken away from them, be restored.[16]

Here is the final wording of the text:

> That the subjects which are Protestants may have Arms for their Defence suitable to their Conditions, and as allowed by Law.[17]

The collective vs. individual rights argument

Note that the word "common" no longer modifies the word "Defence," which clearly indicates an individual, not a collective, right.

Note too the modifying phrases "suitable to their Conditions" and "as allowed by Law," which were added to the final draft in recognition of several sixteenth-century statutes (then still in effect) that had placed certain restrictions upon the types of arms certain subjects could own.

English courts thereafter were to interpret these phrases in terms of the common law, which protected the right of the individual citizen to keep and bear ordinary personal arms in a peaceable manner. Here is a jury instruction from an English trial judge in 1820:

> [The English Bill of Rights] . . . provides that "the subjects which are Protestant may have arms for their defence suitable to their conditions, and as

allowed by law.". . . . But are arms suitable to the condition of people in the ordinary class of life, and are they allowed by law? A man has a clear right to protect himself in his house. A man has a clear right to protect himself when he is going singly or in a small party upon the road where he is travelling or going for the ordinary purpose of business. But I have no difficulty in saying you have no right to carry arms to a public meeting if the number of arms which are carried are calculated to produce terror and alarm.[18]

Additional legislation was to further amplify the right to arms ownership. An act was passed that prohibited Catholics from keeping "any Arms, Weapons, Gunpowder, or Ammunition."[19] But it did permit Catholics to retain those weapons that local justices at Quarter Session thought necessary "for the Defence of his House or Person."[20] This exception is significant in that, even at a time when there was fear of religious war, Catholic Englishmen were permitted the means to defend themselves and their households.

Thus, the ancient right — the individual right — of Englishmen to have arms, coupled with a civic responsibility to train themselves in the use of those arms and be available for service in the militia, was restored.

The individual right to bear arms is restored in England

Reproduced below is a sampling of public writings in the period before 1689, setting forth in various ways the English understanding of the ancient right to keep and bear arms.

SIR JOHN FORTESCUE

An unarmed citizenry would make England prey to all nations

They [the French peasants] grow crooked, and become feeble, not able to fight nor to defend the realm; nor do they have weapons, nor the money to buy them weapons withal. But truly they live in the most extreme poverty and misery, and yet dwell in the most fertile realm of the world. Wherefore the French king hath not men of his own realm to defend it, except the nobles, which bear not such impositions, and therefore are very cautious of risking their bodies; by which cause the said king is compelled to make his armies and retinues for the defence of his land of strangers, as Scots, Spaniards, Arrogoners, Germans, and of other nations, or else his enemies might overrun him; for he hath no defence of his own except his castles and fortresses. If the realm of England, which is an isle, and therefore not likely to get aid of other realms, were ruled under such a law, and under such a prince, it would be a prey to all other nations that would conquer, rob, or devour it.[21]

SIR THOMAS MORE

Nevertheless, men and women alike [of More's race of Utopians] assiduously exercise themselves in military training on fixed days lest they should be unfit for war when need requires. Yet they do not lightly go to war. They do so only to protect their own territory or to drive an invading enemy out of their friends' lands or, in pity for a people oppressed by tyranny, to deliver them by force of arms from the yoke and slavery of the tyrant.[22]

MICHAEL DALTON

If Thieves shall come to a Man's House, to rob or murder him, he may lawfully assemble company to defend his House by force; and if he or any of his company shall kill any of them in defence of Himself, his Family, his Goods or House, This is no Felony, neither shall they forfeit any thing therefore.[23]

Self-defense is no felony

SIR EDWARD COKE

According to the U.S. Supreme Court, Sir (Lord) Edward Coke was "widely recognized by the American colonists as the greatest authority of his time on the laws of England"[24] and on "common-law rule[s]."[25] Two of his works, *Institutes of the Laws of England* and his *Reports,* were commonly found in the libraries of American colonists.[26] Here is what Lord Coke wrote on the right of self-defense in these works, especially regarding the use of deadly force against burglars and robbers:

Some [homicides are fully justified and commendable] without any giving back to a wall, etc. or other inevitable cause [that is, without any retreat or other necessity]. As if a thiefe offer to rob or murder B either abroad, or in his house, and thereupon assault him, and B defend himself without any giving back, and in his defence killeth the thiefe, this is no felony; for a man shall never give way to a thiefe, etc. neither shall he forfeit anything.[27]

A man's house is his castle

That the house of everyone is to him as his castle and fortress, as well for his defence against injury and violence, as for his repose; and although the life of man is a precious thing and favoured in the law; so that although a man kills another in his defence [in spontaneous disputes and brawls], or kills one *per infortun'* [by accident], without any intent, and in such case he shall forget his goods and chattels, for the great regard which the law has to a man's life; but if thieves come to a man's house to rob him, or murder, and the owner or his servants kill any of those thieves in defence of himself and his house, it is not felony, and he shall lose nothing, and therewith agree . . . [citing cases]. So it is held in [citing case], every one may assemble his friends and neighbors to defend his house against violence: but he cannot assemble them to go with him to the market, or elsewhere for his safeguard against violence: and the reason of all this is, because *domus sua cuique est tutissimum refugium* [a home is for everyone his safest refuge].[28]

One is allowed to repel force with force . . . the laws permit the taking of arms against armed persons.[29]

SIR WALTER RALEIGH

[It was a basic principle of a tyrant] to unarm his people of weapons, money, and all means whereby they resist his power.[30]

THOMAS HOBBES

A Covenant not to defend myself from force, by force, is always void. For . . . no man can transfer, or lay down his Right to save himself from Death.[31]

A natural right of self-protection

The Obligation of Subjects to the Sovereign is understood to last as long, and no longer, than the power lasts, by which he is able to protect them. For the right men have by Nature to protect themselves, when none else can protect them, can by no Covenant be relinquished.[32]

JAMES HARRINGTON

The arms of the commonwealth are both numerous, and in posture of readiness, but they consist of her citizens.[33]

Men accustomed unto their arms and their liberties will never endure the yoke.[34]

[A citizenry] trained up unto their arms, which they use not for the defence of slavery but of liberty [composes] the vastest Body of well disciplined militia that is possible in nature.[35]

The distribution of arms [among the citizens prevents a monarch from overcoming a republic].[36]

. . . [W]here the owner of the Plough comes to have the Sword too, he will use it in defence of his own.[37]

JOHN LOCKE

Whosoever *uses force without Right* . . . puts himself into a *state of War* with those, against whom he so uses it, and in that state all former Ties are cancelled, all other Rights cease, and every one has a Right to defend himself, and to *resist* the Aggressor.[38] [Emphasis in original.]

[Private persons] have a right to defend themselves and recover by force what by unlawful force is taken from them. . . .[39]

"The law could not restore life to my dead carcass"

[One may kill an aggressor where there is insufficient time to appeal to the law, for] the law could not restore life to my dead carcass.[40]

[Quoting William Barclay] Self defence is a part of the law of nature; nor can it be denied the community, even against the king himself.[41]

Every one as he is *bound to preserve himself,* and not to quit his station willfully; so by the like reason when his own Preservation comes not in competition ought he, as much as he can, *to preserve the rest of Mankind,* and may not unless it be to do Justice on an Offender, take away, or impair the life, or what tends to the Preservation of the Life, the Liberty, Health, Limb or Goods of another.[42] [Emphasis in original.]

The body of the People may with Respect resist intolerable Tyranny.[43]

STATE TRACTS

[The English liked to boast that they were] the freest subjects under Heaven [because they had the right] to be guarded and defended from all Violence and Force, by their own Arms, kept in their own hands, used at their own charge.[44]

The period from the late seventeenth century until 1760 saw the rise to political power in England of a group of statesmen commonly referred to as "classical Republicans," under the leadership of members of the Whig Party. The Whigs had been largely responsible for the Glorious Revolution of 1688, which established the supremacy of Parliament over the king, and, of course, the Whigs were instrumental in the drafting and enactment of the English Bill of Rights in 1689.

In the years immediately surrounding that date, which you will recall I consider the pivotal point in the history of the right to keep and bear arms in England, there was a flowering of republican expression on this issue from such Whig writers as James Harrington, John Trenchard, Algernon Sidney, Robert Molesworth, Andrew Fletcher, and James Burgh. The political philosophies of these men had been strongly influenced by the writings of Machiavelli and Beccaria; and their writings, in turn, were to exercise a dominant influence upon the framers of the U.S. Constitution.

The flowering of republican expression

The influ-
ence of the
English
Whigs on
political
thought
in the
Colonies
As David T. Hardy observes, "The Whig writings have more than purely historical interest. John Adams estimated that ninety percent of Americans were Whig sympathizers at the time of the American Revolution, and many of these American Whigs were deeply familiar with the writings of their English predecessors. John Adams held special regard for Harrington, although he probably did not endorse the 1779 proposal to change Massachusetts' name to *Oceana* [from the title of Harrington's most celebrated work]. Adams and Madison both studied Molesworth in detail; Jefferson's library boasted copies of Sidney, Molesworth, and Harrington. These works, and those of Fletcher, were also owned by the likes of Benjamin Franklin, John Hancock, and George Mason. When Burgh's *Political Disquisitions* was printed in the Colonies, Benjamin Franklin served as editor, and the subscription list for the first edition included George Washington, John Adams, John Hancock, and John Dickinson."[45]

Reproduced below is a sampling of writings from several leading Whig politicians and other political commentators in the period from the late seventeenth to the middle of the eighteenth century.

JOHN TRENCHARD AND
WALTER MOYLE

And if we inquire how these unhappy nations have lost that precious jewel Liberty, and we as yet preserved it, we shall find their miseries and our happiness proceed from this, that their necessities or indiscretion have permitted a standing army to be kept amongst them, and our situation rather than our prudence, hath as yet defended us from it.[46]

[Arming and training the people] was the only Bulwark of their Liberties and . . . the surest way to preserve them both at home and abroad, the People being secured thereby as well against the Domestick Affronts of any of their own Citizens, as against the Foreign Invasions of ambitious and unruly Neighbours. . . . [The people must be armed to] stand upon [their] own Defence; which if [they] shall never be put upon it, but [their] Swords may grow rusty in [their] hands; for that Nation is the surest to live in Peace, that is most capable of making War, and a Man that hath a Sword by his side, shall have least occasion to make use of it.[47]

The people must be armed

ALGERNON SIDNEY

Nay, all laws must fall, human societies that subsist by them be dissolved, and all innocent persons be exposed to the violence of the most wicked, if men might not justly defend themselves against injustice by their own natural right, when the ways prescribed by publick authority cannot be taken.[48]

Let the danger be never so great, there is a possibility of safety while men have life, hands, arms, and courage to use them; but that people must certainly perish, who tamely suffer themselves to be oppressed.[49]

Every man is armed and disciplined

[I]n a popular or mixed government every man is concerned: Every one has a part according to his quality or merit . . . the body of the people is the publick defence, and every man is armed and disciplin'd.[50]

No numbers of men, tho naturally valiant, are able to defend themselves, unless they be well arm'd, disciplin'd and conducted.[51]

Swords were given to men, that none might be Slaves, but such as know not how to use them . . .[52]

ROBERT MOLESWORTH

The arming and training of all the freeholders of England, as it is our undoubted ancient Constitution, and consequently our Right: so it is the opinion of most Whigs, that it ought to be put in Practice.[53]

ANDREW FLETCHER

He that is armed, is always the master of the purse of him, that is unarmed.[54]

SIR WILLIAM BLACKSTONE

The next commentator I want to present to you is the brilliant jurist William Blackstone. Blackstone was a member of the political opposition to the Whigs, the Tory Party. Yet he agreed with many of the Whig republican philosophies.

Moreover, as Professor Malcolm points out, "the influence of the radical Whigs on Americans of the founding era is generally acknowledged, but the profound impact of a more moderate English author has usually been underestimated. The first volume of William Blackstone's *Commentaries on the Laws of England* did not appear in Britain until 1765, and the fourth and last volume until 1769, yet nearly 2500 copies had been sold in America by the start of the American Revolution in 1775.[55] Blackstone's work not only sold well but was immediately regarded as authoritative. The author of a study of the influence of English and European writers on eighteenth-century American political thought tabulated the frequency with which some thirty-six authors were mentioned by major American political writers between 1760 and 1805. Blackstone was the most cited English writer, second only to Montesquieu.[56] Blackstone's views on the right of individuals to be armed are of great importance, therefore, in penetrating the minds of the American founders."[57]

The most important influence of all was Blackstone's *Commentaries on the Laws of England*

While it can never be proven, it is probable that *every lawyer in the Colonies — which included, of course, most of the Founding Fathers — had learned much of his common law from Blackstone.* It is no wonder, under those circumstances, that in defining and modifying English law to suit the needs of the new Colonies the Founding Fathers' primary and most influential reference would be the words of their mentor. Here is what Blackstone had to say:

The natural right of resistance and self-preservation The fifth and last auxiliary right of the subject, that I shall present mention, is that of having arms for their defence, suitable to their condition and degree and such as are allowed by law. Which is also declared by the same statute W & M st. 2.c.2 [the English Bill of Rights] and it is indeed a public allowance under due restrictions, of the natural right of resistance and self-preservation, when the sanctions of society and laws are found insufficient to restrain the violence of oppression. In these several articles consist the rights, or as they are frequently termed, the liberties of Englishmen. . . .[58]

. . . And we have seen that these rights . . . consist, primarily, in the free enjoyment of personal security, of personal liberty, and of private property. So long as these remain inviolate, the subject is perfectly free; for every species of compulsive tyranny and oppression must act in opposition to one or other of these rights. To preserve these from violation, it is necessary that the constitution of parliaments be supported in it[s] full vigor. . . . And lastly, to vindicate these rights, when actually violated or attacked, the subjects of England are entitled, in the first place, to the regular administration and free course of justice in the courts of law; next to the right of petitioning the king and parliament for redress of grievances; and, *lastly, to the right of having and using arms for self preservation and defence*. And all of these rights and liberties it is our birthright to enjoy entire unless where the laws of our country have laid them under necessary restraints. Restraints in themselves so gentle and moderate, as will appear from further inquiry, that no man of sense of probity would wish to see them slackened. For all of us have it in our choice to do every good thing that a good man would desire to do; and are restrained from nothing, but what would be pernicious either to ourselves or to our fellow citizens.[59] [Emphasis added.]

The liberties of Englishmen include the right of having and using arms for self-defense

In a land of liberty, it is extremely dangerous to make a distinct order of the profession of arms. . . . [N]o man should take up arms, but with a view to defend his country and its laws; he puts not off the citizen when he enters the camp. The laws . . . [of England] know no such state as that of a perpetual standing soldier, bred up to no other profession than that of war.[60]

JEAN L. DeLOLME

But all those privileges of the People, considered in themselves, are but feeble defences against the real strength of those who govern. All those provisions, all those reciprocal Rights, necessarily suppose that things remain in their legal and settled course: what would then be the recourse of the People, if ever the Prince, suddenly freeing himself from all re-

Armed resistance is the resource against the violences of power straint, and throwing himself as it were out of the Constitution, should no longer respect either the person, or the property of the subject, and either should make no account of his conversation with the Parliament, or attempt to force it implicitly to submit to his will? — It would be *resistance*. . . . The question has been decided in favour of this doctrine by the Laws of England, and that resistance is looked upon by them as the ultimate and lawful resource against the violences of Power. [This "resource" was actually guaranteed by a bill of rights that] expressly insured to individuals the right of publicly preferring complaints against the abuses of Government, and moreover, of being provided with arms for their own defence.[61] [Emphasis added.]

JAMES BURGH

No kingdom can be secured otherwise than by arming the people. The possession of arms is the distinction between a freeman and a slave, he, who has nothing, and who himself belongs to another, must be defended by him, whose property he is, and needs no arms. But he who thinks he is his own master, and has what he can call his own, ought to have arms to defend himself, and what he possesses, else he lives precariously, and at discretion.[62]

Had we at this time no standing army, we should not think of forcing money out of the pockets of

three millions of our subjects. We should not think
of punishing with military execution, unconvicted
and unheard, our brave American children, our
surest friends and best customers. . . . We should
not — but there is not an end to observations on
the difference between the measures likely to be
pursued by a minister backed by a standing army,
and those of a court awed by the fear of an armed
people.[63]

ADAM SMITH

Men of republican principles have been jealous of
a standing army as dangerous of liberty. . . . The
standing army of Caesar destroyed the Roman
republic. The standing army of Cromwell turned
the Long Parliament out of doors.[64]

WILLIAM PITT

If I were an American, as I am an Englishman,
while a foreign troop was landed in my country, I
never would lay down my arms — never — never
— NEVER! You cannot conquer America![65]

GRANVILLE SHARPE

No Englishman can be truly loyal who opposed the
principles of English law whereby the people are
required to have arms of defence and peace, for
mutual as well as private defence. . . . The laws of
England always required the people to be armed,
and not only *armed,* but to be *expert in arms.*[66]
[Emphasis added.]

**The laws
of England
always
required the
people to
be armed**

WILLIAM BLIZARD
The Recorder of London
(Chief legal adviser to the Mayor and Council)

An important statement from chief legal counsel to the City of London

It is a matter of some difficulty to define the precise limits and extent of the rights of the people of this realm to bear arms, and to instruct themselves in the use of them, *collectively,* and much more so to point out all acts of that kind, which would be illegal or doubtful in their nature.

The right of his majesty's Protestant subjects, to have arms for their own defence, and to use them for lawful purposes, is most clear and undeniable. It seems, indeed, to be considered, by the ancient laws of this kingdom, not only as a right, but as a *duty;* for all the subjects of the realm, who are able to bear arms, are bound to be ready, at all times, to assist the sheriff, and other civil magistrates, in the execution of the laws and the preservation of the public peace. And that right, which every Protestant most unquestionably possesses, individually, may, and in many cases *must,* be exercised collectively, is likewise a point which I conceive to be most clearly established by the authority of judicial decisions and ancient acts of parliament, as well as by reason and common sense.

It seems to follow, of necessary consequence, that it cannot be unlawful to learn to use them (for such lawful purposes) with safety and effect. For it would be too gross an absurdity to allege, that it is not lawful to be instructed in the use of anything which is lawful to use. . . .

The lawful purposes of which such arms may be used (besides immediate self defence) are the suppression of violent and felonious breaches of the peace, the assistance of civil magistrates in the execution of the laws, and the defence of the kingdom against foreign invaders. . . . [I]n any other situation but that of invasion by a foreign enemy, I should very much doubt not only the propriety, but the legality, of any commissions granted by the crown to armed associations not previously voted by Parliament.

To apply these principles to the case of the London [Military Foot] Association: I can see nothing in their plan or conduct which can justly be considered a violation of the laws. . . .

To strengthen the civil power, and to keep themselves at all times prepared for a vigorous and effectual discharge of their duty as citizens . . . are, in my view, sufficient viable and legal objects for the continuation of the association. . . . I would recommend it to this respectable body, to consider themselves a civil, and not a military, association, and confine themselves, in the present state of things, to those civil objects which will, upon the principles laid down, sufficiently justify them in exercising and perfecting themselves in the use of arms, without any commission whatever.[67] [Emphasis in original.]

Lawful purposes of the use of arms defined

SIR WILLIAM HAWKINS

[The common law rule is that] every private person seems authorized by the Law to arm himself for [various] purposes . . . [among them] killing of dangerous rioters.[68]

. . . that no wearing of arms within the meaning of th[e] [S]tatute [of Northampton, 1328], unless it be accompanied with such circumstances as are apt to terrify the people, from whence it seems to follow, [t]hat persons of quality are in no danger of offending against this statute by wearing common weapons.[69]

THOMAS BABINGTON MACAULEY

[The right to be armed] is the security without which every other is insufficient.[70]

JAMES PATERSON

The right to carry arms is a natural right

In all countries where personal freedom is valued, however much each individual may rely on legal redress, the right of each to carry arms — and these the best and sharpest — for his own protection in case of extremity, is a right of nature indelible and irrepressible, and the more it is sought to be repressed the more it will recur.[71]

***

You will recall that in the last chapter we emphasized that when the right to keep and bear arms made its transition across the English Channel from continental Europe, it was recognized as a dual right: a right of collective protection in the form of militias in service to the state and a right of individual self-protection.

Now, after several hundred years of refinement in the cauldron of political strife in England, as the right travels across to the Atlantic to the Colonies, *its character has not changed.* The colonists clearly understood, thanks to their knowledge of English constitutional history, that the right to keep and bear arms had been and should continue to be a *dual right.*

The dual right to keep and bear arms is unchanged as it comes to America

And, in the Colonies, just as in medieval England, there would be, so the colonists understood, several armed bodies: the standing army, provided by the British; the select fyrd, provided by the colonial militia; and the great fyrd, constituted of the remaining citizens. All citizens, of whatever military class, would be required in one way or another to keep and bear arms for militia duty. And all citizens, at all times and in all circumstances, would retain the English right to keep and bear arms both for militia duty and for the individual protection of themselves and their families.

But as we will see in the next chapter, the colonists soon learned that while these rights required no alteration, a medieval military structure was alien to the functioning of a free republican society. The British standing army proved to be an onerous presence in their midst; and the concept of a select militia proved to be nothing more than a standing army under the guise of another name. Only a general militia, as they saw it, could provide them with the means to protect themselves without sacrificing their right to keep and bear arms.

Lexington and Concord

These circumstances were to become the catalyst for the confrontations at Lexington and Concord when the British army attempted to seize the arms and munitions of the colonists. And those events, in turn, along with other inequities that were being forced upon the colonists by the British monarchy, led not only to the American Revolution, but also to the enactment of state constitutions then being drafted—constitutions containing bills of rights that were to become the models for the Bill of Rights of the U.S. Constitution.

IV

THE DEVELOPMENT
AND DECLARATION
OF THE
RIGHT IN AMERICA

A

DRAFTING AND RATIFICATION
OF THE BILL OF RIGHTS
IN THE COLONIAL PERIOD

A s heirs to the majestic constitutional history of England, the intellectual and political leaders of the new Colonies intended nothing less than to incorporate into their new government the laws and liberties of Englishmen, including the well-established right of the law-abiding citizen to keep and bear arms.

    Colonists were heirs to the constitutional history of England

  Yet, while engaged in bringing about one of the most radical political changes in the history of the Western world, the Founding Fathers remained conservative republicans who valued tradition and their English heritage — the dynasties of the Angles, Saxons, Picts, and Jutes; 1066 and the Norman Conquest; the Magna Carta; the reigns of the Norman, Lancastrian, Plantagenet, Tudor, Stuart, and Hanoverian kings; the Civil Wars; the Restoration; the Glorious Revolution; and, most particularly, the Age of Enlightenment and the Whig philosophies that came to dominate English political thought during the hundred years preceding the American Revolution.

Founding Fathers' knowledge and reverence for English law and customs

They revered English customs and law. Chief Justice Howard Taft observed that

[t]he Framers of our Constitution were born and brought up in the atmosphere of the common law, and thought and spoke its vocabulary. They were familiar with other forms of government, recent and ancient, and indicated in their discussions earnest study and consideration of many of them; but, when they came to put their conclusions into the form of fundamental law in a compact draft, they expressed themselves in terms of the common law, confident that they could be shortly and easily understood.[1]

This analysis by Chief Justice Taft explains, in part, the confusion that has developed, especially in this century, over the interpretation of the language of the Second Amendment. The meaning of such words as "militia," "keep arms," "bear arms," "discipline," "well regulated," and "the people" was the meaning of these words as they were used in the English common law of the sixteenth through the eighteenth centuries — not as they are used today. As Chief Justice Taft further commented:

The language of the Constitution cannot be interpreted safely except by reference to the common law and to British institutions as they were when the instrument was framed and adopted.[2]

Thomas Jefferson, by no means an imprecise thinker, was well aware of this consideration. In commenting upon how the Constitution should properly be read, he said:

On every question of construction let us carry ourselves back to the time when the Constitution was adopted, recollect the spirit manifested in the debates, and instead of trying what meaning can be squeezed out of the text, or invented against it, conform to the probable one which was passed.[3]

Yet despite this clear evidence, gun control and prohibition proponents attempt to squeeze out of the text of the Second Amendment the meaning that only a "collective" — not an individual — right is guaranteed by the amendment. They argue that the words of the amendment allegedly apply only to the group in our society that is "well regulated" and "keeps and bears arms," the National Guard. But they are wrong.

David I. Caplan, who has examined this issue in depth, provides this analysis:

In colonial times the term "well regulated" meant "well functioning" — for this was the meaning of those words at that time, as demonstrated by the following passage from the original 1789 charter of the University of North Carolina: "Whereas in all well regulated governments it is the indispensable duty of every Legislature to consult the happiness of a rising generation . . ." Moreover the Oxford English Dictionary defines "regulated" among other things as "properly disciplined"; and it defines "discipline" among other things as "a trained condition."

Privately kept firearms and training with them apart from formal militia mustering thus was encompassed by the Second Amendment, in order to enable able-bodied citizens to be trained by being familiar in advance with the functioning of firearms. In that way, when organized the militia would be able to function well when the need arose to muster and be deployed for sudden military emergencies.

Therefore, even if the opening words of the Amendment, "A well regulated militia . . ." somehow would be interpreted as strictly limiting "the right of the people to keep . . . arms"; nevertheless, a properly functioning militia fundamentally presupposes that the individual citizen be allowed to keep, practice, and train himself in the use of firearms.

National Guardsmen are prohibited from keeping their own military arms

The National Guard cannot possibly be interpreted as the whole constitutional militia encompassed by the Second Amendment; if for no other reason, the fact that guardsmen are prohibited by law (32 U.S.C. § 105[a][1]) from keeping their own military arms. Instead, these firearms are owned and annually inventoried by the Federal government, and are kept in armories under lock and key.[4]

With this preliminary understanding, let's examine how the Amendment came into being and was then ratified into the U.S. Constitution.

The First Continental Congress, which convened at Carpenters' Hall in Philadelphia on September 5, 1774, was the first major political gathering of the American Colonies. This Congress was to become the de facto revolutionary government that directed the war for independence.

The First Continental Congress

The principal outcome of this first meeting was the issuance of a petition called the Declaration of Rights and Grievances, an appeal to King George III to restore harmony between Britain and the Colonies. At that time, there was considerable discord between them, chiefly because of the passage by the British Parliament in March 1774 of the so-called Intolerable Acts, a series of punitive measures directed against the Colony of Massachusetts for its rebellious conduct, which had been recently evidenced by the Boston Tea Party. Before adjourning, the First Continental Congress also arranged for a second Congress to take place in Philadelphia if the king failed to respond favorably to their petition.

As it turned out, not only did George III fail to respond favorably, he began preparations for war. In August 1775 he issued a proclamation "for suppressing rebellion and sedition" in the Colonies and hired 20,000 Hessian mercenaries, who were soon sent to America.

The Second Continental Congress

The Second Continental Congress convened on May 10, 1775. Delegates to this meeting — including George Washington, Benjamin Franklin, and Thomas Jefferson — began to organize the colonies for war. George Washington was commissioned to organize a continental army, and the Congress formulated regulations for foreign trade, issued paper money, and sent emissaries abroad to negotiate with foreign powers for financial, diplomatic, and military assistance. Jefferson, aided especially by John Adams, drafted and Congress adopted the Declaration of Independence on July 4, 1776; and on November 15, 1777, Congress drafted and adopted the Articles of Confederation, which were ratified by the thirteen colonies in 1781.

During much of this period, armed combat had been taking place between the colonists and the British army and its mercenaries. The conflict ended with the surrender of the British forces at Yorktown on October 19, 1781.

Subsequently, the states recognized that the Articles of Confederation were flawed, impractical, and urgently in need of amendment. Therefore, the States sent delegates to a convention that convened at the State House in Philadelphia on May 25, 1787.

The Convention was attended by 55 delegates from twelve states, all prominent political figures of the time, including such luminaries as James Madison, George Mason, Benjamin Franklin, and Alexander Hamilton. (John Jay and Thomas Jefferson did not attend, as they were on diplomatic missions abroad; nor did Patrick Henry or Samuel Adams, both of whom opposed the formation of a strong central government for the new nation.) The delegates soon realized that merely amending the Articles of Confederation would not solve the problems facing the States and that a new governing document was required.

After four months of debate, the Constitution was drafted, signed, and then sent to the individual states for ratification, as required by its Article VII. This Article provided that the Constitution could become effective only after ratification by at least two-thirds of the states.

Drafting and ratification of the U.S. Constitution

In the months before and after the "Constitutional" Convention, including the ratification period that lasted until June 21, 1788 (when New Hampshire became the ninth state to ratify, fulfilling the two-thirds majority ratification requirement), numerous constitutional debates took place in all the states, accompanied by a steady stream of commentary in the popular press about the issues being debated.

As I began to read the original documents from the period — as you will be doing in this chapter of the primer — it came as no surprise that with all these politicians at work, literally thousands of pages of debate proceedings, records, and suggested amendments were produced.

Reading their words, I tried to imagine what it would be like to be in their company and share in what they must have been feeling. Surely they must have been proud of their stunning victory over the British and full of optimism for their future as free people in a free country. But at the same time, they must have felt humbled, uncertain, and fearful of the momentous task that lay before them. I then began to realize that even though only fourteen years had gone by, for these most determined men it was likely that the smell of gunpowder from Lexington and Concord was still in their noses.

THE FEAR OF STANDING ARMIES

Of all the powerful memories and emotions the Founding Fathers brought to the constitutional debates, apparently none was stronger than their fear of standing armies. As David Young has observed: "The necessity of an armed populace, protection against disarming of the citizenry, and the need to guard against a select militia and assure a real militia which could defend liberty against any standing forces the government might raise were topics interspersed throughout the ratification period."[5]

What kind of militia?

Yet, in the absence of a standing army, how was the nation to defend itself from external or internal aggression? The Founding Fathers understood this would be accomplished by a *militia*. But what kind of militia?

Here is a typical Anti-federalist view, expressed by Richard Henry Lee (writing under the pseudonym "The Federal Farmer"):

> A militia when properly formed, are in fact the people themselves, and render regular troops in great measure unnecessary. The powers to form and arm the militia, to appoint their officers, and to command their services, are very important; nor ought they in a confederated republic to be lodged, solely, in any one member of the government. First, the constitution ought to secure a genuine [ ] and guard against a select militia, by providing that the militia shall always be kept well organized, armed, and disciplined, and include, according to the past and general usage of the states, all men capable of bearing arms; and that all regulations tending to render this general militia useless and defenceless, by establishing select corps of militia, or distinct bodies of military men, not having permanent interests and attachments in the community is to be avoided.
>
> . . . to preserve liberty, it is essential that the whole body of the people always possess arms, and be taught alike, especially when young, how to use them . . .[6]

Regarding the freedom to keep and bear arms, of particular concern to the Anti-federalists was that a central government would, over time, convert and model from the corpus of the general militia (traditionally meaning all able-bodied men between the ages of roughly 16 and 60) a "select"

A concern of the Anti-federalists

militia (men typically between the ages of 18 and 21, say, who would receive more training and be better equipped than the rest of the people).

As far as the Anti-federalists were concerned, such a skilled and select militia would, for all practical purposes, be the same as the standing army that they so feared and detested. They were aware that in 1783 George Washington, and a year later Baron Von Steuben (the Prussian expatriate who had served as Washington's inspector general), had proposed a "peace establishment," which at that time would have been the equivalent of a select militia; and that Alexander Hamilton, one of the leading Federalists, had advocated a select militia in *The Federalist,* No. 29.[7] (It is interesting to note, however, that Hamilton's proposal assumed that the general population would be armed.)

George Washington and Alexander Hamilton had proposed select militias

But if the people were not to maintain a standing army, whence would come their defense against armed aggression? It would come, the Anti-federalists understood, through the existence in each state of a *general* militia, in which every able-bodied man aged 16 to 60, keeping his own arms and ammunition and trained (e.g., well regulated or disciplined) in their use, could answer the call to muster in defense of life and property.

Don B. Kates, one of our leading Second Amendment scholars, observes:

The 'militia' was the entire adult male citizenry, who were not simply *allowed* to keep their own arms, but affirmatively *required* to do so. . . . With slight variations, the different colonies imposed a duty to keep arms and to muster occasionally for drill upon virtually every able-bodied white man between the age of majority and a designated cut-off age. Moreover, the duty to keep arms applied to *every* household, not just to those containing persons subject to militia service. Thus the over-aged and seamen, who were exempt from militia service, were required to keep arms for law enforcement and for the defense of their homes from criminals or foreign enemies.[8] [Emphasis in original.]

The duty to keep arms applied to every household

THE REAL CONTROVERSY BETWEEN THE FEDERALISTS AND ANTI-FEDERALISTS

I initially concluded that the composition of the militia was soon to become the major issue in the struggle that would take place during the ratification period between the Federalists and the Antifederalists over whether the new Constitution should include a Bill of Rights. That appears to be a reasonable conclusion to reach, particularly as one reads the powerful and memorable rhetoric of the Anti-federalists such as that of Richard Henry Lee reprinted above.

But I soon discovered my initial impression was wrong.

I had fallen into the trap that has ensnared so many who have misunderstood the nature of the struggle between the Federalists and the Anti-federalists — and that number includes those who believe in the "collective right" or "states' right" interpretation of what the Second Amendment means; those who believe that the Second Amendment was drafted solely to satisfy the demands of the Anti-federalists for a general militia instead of a standing army.

To be sure, the Anti-federalists unquestionably held strong convictions about the need for a militia to replace a standing army in their new republic. But even more important than that conviction in the Anti-federalist philosophy was the need for a bill of rights.

The Anti-federalists insisted upon a bill of rights

The Anti-federalists — among them Richard Henry Lee, Elbridge Gerry, George Mason, Patrick Henry, and Samuel Adams — were militant advocates of the inclusion of a bill of rights in the Constitution. They were suspicious of the extraordinary powers that were to be granted to the federal government by a Constitution that lacked a bill of rights that would clearly and unequivocally protect certain freedoms.

Don Kates gave me a clearer appreciation of what the controversy between the Federalists and Anti-federalists was all about:

> While none of the Founders *liked* the idea of a standing army, the majority (Madison strongly included) believed it to be necessary. The Second Amendment was not a response to Anti-federalist

criticism of the standing army. *All* the Bill of Rights were added because of a desire to disarm what Madison and the other Federalists saw as an Anti-federalist quibble, a strawman objection to the lack of a Bill of Rights which was intended to excite the fear and passion of the masses but which the statesmen on both sides viewed as negligible. Madison just wrote up a set of principles — of truisms — in which *everybody* believed, and the Congress duly passed it as the Bill of Rights. Two of these truisms that got cobbled into one article were: that there is a natural right to be armed; and that militias are a good thing, a much better thing than a standing army, however necessary it may be.[9] [Emphasis in original.]

The Federalists, whose early leaders in addition to Hamilton included John Jay, James Madison, and George Washington, were no less fearful of standing armies than were the Anti-federalists. However, the Federalists believed that the strong national government that the Constitution provided would be sufficient protection against the evil of a standing army and therefore advocated that it be ratified without change. In fact, some Federalists even believed the Constitution to be a perfect instrument, divinely inspired. There were many Federalists, of course, who did support adding a bill of rights, but unfortunately the rules under which the proposed Constitution had been signed in Philadelphia prohibited any amendment to the document before ratification.

Federalists saw no need for a bill of rights

The Federalists' opposition to the inclusion of a
bill of rights in the Constitution was founded, as
David E. Young explains, upon their belief that
"under the Constitution the people gave Congress
only certain defined powers. It has no other powers.
The powers given by the people were not intended
for the purpose of violating any of the individual
rights protected by the states' bills of rights. In fact,
the powers being given to the federal government
were being taken from the state governments
where their rights are already protected. The total
sum of powers of the new federal government and
the state government would be exactly the same as
the sum of the powers of the old government and
the state government. Therefore a bill of rights in
the federal Constitution would serve no useful purpose as Congress was given no powers to violate the
individual rights of the citizens."[10]

Don Kates continues this line of thought:

[Today] both sides in the modern Second Amendment debate recognize that Madison proposed,
and the Federalist First Congress passed, the Bill
of Rights in response to Anti-federalist criticism of
the Constitution. Unlike the individual right view
[the view of those who believe the Second Amendment protects an "individual" right to keep and
bear arms], however, the states' right view presupposes the Amendment's hostility to parts of the
Constitution to which the Anti-federalists were
deeply opposed. The Anti-federalists had opposed

**The Anti-
federalists
opposed
ratifica-
tion on two
grounds**

ratification of the Constitution on two very different kinds of grounds. One involved deep suspicion about specific provisions, particularly those allowing a standing army and providing for federal supervision of the militia. Entirely independent of those specifics, the Anti-federalists, and many other Americans, were critical of the failure to append to the Constitution a charter of basic human rights that the federal government could not infringe under any circumstances.

The individual right view sees the Second Amendment, and the Bill of Rights in general, as responding to this second kind of criticism. During the ratification debate, the Federalists vehemently denied that the federal government would have the power to infringe freedom of expression, religion, and other basic rights — expressly including the right to arms. In this context, Madison secured ratification by his commitment to support the addition by amendment of a charter that would guarantee basic rights. But that commitment extended only to safeguarding the fundamental rights that all agreed should never be infringed. It did not involve conceding any issue on which the Federalists and Anti-federalists disagreed, i.e., the latter's opposition to specific provisions of the Constitution. Indeed, a few days after their submission, Madison said that he had "deliberately proposed amendments that would not detract from federal powers, among them a right for the citizenry to be armed."[11]

The Second Amendment, then, was a response to the perceived lack of individual rights guaran-

The Second Amendment was a response to the lack of individual rights guarantees

tees, not, as states' right proponents contend, a reaction to the standing army and militia control provisions of [the original Constitution]. The latter source of Anti-federalist wrath was simply not addressed by the Second Amendment. Nothing on the face of the Amendment deals with [those] concerns; certainly Madison did not see it as changing those portions of the Constitution. The Anti-federalists were not placated by the Amendment; when the proposed Bill of Rights reached the Senate, they unsuccessfully attempted to amend or repeal the offending clauses of [the original Constitution].[12]

Little debate about the right to keep and bear arms

It is revealing that in the thousands of pages of proceedings that were published in the course of the debates that took place in the state and federal legislatures before the drafting of the bill of rights and throughout the ratification period, little mention is made of the individual right to keep and bear arms. This indicates, I think it is fair to say, that whatever their disagreements about the inclusion of a bill of rights in the Constitution, the Federalists and Anti-federalists were unanimous in their support of an individual right to keep and bear arms. They were also unanimous in assuming that "the right of the people to keep . . . arms"[13] included the individual right to keep ordinary personal arms for armed self- and community-defense, especially against burglars, robbers, and rapists.

This lack of understanding of the nature of the controversy between the Federalists and the Anti-federalists is one of the two principal reasons, I believe, why the proponents of gun control have reached the erroneous conclusion that the Second Amendment guarantees only a "collective right" or "states' right" to keep and bear arms.

Whatever the merits of the Anti-federalists' cause, we know now that the Federalists persevered in the controversy and the Bill of Rights was added to the Constitution. When the first U.S. Congress convened on March 4, 1789, 103 proposed amendments had been submitted by the states to be considered for inclusion in a bill of rights. Congress reduced that number to twelve, and these were sent back to the states for ratification. Two amendments failed to be ratified, and the remaining ten, now called the Bill of Rights, were ratified on December 15, 1791.

THE RIGHT OF SELF-PROTECTION

The second principal reason that the intent of the framers of the Second Amendment is misunderstood in some quarters today, I think, is the failure to appreciate how vitally important to them was the right to possess arms, not only for service in the militia, but for *self-protection*. (Remember our earlier discussion of the development and migration of these dual rights from Greece to Rome to continental Europe to England?)

To understand how the duty and right of self-protection were viewed by the Founding Fathers — as well as the general population — of the American

The Founding Fathers' view of self-protection

Colonies in the late eighteenth century, it may be helpful to take a look at some of the realities of life at that time. First, as David Young reports,

> Most Americans were accustomed to having their individual rights protected from violation from the government because approximately two thirds of the population of the United States lived in states with constitutional bills of rights. In most of the other states some individual rights were protected in the state constitutions. . . . An armed populace was guaranteed in one way or another in *every* bill of rights of the original states [of those seven states — Virginia, Maryland, Delaware, New Hampshire, Pennsylvania, North Carolina, Massachusetts (and later Vermont, after it was recognized as a separate state in 1791) — that chose to draft one]. These provisions were the early progenitors of the Second Amendment, since it was the state bills of rights which were cited when the necessity of adding a bill of rights limiting the federal government was discussed later during the controversy over ratification of the United States Constitution.[14] [Emphasis in original.]

Second, whether for frontier engagements with hostiles, for hunting, or for duty in the militia, **The entire adult male population was armed** practically the entire adult male population was armed. We know that many of the Founding Fathers, including George Washington, Thomas Jefferson, and George Mason, were gun collectors. Many had served in armed combat during the Revolution and presumably had brought their weapons home upon the cessation of hostilities; a large number, of course, were hunters; and some were even marksmen. James Madison, for example, boasted that he could hit a small target at 100 yards . . . but he admitted that he was far from the best marksman.[15]

Third, there were no police. Just as in England at the time (which had no police force until 1829), America had no police during the colonial period (the first American police force was not organized until 1845). As Don Kates points out, "Even then [in England and America] the police were forbidden arms, under the view that if these were needed they could call armed citizens to their aid. (Ironically, the only gun control in nineteenth century England was the policy of forbidding police to have arms while on duty.)"[16]

There were no police

Fourth, Americans (and their English cousins) were keenly aware of what could befall an unarmed populace. The historical example probably most familiar to eighteenth-century Englishmen and Americans was the persecution that drove thousands of Huguenots to the shores of both countries. As the historian Barbara Tuchman has noted:

> Among the numerous tribulations visited in the 1690s upon the [unarmed] Huguenots in order to compel them to convert [to Catholicism], the most atrocious — and effective — were the *dragonnades,* or billeting of dragoons on Huguenot families with encouragement to behave as viciously as they wished. Notoriously rough and undisciplined, the enlisted troops of the dragoons spread

carnage, beating and robbing the householders,
raping the women, smashing and wrecking and
leaving filth . . .[17]

This Huguenot lesson was reinforced in the Colonies "with the licentious and outrageous behavior
of the military sent among them by the British
during the decade of protest and turmoil that pre-
ceded the Revolution."[18]

Papers throughout the Colonies began printing a
regular series called the "Journal of Occurrences,"
which detailed outrages alleged to have been committed by British troops in Boston:

> Dec. 12, 1768. A Married Lady of this Town was
> the other Evening, when passing from one House
> to another, taken hold of by a Soldier; who other-
> ways behaved to her with great rudeness. . . .
> Another Woman was pursued by a Soldier into a
> House near the North End, who dared to enter the
> same, and behave with great insolence. . . .[19]

**Criminal
offenses
by English
troops**

In fact, "throughout the eighteenth century,
criminal offenses by English soldiers, sailors, and
hired foreign mercenaries in the Colonies were a
constant occurrence and a subject of constant an-
tagonism between Americans and the English military, who refused to punish their men or to turn
them over to local justice. As a result of these
experiences, in the Anglo-American legal tradition, as the Founding Fathers understood it [even
though there was no police force] the very idea of

empowering government to place an armed force in constant watch over the populace was vehemently rejected as being a model of French Catholic despotism."[20]

Fifth, they had learned their law from the English common law, particularly from the writings of one of their principal mentors, William Blackstone. According to Kates,

> [Blackstone] placed the right to arms among the "absolute rights of individuals at common law," those rights he saw as preserving to England its free government and to Englishmen their liberties. Yet, unquestionably, what Blackstone was referring to was the individuals' rights to have and use arms for self-protection. He describes the right to bear arms as being "for self-preservation and defence," and self-defense as being "the primary law of nature [which cannot be] taken away by the law of society" — the "natural right of resistance and self-preservation, when the sanctions of society and laws are found insufficient to restrain the violence of oppression."[21]

They had learned from Blackstone that they had an absolute right to keep and bear arms for their defense

> This background suggests why Blackstone saw political overtones in the right to arms, coupling his discussion of it to rights that are plainly political in nature. It helps to explain why in the Bill of Rights the right of arms [of the Second Amendment] is preceded by the rights of religion, expression, press and petition [of the First Amendment], then followed by the guarantee against quartering soldiers [of the Third Amendment], and then followed, in turn, by protection against unreasonable

searches and seizures [of the Fourth Amendment].[22]

Consider how these first four amendments join together to form an umbrella of individual protection. As Kates concludes, "Not only are these rights phrased in substantially identical terms (the First, Second and Fourth Amendments all speak in terms of rights of 'the people'), but their roots [in the constitutional and common law of England], and the situations in which they were visualized as operating, are closely identified."[23]

Being prepared for self-defense was a moral imperative and a pragmatic necessity

Thus we see that as a result of several powerful influences — their Anglo-American philosophical heritage, their education in the English common law, and the impact of the realities of colonial life upon the daily conduct of their lives — "[t]o the Founders and their intellectual progenitors, being prepared for self-defense was a moral imperative as well as a pragmatic necessity."[24]

In the tradition from which the Second Amendment derives it was not only the unquestioned right, but a crucial element in the moral character of every free man that he be armed and willing to defend his family and community against crime. This duty included both individual acts and joining with his fellows in hunting criminals down when the hue and cry went up, as well as the more formally organized posse comitatus [literally, the power or authority of the county] — a body of persons summoned by the sheriff to assist in preserving the public peace.[25]

And this leads, rather logically and naturally, I think, to the clear and unequivocal words of the Second Amendment. The Founding Fathers intended that the people possess a right to be armed for duty in the general militia, as well as a right to keep and bear arms for their self-protection. In other words, for their generation and all succeeding generations of free Americans,

Every man should be armed

they intended that every man should be armed.

What follows next are the arms-rights provisions from the constitutions of the eight states that enacted a bill of rights prior to the adoption of the U.S. Constitution.

VIRGINIA
(June 12, 1776)

13. That a well-regulated militia, composed of the body of the people, trained to arms, is the proper, natural, and safe defence of a free state; that standing armies, in time of peace, should be avoided, as dangerous to liberty; and that in all cases, the military should be under strict subordination to, and governed by, the civil power.[26]

DELAWARE
(September 11, 1776)

18. That a well-regulated militia is the proper, natural and safe defence of a free government.[27]

PENNSYLVANIA
(September 28, 1776)

The people have a right to bear arms XIII. That the people have a right to bear arms for the defence of themselves and the state; and as standing armies in the time of peace are dangerous to liberty, they ought not to be kept up; and that the military should be kept under strict subordination to, and governed by, the civil power.[28]

MARYLAND
(November 11, 1776)

XXV. That a well-regulated militia is the proper and natural defence of a free government.[29]

NORTH CAROLINA
(December 18, 1776)

The people have a right to bear arms XVII. That the people have a right to bear arms, for the defence of the State; and, as standing armies, in time of peace, are dangerous to liberty, they ought not to be kept up; and that the military should be kept under the strict subordination to, and governed by, the civil power.[30]

VERMONT
(July 8, 1777)

XV. That the people have the right to bear arms for the defence of themselves and the State . . .[31]

MASSACHUSETTS
(October 25, 1780)

XVII. The people have a right to keep and bear arms for the common defence.[32]

NEW HAMPSHIRE
(June 2, 1784)

XXIV. A well regulated militia is the proper, natural, and safe defence of a state.[33]

In addition to these legislative enactments of bills or declarations of rights, there were numerous other proclamations being promulgated. For example:

Other proclamations and writings

INSTRUCTIONS OF TOWN MEETING, PRESTON, CONNECTICUT
(November 26, 1787)

It is our ardent wish that an efficient government may be established over these states so constructed that the people may retain all liberties, privileges, and immunities usual and necessary for citizens of a free country and yet sufficient provision made for carrying into execution all the powers vested in government. We are willing to give up such share of our rights as to enable government to support, defend, preserve the rest. It is difficult to draw the line. All will agree that the people should retain so much power that if ever venality and corruption should prevail in our public councils and government should be perverted and not answer the end of the institution, viz., the well being of society and the good of the whole, in that case the people may resume their rights and put an end to the wantonness of power. In whatever government the people neglect to retain so much power in their hands as to be a check to their rulers, depravity and the love of power is so prevalent in the humane mind, even of the best of men, that tyranny and cruelty will inevitably take place.[34]

MINORITY OF THE PENNSYLVANIA CONVENTION
(December 12, 1787)

The people have a right to bear arms

That the people have a right to bear arms for the defence of themselves and their own state, or the United States, or for the purpose of killing game; and no law shall be passed for disarming the people or any of them, unless for crimes committed, or real danger of public injury from individuals.[35]

DEBATES OF THE MASSACHUSETTS CONVENTION
(February 6, 1788)

Congress shall never prevent the keeping of arms

And that the said Constitution be never construed to authorize Congress to infringe the just liberty of the press, or the rights of conscience; or to prevent the people of the United States, who are peaceable citizens, from keeping their own arms.[36]

NEW HAMPSHIRE
RATIFICATION CONVENTION
(June 21, 1788)

Congress shall never disarm any citizen, unless such as are or have been in actual rebellion.[37]

Congress shall never disarm any citizen

VIRGINIA CONVENTION
(June 27, 1788)

17th. That the people have a right to keep and bear arms; that a well-regulated militia, composed of the body of the people trained to arms, is the proper, natural, and safe defence of a free state; that standing armies, in time of peace, are dangerous to liberty, and therefore ought to be avoided, as far as the circumstances and protection of the community will admit; and that, in all cases, the military should be under strict subordination to, and governed by, the civil power.[38]

The people have a right to bear arms

NEW YORK CONVENTION
(July 7, 1788)

That the militia should always be kept well organized, armed and disciplined, and include, according to past usages of the states, all the men capable of bearing arms, and that no regulations tending to render the general militia useless and defenceless, by establishing select corps of militia, of distinct bodies of military men, not having permanent interests and attachments to the community, ought to be made.[39]

NEW YORK CONVENTION
(July 26, 1788)

The people have a right to bear arms   That the people have the right to keep and bear arms; that a well-regulated militia, including the body of the people *capable of bearing arms,* is the proper, natural, and safe defence of a free state.[40] [Emphasis in original.]

RHODE ISLAND RATIFICATION CONVENTION
(May 29, 1790)

The people have a right to bear arms   XVII. That the people have a right to keep and bear arms; that a well-regulated militia, including the body of the people capable of bearing arms, is the proper, natural, and safe defence of a free state.[41]

We turn next to the public expressions of a number of statesmen, writers, and political philosophers of the colonial and post-colonial periods. These men were at the very top of the political and intellectual society of their time: many had been members of the Continental Congresses, four would go on to become president, one to become chief justice of the Supreme Court, and all were to enjoy long and distinguished careers of public service to their country. Obviously their views on constitutional issues had great influence on public opinion.

THOMAS PAINE

The peaceable part of mankind will be continually overrun by the vile and abandoned while they neglect the means of self-defence. The supposed quietude of a good man allures the ruffian; while on the other hand, arms like laws discourage and keep the invader and the plunderer in awe, and preserve order in the world as well as property. The balance of power is the scale of peace. The same balance would be preserved were all the world destitute of arms, for all would be alike; but since some *will* not, others *dare* not lay them aside. . . . Horrid mischief would ensue were one half the world deprived of the use of them; . . . the weak will become prey to the strong.[42] [Emphasis in original.]

The weak will become prey to the strong

THOMAS JEFFERSON

A strong body makes a strong mind. As to the species of exercises, I advise the gun. While this gives moderate exercise to the body, it gives boldness, enterprise and independence to the mind. Games played with the ball and others of that nature, are too violent for the body and stamp no character on the mind. Let your gun therefore be the constant companion of your walks.[43]

No Free man shall ever be debarred the use of arms.[44]

[W]hat country can preserve it[]s liberties if their rulers are not warned from time to time that their people preserve the spirit of resistance? Let

The tree of liberty must be refreshed with the blood of patriots

them take arms, the remedy is to set them right as to facts, pardon & pacify them. What signify a few lives lost in a century or two? The tree of liberty must be refreshed from time to time with the blood of patriots & tyrants. It is nature's manure.[45]

PATRICK HENRY

The militia, sir, is our ultimate safety. We can have no security without it. . . . The great object is, that every man be armed. . . . Everyone who is able may have a gun.[46]

Congress, by the power of taxation, by that of raising an army, and by their control over the militia, have the sword in one hand, and the purse in the other. Shall we be safe without either? Congress have an unlimited power over both: they

No nation ever retained its liberty after the loss of the sword and the purse

are entirely given up by us. Let him candidly tell me, where and when did freedom exist, when the sword and purse were given up from the people? Unless a miracle in human affairs interposed, no nation ever retained its liberty after the loss of the sword and the purse.[47]

GEORGE WASHINGTON

Mercenary armies . . . have at one time or another subverted the liberties of almost all the Countries they have been raised to defend . . .[48]

JOHN ADAMS

Arms in the hands of citizens [may] be used at individual discretion . . . in private self-defence.[49]

SAMUEL ADAMS

. . . and that the said Constitution be never construed to infringe the just liberty of the press or the
rights of conscience; or to prevent the people of the
United States who are peaceable citizens from
keeping their own arms; or to raise standing armies,
unless when necessary for the defence of the United
States or of some one or more of them; or to prevent
the people from petitioning, in a peaceful and or-
derly manner, the Federal Legislature for a redress
of grievances; or to subject the people to unreasonable searches and seizures of their persons, papers,
or possessions.[50]

JAMES MADISON

As the greatest danger is that of disunion of the
states, it is necessary to guard against it by sufficient powers to the common government; and as
the greatest danger to liberty is from large standing
armies, it is best to prevent them by an effectual
provision for a good militia.[51]

Let a regular army, fully equal to the resources *The*
of the country, be formed; and let it be entirely at *Federalist,*
the devotion of the federal government; still it *No. 46*
would not be going too far to say, that the state
governments with the people on their side would
be able to repel the danger. The highest number to
which, according to the best computation, a standing army can be carried in any country, does not
exceed one hundredth part of the whole number of

souls; or one twenty-fifth of the number able to bear arms. This proportion would not yield in the United States an army of more than twenty-five or thirty thousand men. To these would be opposed a militia amounting to near half a million of citizens with arms in their hands, officered by men chosen from among themselves, fighting for their common liberties, and united and conducted by governments possessing their affections and confidence. It may well be doubted whether a militia thus circumstanced could ever be conquered by such a proportion of regular troops. Those who are best acquainted with the late successful resistance of this country against the British arms will be most inclined to deny the possibility of it. *Besides the* **Americans** *advantage of being armed, which the Americans* **possess** *possess over the people of almost every other* **the** *nation,* the existence of subordinate governments **advantage** to which the people are attached, and by which the **of being** militia officers are appointed, forms a barrier **armed** against the enterprises of ambition, more insurmountable than any which a simple government of any form can admit of. *Notwithstanding the military establishments in the several kingdoms of Europe, which are carried as far as the public resources will bear, the governments are afraid to trust the people with arms. And it is not certain that with this aid alone [mere quiet private possession of ordinary personal firearms], they would not be able to shake off their yokes.*[52] [Emphasis added.]

Of all the grievances catalogued by Jefferson in the Declaration of Independence, none were more grievous than those connected with the British military rule in the Colonies. The basic objection of the Colonists was to the existence in their midst of a large standing army, which included a number of foreign mercenaries, including the despised Hessians. It is no accident that the wheat farmers of Virginia dubbed a destructive insect the "Hessian fly."[53]

I believe there are more instances of the abridgment of the freedom of the people by gradual and silent encroachments of those in power than by violent and sudden usurpations.[54]

Freedom is abridged by silent encroachment

ALEXANDER HAMILTON

Little more can reasonably be aimed at with respect to the people at large than to have them properly armed and equipped; . . . This will not only lessen the call for military establishments; but if circumstances should at any time oblige the government to form an army of any magnitude, that army can never be formidable to the liberties of the people, while there is a large body of citizens, little, if at all, inferior to them in discipline and the use of arms, who stand ready to defend their rights and those of their fellow citizens.[55]

GEORGE MASON

To disarm the people [is] the best and most effectual way to enslave them . . .[56]

Who are the militia? They consist now of the whole people, except a few public officers.[57]

An instance within the memory of some of this House, will show us how our militia may be destroyed. Forty years ago, when the resolution of enslaving America was formed in Great Britain, the British Parliament was advised by an artful man [Sir William Keith], who was governor of Pennsylvania, to disarm the people; that was the most effectual way to enslave them; but they should not do it openly; but to weaken them, and let them sink gradually, by totally disusing and neglecting the militia.[58]

FEDERAL FARMER
(RICHARD HENRY LEE)

The yeomanry of the country possess the arms

It is true, the yeomanry of the country possess the lands, the weight of property, possess arms, and are too strong a body of men to be openly offended — and, therefore, it is urged, they will take care of themselves, that men who shall govern will not dare pay any disrespect to their opinions. [But] they may in twenty or thirty years be by means imperceptible to them, totally deprived of that boasted weight and strength: This may be done in great measure by Congress, if disposed to do it, by modeling the militia. Should one fifth, or one eighth part of the men capable of bearing arms, be made a select militia, as has been proposed, and those the young and ardent part of the community, possessed of but little or no property, and all the others put upon a plan that will render them of no importance, the former will answer all the purposes of an army, while the latter will be defenceless.[59]

JOEL BARLOW

Only admit the original, unalterable truth, that all men are equal in superstructure requires no effort but that of natural deduction. Then their rights, and the foundation of everything is laid; to build the first necessary deduction will be, that, the people will form an equal representative government. . . . Another deduction follows, that the people will be universally armed. . . . A people that legislate for themselves ought to be in the habit of protecting themselves, or they will lose the spirit of both.[60]

ELBRIDGE GERRY

What, sir, is the use of a militia? It is to prevent the establishment of a standing army, the bane of liberty.[61]

A standing army is the bane of liberty

ZACHARIAH JOHNSTON

The people are not to be disarmed of their weapons. They are left in full possession of them.[62]

TENCH COXE

[Should tyranny threaten, the] friends . . . of liberty . . . using those arms which Providence has put into their hands, will make a solemn appeal to *"the power above"*. . . . The militia, *who are in fact the effective part of the people at large,* will render many troops *quite unnecessary*. They will form a *powerful check* upon the regular troops, and will generally be sufficient to *overawe* them.[63] [Emphasis in original.]

ST. GEORGE TUCKER

The Second Amendment is the true palladium of liberty

This [Amendment] may be seen as the true palladium [safeguard] of liberty. The right of self defence is the first law of nature; in most governments it has been the study of rulers to confine this right within the narrowest limits possible. Wherever standing armies are kept up, and the right of the people to keep and bear arms is, under any color or pretext whatsoever, prohibited, liberty, if not already annihilated, is on the brink of destruction. In England, the people have been disarmed, generally under the specious pretext of preserving the game; . . . True it is, their bill of rights seems at first view to counteract this policy, but the right of bearing arms is confined to Protestants, and the words "suitable to their condition or degree" have been interpreted to authorize the prohibition of keeping a gun or other engine for the destruction of game, to any farmer, or inferior tradesman, or other person not qualified to kill game . . . so that not one man in five hundred can keep a gun in his house without being subject to a penalty.[64]

HENRY ST. GEORGE TUCKER

The right of bearing arms — which with us is not limited and restrained by an arbitrary system of game laws as in England; but, is particularly enjoyed by every citizen, and is among his most valuable privileges, since it furnishes the means of resisting as a freeman ought, the inroads of usurpation.[65]

Now the natural right of self defence is nothing more than the liberty which the law of nature allows us of defending ourselves from an attack which is made upon our persons or of taking such measures as may guard against any injuries we are likely to suffer from another . . .

. . . [A]s the law of nature allows us to defend ourselves, and imposes no limit upon the right, the only limit we can impose is the necessity of the case. Whatever means are necessary must be lawful; for the rule is general, that where a right is absolutely given, the mean to exercise it must also follow.[66]

A CITIZEN OF AMERICA
(NOAH WEBSTER)

Before a standing army can rule, the people must be disarmed; as they are in almost every kingdom in Europe. The supreme power in America cannot enforce unjust laws by the sword; because the whole body of the people are armed, and constitute a force superior to any bands of regular troops that

Before a standing army can rule, the people must be disarmed

can be, on any pretence, raised in the United States.[67]

WILLIAM RAWLE

In the Second Article, it is declared, that a *well regulated militia is necessary to the security of a free state;* a proposition from which few will dissent. Although in actual war, the services of regular troops are confessedly more valuable; yet while peace prevails, and in the commencement of a war before a regular force can be raised, the militia form the palladium [safeguard] of the country. . . .

The corollary from the first position is, that *the right of the people to keep and bear arms shall not be infringed*. [Emphasis in original.]

No clause in the Constitution could be conceived to give Congress the power to disarm the people

No clause in the Constitution could by any rule of construction be conceived to give the Congress a power to disarm the people. Such a flagitious [infamous or scandalous] attempt could only be made under some general pretence by a state legislature. *But if in any blind pursuit of inordinate power either should attempt it, this amendment may be appealed to as a restraint on both*. [Emphasis added.]

In most of the countries of Europe, this right does not seem to be denied, although it is allowed more or less sparingly, according to circumstances. In England, a country which boasts so much of its freedom, the right was assured to Protestant subjects only, on the revolution of 1688, and it is cautiously described to be that of bearing arms for their defence "suitable to their conditions, and as allowed by law." An arbitrary code for the preservation of game in that country has long disgraced them.[68]

JOSEPH STORY

The importance of this article will scarcely be doubted by any persons who have duly reflected upon the subject. The militia is the natural defense of a free country. . . . The right of the citizens to keep and bear arms has justly been considered, as the palladium [safeguard] of the liberties of a Republic; since it offers a strong moral check against the usurpation and arbitrary power of rulers; and will generally, even if these are successful in the first instance, enable the people to resist and triumph over them. . . .

The right to keep and bear arms is a strong moral check against the arbitrary power of rulers

A similar provision in favor of Protestants (for to them it is confined) is to be found in the bill of rights of 1688, it being declared "the subjects, which are Protestants, may have arms for their defense suitable to their condition, and as allowed by law." But under various pretenses the effect of this provision has been greatly narrowed; and it is at present in England more nominal than real as a defensive privilege.[69]

THOMAS M. COOLEY

The second amendment . . . like most other provisions in the Constitution, has a history. It was adopted, with some modification and enlargement, from the English Bill of Rights of 1689, where it stood as a protest against the arbitrary action of the overturned dynasty in disarming the people, and as a pledge of the new rulers that this tyrannical action should cease . . .

The right declared was meant to be a strong moral check against the usurpation and arbitrary power of rulers, and as a necessary and efficient means of regaining rights when temporarily overturned by usurpation.

The right is general. *It may be supposed from the phraseology of this provision that the right to keep and bear arms was only guaranteed to the militia; but this would be an interpretation not warranted by the intent.* The militia, as has been explained elsewhere, consists of those persons who, under the laws, are liable to the performance of military duty, and are officered and enrolled for service when called upon. . . . [I]f the right were limited to those enrolled, the purpose of the guarantee might be defeated altogether by the action or the neglect to act of the government it was meant to hold in check. *The meaning of the provision undoubtedly is, that the people, from whom the militia must be taken, shall have the right to keep and bear arms, and they need no permission or regulation of law for the purpose.* But this enables the government to have a well regulated militia; for to bear arms implies something more than mere keeping; it implies the learning to handle and use

The people need no permission to keep and bear arms

them in a way that makes those who keep them ready for their efficient use; in other words, it implies the right to meet for voluntary discipline in arms, observing in so doing the laws of public order.[70] [Emphasis added.]

Of the documents reproduced on the preceding pages, none was more influential than Madison's *The Federalist,* No. 46. Madison was the most important political leader in the constitutional debates that were to decide, first, whether there would be amendments added to the Constitution; second, what rights would be enumerated; and third, what the specific language of each proposed amendment would be.

It is ironic that Madison, a staunch Federalist, became the drafter of the Bill of Rights after his initial strong opposition to having the Constitution amended in any way. But during the bitter ratification debates, recognizing the growing popularity of the Anti-federalist cause and fearful of not being elected to the House of Representatives if he continued to endorse the increasingly unpopular Federalist position, Madison changed his viewpoint and pledged to work for an adoption of the Bill of Rights in the first Congress.

And as we know, indeed he did. Further, given **Madison** Madison's considerable skills as a precise legal **drafts the** draftsman, just how he went about drafting the **Bill of** provisions regarding the right to keep and bear **Rights** arms, as well as the exact language he used, is compelling evidence of what he understood that right to mean. As David Hardy points out:

> Madison's initial Bill of Rights proposals have two features which merit comment. First, contrary to some claims that "right of the people" connoted a state rather than an individual right, Madison's plan used "right of the people" to describe freedom of speech, press and other clearly individual rights.
>
> A second noteworthy aspect of Madison's plan is organization. Today, of course, we are accustomed to a Bill of Rights structured as a number of amendments, generally printed following the Constitution. But Madison envisioned amendments written to be inter-lineated with the Constitution's text. Thus we can determine exactly what the context in which each right was seen. If Madison had seen the right to bear arms as primarily restricting federal power over state militia, he probably would have designated it as an amendment to Article I, sec. 8, which contains the federal power to organize and call out the militia. Instead, he grouped the right to keep and bear arms with freedom of speech and similar rights and placed it after Article I, sec. 9. There, it would follow the guarantees of individual rights in the original Constitution (viz., limitations on suspension of habeas corpus and enactment of bills of attainer or ex post facto laws).[71]

Madison places the right to keep and bear arms alongside our other individual freedoms

Or, as Professor Nicholas J. Johnson observes:

> Indeed, it is hardly credible to assume that the term "the People" was intended [by Madison] to protect the rights of private individuals to assemble

peaceably and petition the government in the First Amendment, was somehow transformed in the Second into a right of states, and then miraculously was returned to a right of private individuals to be secure in their persons, houses, papers and effects in the Fourth Amendment.[72]

Or, in the words of Professor William Van Alstyne:

The postulation of a "right of the people to keep and bear Arms" would make sense standing alone, however, even if it necessarily left some questions still to be settled. It would make sense in just the same unforced way we understand even upon a first reading of the neighboring clause in the Bill of Rights, which uses the exact same phrase in describing something as "the right of the people" that "shall not be violated" (or "infringed"). Just as the Second Amendment declares that "the right of the people to keep and bear Arms[] shall not be infringed," so, too, the Fourth Amendment declares:

> The right of the people to be secure in their persons, houses, papers, and effects, against unreasonable searches and seizures, shall not be violated. . . .

Here, in the familiar setting of the Fourth Amendment, we are not at all confused in our take on the meaning of the amendment; it secures to each of us personally (as well as to all of us collectively) a certain right — even if we are also uncertain of its scope. Nor are we confused in turning to other clauses. For example, the Sixth Amendment provides:

> In all criminal prosecutions, the accused shall enjoy the right of a speedy and public trial. . . .

The right of the people to keep and bear arms is equal to their right to be secure in their homes . . .

. . . the right to a speedy trial . . .

**... and
the right
to trial
by jury**

And so, too, the Seventh Amendment provides:

> In Suits at common law, where the value in
> controversy shall exceed twenty dollars, the right
> of trial by jury shall be preserved. . . .

That each of these rights — that all of these rights
— are examples of personal rights protected by the
Bill of Rights seems perfectly clear.[73]

How incontrovertible does the meaning of the
Second Amendment become with the benefit of
these insights!

If you will permit the italics I am going to supply,
let's read the Amendment again:

**A reading
of the
Second
Amendment
as the
Founding
Fathers
must have
understood
it to mean**

A well regulated militia [*that is, well functioning, and well trained in the use of ordinary personal firearms*] **being necessary to the security
of a free state** [*we have seen all the evils atten-
dant to the existence of a standing army and know
that our personal and community safety and security, as well as our freedom, must come from
ourselves, equipped with our own arms and ammunition, trained (or well regulated) by ourselves,
organized and led by ourselves*], **the right of the
people** [*an individual right just as we possess
in the First, Fourth, Sixth, and Seventh Amendments; not the state's collective right to form a
select militia that might become, under certain
circumstances, the equivalent of a standing army
in our midst*] **to keep and bear arms shall not be
infringed.**

B
A SELECTION OF SECOND AMENDMENT COMMENTARY APPEARING IN THE POPULAR PRESS IN COLONIAL TIMES

As I studied the debates that took place during the colonial period regarding the purpose and meaning of a federal bill of rights, I came to perceive a close, and at first glance unusual, conjunction between the First and Second Amendments. Now, why should that be? After all, in one way or another, all of the amendments in the Bill of Rights — certainly the first eight, anyway — specifically ratify various individual civil liberties. So why did the First and Second Amendments seem to the colonists to be allied in some special way? I believe that it was because they recognized that these rights, before all others, were absolutely critical to the survival of their new republic; that without these rights liberty was not possible. It was not by accident, I think, that in the final draft that was adopted and ratified, the framers of the Bill of Rights chose to position the freedoms of speech and arms-bearing as the first two amendments in the document.

The relationship between the First and Second Amendment

You see, we know that the Founding Fathers were well aware of the significance of an event that had occurred 56 years earlier, in 1735 (when Jefferson and Madison were yet to be born and George Washington was only three years old). That event was the trial in New York City of John Peter Zenger, printer of the *New-York Weekly Journal,* for seditious libel based upon a series of attacks Zenger had made in his paper upon the character of William Cosby, governor of the colony of New York. The trial judge accurately instructed the jury that under the common-law definition Zenger's printed criticisms were considered seditious libel. But after hearing the defense's argument that the cause of liberty demanded the press have the right to speak and write the truth, the jury ignored the judge's instructions and found Zenger not guilty. His acquittal was to become a dominant symbol of the colonist's right to maintain a free press.[1]

Peter Zenger's acquittal on a charge of libel became a symbol of the right to a free press

And how free (and freewheeling) these colonial newspapers were! Today, for fear of lawsuits, our newspapers and television networks generally opt for safety and blandness. But the early colonial newspapers — chief among them the *Boston Evening Post, Boston Gazette, Boston Newsletter, Providence Gazette & Country Journal, New York Courier and Enquirer, New York Statesman and Evening Advertiser, New York Gazette and Mercury,* and *Pennsylvania Gazette* — were aggressive, rude, unabashedly partisan, and tremendously influential.

"The influence and circulation of [colonial] newspapers is great beyond any thing ever known in Europe," an English visitor wrote. "Newspapers penetrate to every crevice of the [country]."[2] And these newspapers were carrying not only news about America but crucial editorial commentary about America's new government.

For as English editor and censor Roger L'Estrange cautioned in 1663, "A public newspaper makes the multitude too familiar with the actions and counsels of its superiors, too pragmatical and censorious, and gives them, not only an itch, but a kind of colourable right and licence to be meddling with the government."[3]

"In the decade leading up to the American Revolution," wrote Mitchell Stephens, "a hostile press certainly created unrest and helped dissolve whatever union of opinion had existed between British officials and their American subjects. But the true power of the pre-Revolutionary press is not to be found in its ability to wound the British. The true power of this press was its ability to enfranchise and unify the Americans. . . . It helped the inhabitants of the colonies imagine themselves Americans."[4]

The true power of the press was to unify Americans

The colonial newspapers were to become the most powerful weapon in the struggle to persuade the people to join in what John Adams called "the real American revolution,"[5] a conviction later to be echoed by these words of James Madison: "A popular government without popular information, or the means of acquiring it, is but a prologue to farce or a tragedy."[6]

Of course, in colonial times there was no radio or television. Newspapers — particularly those in the major urban centers of Boston, New York, and Philadelphia — were the only means for literate members of the population to acquire news and informed opinion. Throughout the entire colonial period, major newspapers enjoyed substantial circulation growth, year after year, and there is ample evidence that their pages were avidly read and discussed. Of particular interest to readers were editorials on the debates then being conducted, debates over whether the Constitution should be amended to include a bill of rights, and more specifically, debates over an amendment restricting the federal government from forming select militias and at the same time enunciating the right of free and law-abiding citizens to keep and bear arms.

Here is a representative sampling of commentary on Second Amendment issues that appeared in the popular press at the time.

BOSTON JOURNAL OF THE TIMES

Instances of the licentious and outrageous behavior of the *military conservators* still multiply upon us, some of which are of such nature, and have been carried to such lengths, as must serve fully to evince that a late vote of this town, calling upon its inhabitants to provide themselves with arms for their defence, was a measure as *prudent* as it was *legal* . . . It is a natural right which the people have reserved to themselves, confirmed by the [English]

It was prudent and legal for citizens to arm themselves for their defense

Bill of Rights to keep arms for their own defence; and as Mr. Blackstone observes: it is to be made use of when the sanctions of society and law are found insufficient to restrain the violence of oppression. [Emphasis in original.]

1768

BOSTON EVENING POST
(Unknown author, defending a vote by Boston colonists requesting their fellow citizens to purchase arms)

Nor is there a person either in or out of Parliament, who has justly stated and proved one single act of that town, as a public body, to be, we will not say treasonable or seditious, but even at all illegal. . . . For it is certainly beyond human art and sophistry, to prove the British subjects, to whom the *privilege* of bearing arms is expressly recognized by the [English] Bill of Rights, and who live in a Province where the law requires them to be equipped with *arms,* &c. are guilty of an *illegal act,* in calling upon one another to be supplied with them, as the law *directs*. [Emphasis in original.]

One who is required to bear arms cannot be guilty of asking another to be supplied with them

April 3, 1769

NORTH CAROLINA GAZETTE
(NEWBURN)

[I]t is the Right of every English subject to be prepared with Weapons for his Defence.

July 7, 1775

BOSTON INDEPENDENT CHRONICLE

It was in the law of nature for every man to defend himself

It was absolutely necessary to carry arms for fear of pirates, &c. and . . . their arms were all stamped with peace, that they were never to be used but in case of hostile attack, that it was in the law of nature for every man to defend himself, and unlawful for any man to deprive him of those weapons of self defence.

October 25, 1787

NEW YORK JOURNAL
(Unknown author, writing under the pseudonym "Brutus")

When a building is to be erected which is intended to stand for ages, the foundation should be firmly laid. The constitution proposed to your acceptance, is designed not for yourselves alone, but for generations yet unborn. The principles, therefore, upon which the social compact is founded, ought to have been clearly and precisely stated, and the most express and full declaration of rights to have been made. . . .

. . . The common good, therefore, is the end of civil government, and common consent, the foundation on which it is established.

To effect this end, it was necessary that a certain portion of natural liberty should be surrendered, in order, that what remained should be preserved. . . .

But it is not necessary, for this purpose, that individuals should relinquish all their natural rights. Some are of such a nature that they cannot be surrendered. Of this kind are the rights of conscience, the right of enjoying and defending life, &c. [S]o in forming a government on its true principles, the foundation should be laid in the manner I before stated, by expressly reserving to the people such of their essential rights, as are not necessary to be parted with.

November 1, 1787

BOSTON HERALD AMERICAN
(Unknown Anti-federalist author, writing under the pseudonym "John De Witt")

It is asserted by the most respectable writers upon the Government, that a well regulated militia, composed of the yeomanry of the country have ever been considered as the bulwark of a free society. . . .

. . . Every writer upon government — Locke, Sidney, Hamden, and a list of others — have uniformly asserted, that standing armies are a solecism [mistake] in any government, that no nation ever supported them, that did not resort to, rely on, and finally become a prey to them. . . .

. . . [T]he first policy of tyrants has been to annihilate all other means of national activity and defence, and to rely solely upon standing troops. . . .

Every writer upon government has asserted that standing armies are a mistake

. . . Pisistratus in Greece, and Dionysius in Syracuse, Charles in France, and Henry in England, all cloaked their villainous intentions under an idea of raising a small body for a guard to their persons.

December 3, 1787

CONNECTICUT COURANT
(HARTFORD)
(Unknown author, writing under the pseudonym "the Republican")

Oppressed and dispirited people neither possess arms nor know how to use them

In countries under arbitrary government, the people oppressed and dispirited neither possess arms nor know how to use them. Tyrants never feel secure until they have disarmed the people. They can rely upon nothing but standing armies of mercenary troops for the support of their power. But the people of this country have arms in their hands; they are not destitute of military knowledge; every citizen is required by law to be a soldier; we are marshaled into companies, regiments, and brigades for the defence of our country. This is a circumstance which increases the power and consequence of the people; and enables them to defend their rights and privileges against every invader.

January 7, 1788

PENNSYLVANIA GAZETTE
(PHILADELPHIA)
(Tench Coxe, writing in support of the proposed
Constitution, under the pseudonym
"a Pennsylvanian")

The power of the sword, say the minority of Pennsylvania, is in the hands of Congress. My friends
and countrymen, it is not so, for THE POWERS **The powers**
OF THE SWORD ARE IN THE HANDS OF **of the**
sword are
THE YEOMANRY OF AMERICA FROM SIX- **in the**
TEEN TO SIXTY. The militia of these free com- **yeomanry**
monwealths, entitled and accustomed to their
arms, when compared to any possible army must
be *tremendous and irresistible*. Who are these
militia? [A]re they not our selves. Is it feared, then,
that we shall turn our arms *each against his own*
bosom. Congress have no power to disarm the
militia. Their swords, and every other terrible implement of the soldier, are *the birthright of an*
American. . . . [T]he unlimited power of the sword
is not in the hands of either the *federal or state*
governments, but, where I trust in God it will ever
remain, *in the hands of the people*. [Emphasis in
original.]

February 20, 1788

WINCHESTER GAZETTE (VIRGINIA)

There are other things so clearly out of the power
of Congress, that the bare recital of them is suffi-

cient. I mean "rights of conscience, or religious liberty — the rights of bearing arms for defence, or for killing game — the liberty of fowling, hunting and fishing . . ."

February 22, 1788

FREEMAN'S JOURNAL
(PHILADELPHIA)

It is very difficult to regain freedom once lost

The freemen of America will remember, that it is very easy to change a *free* government into an arbitrary, despotic, or *military one:* but it is very difficult, almost impossible to reverse the matter — very difficult to regain *freedom* once lost. [Emphasis in original.]

March 5, 1788

PENNSYLVANIA GAZETTE
(PHILADELPHIA)
(Unknown author, writing under the pseudonym "Philodemos")

Every free man has *a right to the use of the press*, so he has to *the use of his arms*. [B]ut if he commits [libel], he abuses his privilege, as unquestionably as if he were to plunge his sword into the bosom of a fellow citizen. [Emphasis in original.]

March 8, 1788

STATE GAZETTE OF SOUTH CAROLINA
(CHARLESTON)
(Unknown author, writing under the pseudonym "M.T. Cicero")

No free government was ever founded, or ever preserved in its liberty, without uniting the characters of the citizen and soldier in those destined for the defence of the state. . . . Such are a well regulated militia, composed of the freeholders, citizen and husbandman, who take up arms to preserve their property, *as individuals,* and their rights as freemen. [Emphasis added.]

The characters of the citizen and the soldier are united for defense of the state

September 8, 1788

PENNSYLVANIA GAZETTE
(PHILADELPHIA)
(Reverend Nicholas Collin, writing under the pseudonym "Foreign Spectator")

While the people have property, arms in their hands, and only a spark of a noble spirit, the most corrupt congress must be mad to form any project of tyranny.

November 7, 1788

FEDERAL GAZETTE (PHILADELPHIA)
(Tench Coxe, writing in support of the proposed
Bill of Rights, under the pseudonym
"a Pennsylvanian")

As civil rulers, not having their duty to the people duly before them, may attempt to tyrannize, and as the military forces which must be occasionally raised to defend our country, might pervert their power to the injury of their fellow-citizens, the people are confirmed by the next article [the Second Amendment] in their right to keep and bear their private arms.

June 18, 1789

FEDERAL GAZETTE (PHILADELPHIA)
(Unknown author, writing under the pseudonym
"One of the People")

Let these truths sink deep into our hearts: that the people are the masters of their rulers and that rulers are the servants of the people — that men cannot *give* to themselves what they *own* from nature — that a free government is no more than a few plain directions to a number of servants, how to take care of a part of their master's property — and that a master reserves to himself the exclusive care of all that property, and of *every thing else* which he has not committed to the care of those servants. [Emphasis in original.]

A free government is no more than a few plain directions to a number of servants

July 2, 1789

PHILADELPHIA INDEPENDENT GAZETTEER
(Samuel Bryan, prominent Anti-federalist,
writing under the pseudonym "Centinel")

It is remarkable that this article (the Second Amendment) only makes the observation, "that a well regulated militia, composed of the *body* of the people, is the best security of a free state;" *it does not ordain, or constitutionally provide for, the establishment of such a one.* The absolute command vested by other sections [of the Constitution] in Congress over the militia, are not in the least abridged by this amendment. The militia may still be subjected to martial law . . . may still be marched from state to state and made the unwilling instruments of crushing the last efforts of expiring liberty. [Emphasis added.]

The Second Amendment does not ordain, or constitutionally provide for, the establishment of a militia

September 9, 1789

GAZETTE OF THE UNITED STATES
(NEW YORK)
(Extract of letter from Fayetteville, North
Carolina, dated September 12, 1789)

The right of the people to keep and bear arms has been recognized by the General Government; but the best security of that right after all is that military spirit, that taste for martial exercises, which has always distinguished the free citizens of these

Such men form the best barrier to the liberties of America States. . . . Such men form the best barrier to the liberties of America.

October 14, 1789

BOSTON INDEPENDENT CHRONICLE
(Reporting a speech delivered by George Washington to Congress on January 7, 1790)

A free people ought . . . to be armed . . .

January 8, 1790

PROVIDENCE GAZETTE &
COUNTRY JOURNAL
(Reporting on the proposed Bill of Rights)

. . . that the right of the citizens to bear arms in defence of themselves and the State, and to assemble peaceably together . . . shall not be questioned.

January 30, 1790

PROVIDENCE GAZETTE &
COUNTRY JOURNAL
(Reporting on the proposed Bill of Rights)

. . . the people have a right to keep and bear arms . . . [and] . . . that a well-regulated militia include[s] the body of the people capable of bearing arms.

June 5, 1790

PHILADELPHIA
INDEPENDENT GAZETTEER
(Unknown author, writing under the pseudonym
"a Farmer")

Whenever people . . . [i]ntrust the defence of their country to a regular, standing army, composed of mercenaries, the power of that country will remain under the direction and influence of the most wealthy citizens.

January 29, 1791

With a standing army, power will remain under the direction and influence of the most wealthy citizens

C
THE STATE
OF THE LAW

S ince I began working on this book in 1995,
whenever the opportunity presented itself I
have been asking people what they know about the
Second Amendment and the issue of gun control in
this country. And what I learned is that most of
them, surprisingly, had no idea that the Second
Amendment standing alone may provide no protection whatsoever from the enactment of gun control or prohibition laws by states and other local
legislative bodies.

Apparently these people believe that because
the Supreme Court has employed the Fourteenth
Amendment to create an umbrella of federal protection to restrain states from interfering with many
of our individual rights, the right to keep and bear
arms is included among them. That just isn't so,
yet. Let's review how this came to be.

When the U.S. Constitution, including its Bill of
Rights, was drafted and ratified it was a *federal*
instrument, setting forth the powers (along with
restraints against the power) of the federal government. Other than a few minor exceptions and one
clearly stated mandate, "The Citizens of each State
shall be entitled to all Privileges and Immunities of
Citizens in the several States,"[1] the document

**Many do
not realize
that the
Bill of
Rights
was enacted
to restrain
only
federal
action**

mentions nothing of state laws as relating to individual freedoms. Obviously none of the individual rights contained in the Bill of Rights were intended by the framers of the Constitution to have any force and effect upon state law.

Many states enacted their own bills of rights

Of course, in the colonial period many states had enacted state bills of rights or constitutions that included guarantees of many of the rights that were also set forth in the federal Bill of Rights. Individuals residing in such states therefore enjoyed protection against the infringement of only the rights that had been guaranteed to them under their state law. But not all states guaranteed all the federal rights; and in fact, some states provided no individual rights protection whatsoever. Furthermore, from state to state there was no uniformity of the rights protected, nor was there uniformity of the constitutional language defining them.

This was the situation until "black codes" were passed during the Reconstruction period

This was the state of our constitutional law for roughly the next eighty years after ratification of the Constitution in 1789 and ratification of its Bill of Rights in 1791. But after Appomattox, dramatic events began taking place during the Reconstruction period that were to cause a substantial change in our constitutional law.

"After the Civil War," as Michael Quinlan reports, "a number of Southern states passed laws that sought to limit the rights of newly freed slaves. These 'black codes' were little more than reincarnations of the former slave codes. The killings, hangings, beatings, and denials of civil rights (including the right to keep and bear arms) committed by the Ku Klux Klan and other radical groups to keep newly freed black citizens shackled to their former slave status demanded federal intervention. In reaction to these oppressive state laws and civil rights violations, Congress enacted both the Civil Rights Act and the Freedman's Bureau Act in 1866 to secure the federal constitutional rights of African-Americans."[2] It also enacted the Thirteenth Amendment, which prohibits slavery or involuntary servitude except as a punishment for crime (ratified December 6, 1865); and the Fourteenth Amendment (ratified July 9, 1868). Of all of this legislation, by far the most profound in terms of its influence on constitutional law is the Fourteenth Amendment.

The Fourteenth Amendment covers a variety of governmental matters, but its most important section is the first, which reads as follows:

The Fourteenth Amendment was passed to extend federal protection to citizens of every state

All persons born or naturalized in the United States, and subject to the jurisdiction thereof, are citizens of the United States and of the State wherein they reside. No State shall make or enforce any law which shall abridge the privileges and immunities of citizens of the United States; nor shall any State deprive any person of life, liberty, or property, without due process of law; nor deny to any person within its jurisdiction the equal protection of the laws.

These words set forth broadly stated powers with far-reaching implications. So, as you might imagine, the interpretation of this section by the Supreme Court — particularly its three principal clauses, the "privileges and immunities" clause; the "due process" clause; and the "equal protection" clause — has been a matter of considerable controversy and constitutional litigation throughout the last hundred years.

The doctrine of incorporation

Beginning in 1897, the Supreme Court began selectively to "incorporate" certain of the individual rights contained in the Bill of Rights into the Fourteenth Amendment, thus requiring states to observe each of the selected rights.

There is no question that the framers of the Fourteenth Amendment fully intended it to be used as a vehicle for incorporation. According to Stephen P. Halbrook:

> A chief exponent of the amendment, Senator Jacob M. Howard (R. Mich.), in referring to "the personal rights guaranteed and secured by the first eight amendments of the Constitution; such as freedom of speech and the press; . . . *the right to keep and bear arms* . . ." argued that the adoption of fourteenth amendment protection was necessary to protect these rights against state legislation. "The great object of the first section of the amendment is, therefore, to restrain the power of the States and compel them at all times to respect these great fundamental guarantees."[3] [Emphasis added.]

And who could be better qualified to define the meaning of Section 1 than its drafter, Representative John A. Bingham (R. Ohio)? Halbrook provides us this important excerpt from Bingham's speech from the floor of the House:

> Mr. Speaker, that the scope and meaning of the limitations imposed by the first section, fourteenth amendment of the Constitution may be more fully understood, permit me to say that the privileges and immunities of citizens of the United States . . . are chiefly defined in the first eight amendments to the Constitution of the United States. Those eight amendments are as follows. [Bingham then goes on to recite the first eight amendments.] These eight articles I have shown never were limitations upon the power of the States, until made so by the fourteenth amendment. The words of that amendment . . . are an express prohibition upon every state in the Union.[4]

"The words of the Fourteenth Amendment are an express prohibition upon every state"

"This is a most explicit statement of the incorporation thesis by the architect of the Fourteenth Amendment," comments Halbrook. "[Although] Representative Bingham based his theory of incorporation on the privileges and immunities clause and not the due process clause as did subsequent court decisions . . . the legislative history supports the view that the incorporation of amendments I through VIII was clear and unmistakable in the minds of the framers of the Fourteenth Amendment."[5]

The Supreme Court has incorporated many rights into state law

Through a number of landmark decisions during the first half of the twentieth century, the Supreme Court began applying the due process clause of the Fourteenth Amendment to incorporate into state law most of the individual rights guaranteed by the Bill of Rights, among them the rights of free speech, religion, petition, and assembly; the right to protection from unreasonable searches and seizures; the right to trial by jury, to the assistance of legal counsel, and to the confrontation of witnesses; the right to protection from self-incrimination and double jeopardy; and the right to protection from cruel and unusual punishments.

Despite the unmistakable legislative intent of Congress as indicated by the statements of Senator Howard and Representative Bingham, notably absent from the list of individual rights the Supreme Court has chosen to incorporate is the Second Amendment (as well as the Third and Seventh Amendments, the right to indictment under the Fifth Amendment, and protection from excessive bail under the Eighth Amendment).

But notably absent is the Second Amendment

And of the rights that have yet to be incorporated, none has generated as much controversy as the Second Amendment. Given the ample opportunities that the Supreme Court has had to engage Second Amendment issues — not only the general question of whether its guarantee of rights should be incorporated into state law by means of the due process clause of the Fourteenth Amendment, but also important specific questions such as the meaning of each of its words (what are constitutionally protected private "arms," for example?) — it is difficult to understand the Court's lack of interest.

Professor Van Alstyne comments:

> That each of these rights — that all of these rights [that have been incorporated into state law through the due process clause] — are examples of personal rights protected by the Bill of Rights seems perfectly clear. . . .
>
> [I]n addressing [the meaning of these other rights] the Supreme Court [has not] found it intractable and certainly none of these other clauses have been disparaged, much less have they been ignored. To the contrary, with respect to each, a strong, supportive case law has developed in the courts, albeit case law that has developed gradually, over quite a long time.
>
> In startling contrast, during this same time, however, the Second Amendment has generated almost no useful body of law. Indeed, it is substantially accurate to say that the useful case law of the Second Amendment, even in 1994, is mostly just missing in action.[6]

Case law of the Second Amendment is missing in action

There are only six cases — five in the nineteenth century and one in the twentieth — in which the Supreme Court has mentioned the Second Amendment, and all have proven to be of little consequential meaning or validity today.

The five nineteenth-century cases, *Scott v. Sandford,*[7] *United States v. Cruikshank,*[8] *Presser v. Illinois,*[9] *Miller v. Texas,*[10] and *Robertson v.*

Baldwin,[11] address the Second Amendment in only a peripheral way and are largely inapplicable now since they were decided before the Supreme Court began incorporating much of the Bill of Rights into the Fourteenth Amendment.

Only one twentieth-century Supreme Court decision: *United States v. Miller*

The twentieth-century case is *United States v. Miller*,[12] a case that is seriously flawed on a number of complicated legal grounds that we won't get into here. But the central finding of that case is this: After reviewing the trial court's decision to dismiss the defendants' indictment for violation of the National Firearms Act of 1934 in that they had transported through interstate commerce a shotgun with a barrel of less than eighteen inches in length without a tax-stamp affixed as required by the statute, the Supreme Court reinstated the indictment. Its reasoning was that "it is not within judicial notice that a [sawed-off shotgun] is any part of the ordinary military equipment or that its use could contribute to the common defense."[13]

Nelson Lund provides this analysis of *Miller:*

The logic of *Miller* would lead to absurd results

The [decision] is incomplete, since its logic would lead to absurd results. The most problematic weapons, for the purpose of private possession, are those that are *most* obviously used in a military context — for example, automatic rifles, artillery, portable rocket launchers, and nuclear devices.

Nevertheless, despite the shortcomings of the *Miller* opinion, the Supreme Court correctly concluded that the Second Amendment protects an individual's right to keep and bear arms and thus rejected the untenable collective right theory: "[The historical sources] show plainly that the Militia comprised all males physically capable of acting in concert for the common defense. . . . And further, that ordinarily when called for service these men were expected to appear bearing arms supplied by themselves and of the kind in common use today."[14] [Emphasis in original]

Let's summarize the situation. We have learned that, in Professor Van Alstyne's words, "[t]he main reason there is such a vacuum of useful Second Amendment understanding . . . is the arrested jurisprudence of the subject as such, a condition due substantially to the Supreme Court's own inertia."[15]

We have also learned that although it has incorporated most of the rights guaranteed by the Bill of Rights into state law through the medium of the Fourteenth Amendment, the Supreme Court has not granted the Second Amendment rights the same status.

So where does that leave us? That leaves us, first, with our local laws. It has been estimated that there exist in this country more than *20,000* gun control statutes in our local jurisdictions — towns, cities, counties, and states.

More than 20,000 local gun control laws

A large majority of the state constitutions include a right to bear arms for a variety of purposes, expressed in a variety of ways. David Caplan has organized this data for us:

> . . . three states (Arkansas, Massachusetts, and Tennessee) contain a "common defense" limitation upon the right to keep and bear arms (a limitation, incidentally, that was rejected by the first Senate of the United States). . . .
>
> . . . 13 states (Alabama, Arizona, Colorado, Connecticut, Illinois, Maine, Mississippi, Missouri, Montana, New Mexico, Oklahoma, Texas, and Washington) clearly refer to the individual's right to keep and bear arms for defensive purposes. . . .
>
> . . . five states (Colorado, Mississippi, Missouri, Montana, and Oklahoma) protect the individual's right to keep arms for the defense of his home, person, and property. . . .
>
> . . . 12 states (Colorado, Florida, Georgia, Idaho, Illinois, Kentucky, Louisiana, Mississippi, Missouri, Oklahoma, Texas, and Utah) have found it necessary to add a state constitutional proviso to the effect that the state legislature may regulate or forbid the carrying of concealed (but not merely concealable) weapons, thus suggesting an individual right to keep and carry arms even if these arms are concealable. . . .[16]

Literally thousands of statutes and ordinances

And at the county and city levels of government, there are literally thousands of statutes and ordinances controlling and prohibiting firearms in all sorts of ways: prohibitions against handguns and machine guns; concealed weapons; against carrying a firearm in public or on another person's property; against hunting; against discharging a firearm within city limits; against using firearms in connection with organizing a private army; against gun possession by certain classes of people including felons and illegal aliens.

At the federal level, while no gun control legislation was enacted by Congress before this century, since the 1930s seven major federal firearm control and prohibition statutes have been enacted, six that control arms and one that reaffirms the right of citizens to keep and bear them. A brief description of the principal provisions of each statute follows:

Seven major federal gun control laws

The National Firearms Act (NFA) of 1934,[17] which is actually a part of the Internal Revenue Code, imposes a tax on importers, manufacturers, dealers, and "transferors" of short-barreled rifles and shotguns, machine guns, and silencers. It requires the registration of such firearms, and prohibits their unauthorized importation.

The Federal Firearms Act (1938)[18] prohibits the interstate shipment or receipt of firearms to or by felons or fugitives from justice and prohibits the shipment of stolen firearms. It requires that firearm manufacturers and dealers obtain a license for the regular shipment of firearms. This statute was repealed by the Gun Control Act of 1968.

The Gun Control Act of 1968 (GCA)[19] prohibits a non-firearms dealer from selling or giving any firearm to a resident of a state other than his own. It requires that persons who engage in the business of buying or selling firearms or ammunition acquire a federal firearms license. It prohibits the possession of a shotgun with a barrel of less than 18 inches or a firearm that fires more than once with a single depression of the trigger. It **Gun Control** prohibits the sale of a rifle or shotgun to anyone **Act of 1968** under 18 years of age and the sale of a handgun and matching ammunition to anyone under 21 years of age. It absolutely prohibits the mere possession of a firearm by various classes of citizens: those who have been convicted of a felony, veterans who received a dishonorable discharge, mental incompetents, illegal aliens, persons who have renounced their citizenship, and users of illegal drugs (including marijuana).

The Firearm Owners' Protection Act (1986)[20] states: "The Congress finds that — (1) the rights of citizens — (A) to keep and bear arms under the second amendment to the United States Constitution; (B) to security against illegal and unreasonable searches and seizures under the fourth amendment; (C) against uncompensated taking of property, double jeopardy, and assurance of due process of law under the fifth amendment; and (D) against unconstitutional exercise of authority under the ninth and tenth amendments; require additional legislation to correct existing firearms statutes and enforcement policies; and (2) additional legislation is required to reaffirm the intent of the Congress, as expressed in section 101 of the Gun Control Act of 1968, that 'it is not the purpose of this title to place any undue or unnecessary Federal restrictions or burdens on law-abiding citizens with respect to the acquisition, possession, or use of firearms appropriate to the purpose of hunting, trap-shooting, target shooting, personal protection, or any other lawful activity, and that this title is not intended to discourage or eliminate the private ownership or use of firearms by law-abiding citizens for lawful purposes.' "

The Undetectable Handgun Law of 1988[21] makes it illegal to possess a newly made handgun that cannot be easily detected by metal detection devices.

The Brady Handgun Violence Prevention Act (1993)[22] mandates a five-day waiting period for all handgun purchases from federally licensed dealers, during which time local law enforcement officers must make a reasonable effort to check the purchaser's personal history. (In June 1996, the Supreme Court indicated it will review whether the employment of local police to check the criminal background of prospective handgun purchasers is an unconstitutional extension of congressional powers and a violation of state sovereignty under the Tenth Amendment.)

The Brady Act

**The 1994 Public Safety and Recrea-
tional Firearms Use Protection Act (the
"Crime Bill")** [23] bans the manufacture or importation of certain newly manufactured firearms,
which include nineteen semiautomatic firearms by
name and scores of additional firearms by definition.

(Incidentally, the Gun-Free School Zones Act of
1991, which makes it illegal to possess a firearm
within 1,000 feet of a school under the justification
that federal authority is applicable under Congress'
constitutional jurisdiction over interstate commerce, was recently declared unconstitutional by
the Supreme Court in *United States v. Lopez*).[24]

To those of us who believe that the Second
Amendment should take its proper place alongside the other individual personal rights that have
been incorporated into the fabric of state law
through the Fourteenth Amendment, two recent
Supreme Court cases provide at least a small measure of hope.

In *United States v. Verdugo-Urquidez,* a decision handed down by the Court in 1990, Chief
Justice Rehnquist observed that " '[T]he people'
protected by the Fourth Amendment, and by the
First and *Second* Amendments . . . refer to a class
of persons who are a part of a national community
or who have otherwise developed sufficient connection with this country to be considered part of that
community."[25] [Emphasis added.]

**Two recent
Supreme
Court
decisions
provide a
small
measure
of hope**

The second is a 1992 decision, *Planned Parenthood v. Casey*, which includes this statement: "It is tempting, as a means of curbing the discretion of federal judges, to suppose that liberty encompasses no more than those rights already guaranteed to the individual against federal interference by the express provisions of the first *eight* amendments of the Constitution."[26] [Emphasis added.]

Here, then, is a Supreme Court that in 1990 can find in *United States v. Verdugo-Urquidez* that "the people" are protected by the First, *Second*, and Fourth Amendments and in 1992 can find in *Planned Parenthood v. Casey* that "liberty encompasses no more than those rights already guaranteed to the individual against federal interference by the express provisions of the first eight amendments of the Constitution." Is it too much to hope that this same Supreme Court will now, at long last, turn its attention to the Second Amendment and provide us with its definition of "this right most valued by free men"?

Is it too much to hope that the Supreme Court will now give us its definition of "this right most valued by free men"?

D
A SELECTION OF
CONTEMPORARY
COMMENTARY

AKHIL REED AMAR

The ultimate right to keep and bear arms belongs to "the people," not the "states." As the language of the Tenth Amendment shows, these two are of course not identical and when the Constitution means "states," it says so. Thus, the "people" at the core of the Second Amendment are the same "people" at the heart of the Preamble and the First Amendment, namely Citizens. What's more, the "militia" as used in the Amendment, and in [U.S. Const., Art I, Sect. 8] clause 16, had a very different meaning 200 years ago than in ordinary conversation today. Nowadays, it is quite common to speak loosely of the National Guard as "the state militia," but 200 years ago, any band of paid, semiprofessional, part-time volunteers, like today's Guard, would have been called a "a *select corps*" or "*select* militia" — and viewed in many quarters as little better than a standing army. In 1789, when used without any qualifying adjective, "the militia" referred to all Citizens capable of bearing arms. The seeming tension between the dependent and the main clauses of the Second Amendment thus evaporates on closer inspection — the "militia" is

"Militia" had a very different meaning 200 years ago

identical to the "people" in the core sense described above. Indeed, the version of the Amendment that initially passed in the House, only to be stylistically shortened in the Senate, explicitly defined the "militia" as "composed of the body of the People." This is clearly the sense in which *the* militia" is used in clause 16 and throughout *The Federalist Papers,* in keeping with standard usage confirmed by contemporaneous dictionaries, legal and otherwise.[1] [Emphasis in original.]

The most dramatic evidence, however, comes from the [1866] Civil Rights Act's Siamese twin, the Freedman's Bureau Act. Initially introduced as a single act, the two bills were later split, but were understood as *in pari materia* [as like subject matter]. As finally adopted, the Freedman's Bureau Act spoke of the "full . . . benefit of all laws and proceedings concerning personal liberty, personal security, and [property], *including the constitutional rights to bear arms.*"[2] [Emphasis added.]

JAMES L. BUCKLEY

The Founding Fathers recognized the need to protect citizens from government itself

At the time of the adoption of the Bill of Rights, this country's statesmen were concerned with the need to protect citizens from government itself, and the passage of almost two centuries has not negated the validity of this concern. The fact that Article I, Section 8, clause 16 of the Constitution grants Congress the power to organize, arm and discipline the militia clearly indicates a quite different intention for the Second Amendment.[3]

ALAN DERSHOWITZ

Foolish liberals who are trying to read the Second Amendment out of the Constitution by claiming it's not an individual right or that it's too much of a safety hazard don't see the danger of the big picture. They're courting disaster by encouraging others to use the same means to eliminate portions of the Constitution they don't like.[4]

Foolish liberals don't see the danger of the big picture

GEORGE FLETCHER

The nearly forgotten Second Amendment in the Bill of Rights protects this right [to keep and bear arms]; even though the prevailing interpretation is that the amendment merely guarantees a right of the states to maintain a militia, convincing evidence indicates that the framers had an individual right in mind.[5]

MAHATMA GANDHI

Among the many misdeeds of the British rule in India, history will look upon the Act depriving a whole nation of arms as the blackest.[6]

GERMAN FIREARMS ACT OF 1937

[Firearms licenses] will not be granted [to] Jews [or persons] suspected of acting against the state. Those who do not require permission to purchase or carry weapons [include] the whole SS [paramilitary adjunct of the Gestapo] and SA [Storm

Troopers], including the Deaths Head group and officers of the Hitler Youth.[7]

STEPHEN P. HALBROOK

No writing stating a "collective right" thesis survives the ratification period

In recent years, it has been suggested that the Second Amendment protects the "collective right" of states to maintain militias, while it does not protect the right of "the people" to keep and bear arms. If anyone entertained this notion in the period during which the Constitution and Bill of Rights were debated and ratified, it remains one of the most closely guarded secrets of the eighteenth century, for no writing surviving from the period between 1787 and 1791 states such a thesis.[8]

CHARLTON HESTON

And if you want to feel the warm breath of freedom on your neck . . . if you want to touch the pulse of liberty that beat in our founding fathers, you may do so through the majesty of the Second Amendment.

Because there, in that wooden stock and blued steel, there lies what gives the most common of men the most uncommon of freedoms. When ordinary hands are free to own this extraordinary symbol, representing the full measure of human dignity and liberty, that is as good as you can have it.

It doesn't matter whether its purpose is to defend our shores or your front door . . . whether it is a rite of passage for a young man or a tool of survival for a young woman . . . whether it brings meat for the table or trophies for the shelf . . . without respect to age, or gender, or race, or class, the Second Amendment right to keep and bear arms connects us all — with all that is right.

And to those who say the Second Amendment doesn't mean what we say it means: Let's settle that right now. The purpose of every line of the Bill of Rights was to protect people from the state. Our founders refused to ratify a Constitution that didn't protect individual liberties. They were just a bunch of old dead white guys, but they invented this country, and they meant what they said. The Second Amendment isn't about the National Guard or the police or any other government entity. It is about law-abiding, private U.S. citizens. Period.[9]

They were just a bunch of old dead white guys . . . but they meant what they said

ADOLF HITLER

The most foolish mistake we could possibly make would be to allow the subjected people to carry arms; history shows that all conquerors who have allowed their subjected people to carry arms have prepared their own fall.[10]

HUBERT H. HUMPHREY

The right of citizens to bear arms is just one more guarantee against arbitrary government, one more safeguard against the tyranny which now appears remote in America, but which historically has proved to be always possible.[11]

NICHOLAS J. JOHNSON

The situation [the banning or licensing of guns] would be much like telling a climber that all ropes will be collectively controlled. If he begins to fall, then he need only call and an agent of the government will be dispatched to bring the rope that will prevent his injury or death. Unfortunately, once the need for the resource arises, assistance will in many instances be too late. Taking the analogy further, to incorporate the additional problem of limited resources by assuming that there are at any one time one hundred actual climbers, thousands of potential climbers and only five rope administrators, together with the acute nature of the need, we should question the wisdom of the decision which prohibited self-help and individual ownership of ropes.[12]

Placed in the position of the Japanese-American internees in World War II, a framer of the Constitution would have chosen to fight and die

Many in the mainstream might consider the alternative of armed resistance [by Japanese-Americans who, during World War II, had their property seized and were interned in concentration camps] to be useless and counterproductive. From the perspective of the victim, the choice between submitting to such grave depredations or fighting, even without the hope of prevailing, might weigh out differently. Certainly, we would expect that any one of the framers [of the Constitution] who found himself suddenly in the circumstances faced by many Japanese internees would have chosen to fight and die rather than submit his life and property to such an unrestrained exercise of collective power. Indeed, the abuses that were used to rationalize the Colonies' revolt against England pale in comparison.[13]

[It is] difficult to justify permitting government agents, whom we ideally characterize as servants, to enjoy a level of security, provided in part by firearms, unavailable to the general population. Such a result leads to the conclusion that those in positions of power in government are distinct from servants whose lives are somehow worth more than the lives of citizens. It then follows that our constitutional system is designed to tolerate a tier of elite whose interest in personal security exceeds that of citizens merely because of their positions in government. Our constitutional tradition, based on the concepts of limited government serving the citizenry and legitimate fear of the power vested in government, seems at odds with such conclusions.[14]

SANFORD LEVINSON

It is simply silly to respond [to the value of an armed citizenry] that small arms are irrelevant against nuclear-armed states: Witness contemporary Northern Ireland and the territories occupied by Israel, where the sophisticated weaponry of Great Britain and Israel have proved almost totally beside the point. The fact that these may not be pleasant examples does not affect the principal point, that a state facing a totally disarmed population is in a far better position, for good or for ill,

It is simply silly to argue that small arms are irrelevant against nuclear-armed states

to suppress popular demonstrations and uprisings than one that must calculate the possibilities of its soldiers and officials being injured or killed.[15]

JOYCE LEE MALCOLM

The Second Amendment was meant to accomplish two distinct goals. . . . First, it was meant to guarantee the individual's right to have arms for self defense and self preservation. . . . These privately owned arms were meant to serve a larger purpose as well . . . and it is the coupling of these two objectives that has caused the most confusion. The customary American militia necessitated an armed public . . . the militia [being] . . . the body of the people. . . . The argument that today's National Guardsmen, members of a select militia, would constitute the *only* persons entitled to keep and bear arms has no historical foundation.[16] [Emphasis in original.]

The argument that National Guardsmen are the only persons entitled to keep and bear arms has no historical foundation

DANIEL D. POLSBY

[A]lmost all qualified historians and constitutional-law scholars who have studied the subject [concur]. The overwhelming weight of authority affirms that the Second Amendment establishes an *individual* right to bear arms, which is not dependent upon joining the National Guard. It goes without saying that like all constitutional rights, the right to keep and bear arms is subject to reasonable regulation consistent with its purposes.[17] [Emphasis in original.]

SA OBERFÜHRER OF BAD TÖLZ, GERMANY

The associations of the national revival, SA [Storm Troopers], SS [para-military adjunct of the Gestapo], and Stahlhelm [a non-Nazi lunatic fringe para-military organization], give every responsible citizen the opportunity of campaigning with them. Therefore anyone who does not belong to one of the above-named organizations and who unjustifiably nevertheless keeps his weapon . . . must be regarded as an enemy of the national government and will be brought to account without compunction and with the utmost severity.[18]

JEFFREY R. SNYDER

What we certainly do not need is more gun control. Those who call for the repeal of the Second Amendment so that we can really begin controlling firearms betray a serious misunderstanding of the Bill of Rights. The Bill of Rights does not *grant* rights to the people, such that its repeal would legitimately confer upon government the powers otherwise proscribed. The Bill of Rights is the list of the fundamental, inalienable rights, endowed in man by his Creator, that define what it means to be a free and independent people, the rights which must exist to ensure that government governs only with the consent of the people.[19] [Emphasis in original.]

What we certainly do not need is more gun control

WILLIAM VAN ALSTYNE

The essential claim (certainly not every claim — but the essential claim) advanced by the NRA with respect to the Second Amendment is extremely strong. Indeed, one may fairly declare, it is at least as well anchored in the Constitution in its own way as were the essential claims with respect to the First Amendment's protection of freedom of speech as first advanced on the Supreme Court by Holmes and Brandeis, seventy years ago. And until the Supreme Court manages to express the central premise of the Second Amendment more fully and far more appropriately than it has done thus far, the constructive role of the NRA today, like the role of the ACLU in the 1920s with respect to the First Amendment (as it then was), ought itself not lightly to be dismissed. Indeed, it is largely by the "unreasonable" persistence of just such organizations in this country that the Bill of Rights has endured.[20]

It is largely by the "unreasonable" persistence of such organizations as the NRA that the Bill of Rights has endured

EARL WARREN

Our War of the Revolution was, in good measure, fought as a protest against standing armies. . . . Despite [all] safeguards, the people were still troubled by the recollection that prompted the charge of the Declaration of Independence that the King had "effected to render the military independent and superior to the civil power." They were reluctant to ratify the Constitution without further assurances, and thus we find in the Bill of Rights

Amendments 2 and 3, specifically authorizing a decentralized militia, guaranteeing the right of the people to keep and bear arms, and prohibiting the quartering of troops in any house in time of peace without the consent of the owner.[21]

The Bill of Rights guarantees the right to keep and bear arms

A FINAL WORD

I n his essay which you will be reading in the Appendix, Professor Van Alstyne points out that the Second Amendment right to keep and bear arms has not enjoyed as benign an interpretive history as have most of our other personal rights that are preserved in the Constitution. He then goes on to make this comparison between the Supreme Court's treatment of the First and Second Amendments:

> . . . the Second Amendment has generated almost no useful body of law. Indeed, it is substantially accurate to say that the useful case law of the Second Amendment, even in 1994, is mostly just missing in action. In its place, what we have is roughly of the same scanty and utterly underdeveloped nature as was characteristic of the equally scanty and equally underdeveloped case law (such as it then was) of the First Amendment in 1904, as of which date there was still to issue from the Supreme Court a single decision establishing the First Amendment as an amendment of anv genuine importance at all. In short, what was true of the First Amendment as of 1904 remains true of the Second Amendment even now.[1]

> . . . The main reason there is such a vacuum of useful Second Amendment understanding . . . is the arrested jurisprudence of the subject as such, a condition due substantially to the Supreme Court's own inertia — the same inertia that simi-

The Second Amendment has generated almost no useful body of law

larly afflicted the First Amendment virtually until
the third decade of this twentieth century when
Holmes and Brandeis were moved personally to
take the First Amendment seriously (as it previously scarcely ever was).[2]

Now, of course, we know that there exist certain
limitations on the right to free speech. It is by no
means an absolute right. The First Amendment
provides no protection, for example, for certain
types of hate speech, speech inciting lawless action,
speech advocating overthrowing the government
with violence, speech associated with blackmail,
extortion, "hard-core" or child pornography, libel,
or slander. Or to use a popular example, no reasonable person argues today that the right to free
speech includes the right for someone to yell
"Fire!" falsely in a crowded movie theater and
cause a panic.

Are there limita-tions on our Second Amendment rights? Is there a "Fire!" exception or, let's say, a "hard-core" or child pornography-type exception to the Second Amendment?[3] One of our leading Second Amendment commentators, David I. Caplan, an-swers that question this way:

> Of course there is. Certainly the keeping of nuclear
> bombs, warplanes, artillery pieces, tanks, and
> similar weapons would not gain judicial approval
> on either constitutional or simple common-sense
> grounds. (Besides, all of these weapons are too
> large to be held in the hand, and are therefore
> incapable of being borne by an individual.) There's
> nothing new about this, of course. In colonial times,

cannons were kept only collectively in community armories. But on the other hand, the private keeping of hand-held firearms (shotguns, pistols and revolvers, and rifles, whether single shot or semiautomatic) by law-abiding citizens for legitimate purposes (hunting, target shooting, self protection, etc.) is clearly protected by the Second Amendment. It can be argued that the possession of machine guns, sawed-off shotguns and rifles, and weapons equipped with silencers — in fact, all hand-held firearms — should similarly enjoy protection from governmental control. However, passage of the National Firearms Act of 1934,[4] mandating that these type firearms can only be acquired by importers, manufacturers, and dealers who have submitted to an expensive and complicated federal tax and registration procedure, removed them from under Second Amendment protection.[5]

Of course, it is — and properly should be — a difficult job for Congress and our courts to place limitations upon rights that are absolutely guaranteed to the people by the Bill of Rights. Whenever you are considering having to limit a constitutionally mandated freedom to meet a perceived need to protect the general welfare of society, you are inevitably going to be in the business of making close calls. Regarding child pornography, for example, what is the age limit of a "child"? Where is the precise demarcation line between "hard-core" and "soft-core" pornography? Should the government bring a prosecution against a person who yells

It should be a difficult job for Congress to place limitations upon constitutionally mandated freedoms

"Fire!" in a crowded theater in the mistaken belief that a fire actually exists? How do you distinguish merely vituperative speech from actionable libel? The history of the First Amendment jurisprudence in the twentieth century is replete with tough questions like this. But, as Caplan remarks, "that hardly means that the First Amendment has become a nullity in our society, nor has the Second."[6]

The Second Amendment presents controversial issues that the Supreme Court and Congress will have to address

The Second Amendment similarly presents controversial issues that will require "close calls."[7] For example, precisely what are "constitutionally protected personal arms"? In the years to come, Congress and the courts will need to address such questions. But thus far, the Supreme Court apparently has been unwilling to tackle them. Meanwhile, Congress is enacting ineffective "paper-tiger" gun control and prohibition measures that provide society with only the marginal benefit of helping those of our citizens who are poorly informed to sleep more comfortably at night — more comfortably, that is, until they are rudely awakened by a vicious robber or serial rapist.

Until the Supreme Court focuses its attention on these issues, and unless we, the people, decide to amend the Constitution, in the coming years we should not allow our government to weaken or substantially alter — to infringe — our Second Amendment, our guaranteed right to keep and bear arms.

*   *   *

As I became personally involved in this issue, the Court's failure to give serious attention to Second Amendment issues became a compelling reason for me to spend the time to prepare this Primer. For I believe that the more *informed political support* the Congress and the courts have from the people — a people who have learned the facts about the issue of firearms control and prohibition; a people who have been able finally to place into retirement the flawed arguments of the gun control advocates that the Second Amendment means something other than what it says in plain English; a people moreover who, in Senator Orrin Hatch's words, recognize that our right to keep and bear arms is the "right most valued by free men"[8] — the better are our nation's chances that long after 1789 when the right was first enunciated, in this year of 1996, or 2096, or indeed ever, *it will not have been infringed.*

The more informed the American people, the better our chances of retaining our Second Amendment rights

APPENDIX

❧❧❧

A Selection of Recent Scholarly Articles
Confirming the Proposition
That the Second Amendment to the
U.S. Constitution
Guarantees to the American Citizen the
Right to Keep and Bear Arms

As we discussed at the beginning of this book, a good deal of the confusion about the meaning of the Second Amendment exists today because of the lack of interest in the issue that existed throughout the American legal community during the nineteenth and twentieth centuries. Within the last decade, however, likely because of the attention being given to the increase of gun violence in our society, coupled with the well-publicized disagreement over the issue between the National Rifle Association and various groups of gun control proponents, the right of Americans to keep and bear firearms is now receiving well-deserved attention in the popular press as well as in intellectual journals.

The issue is beginning to receive well-deserved attention

During the last decade, for example, three superlative articles have been published in the scholarly press — two in law reviews, one in a journal of political thought. All three pieces, therefore, have thus far enjoyed only a small and limited audience.

But each, in its own way, deserves to be read by every American interested in this issue, and for that reason I have chosen to include them in these pages.

Three unique insights

With the permission of the authors, to make for easier reading the lengthy footnotes that appeared on each page of the original articles have been moved to the back of the book where they appear as endnotes. Otherwise, no changes have been made. You will find that the articles are relatively short and quite readable. I hope you will take the time to read them, for they are, I can assure you, worthy of your time and attention. In fact, if you take away nothing else from this book than the unique insights each of these thoughtful writers brings to the Second Amendment issue, I'll be amply rewarded for whatever labor I have expended in putting together this little Primer for you.

THE SECOND AMENDMENT AND THE PERSONAL RIGHT TO ARMS

William Van Alstyne *

INTRODUCTION

Perhaps no provision in the Constitution causes one to stumble quite so much on a first reading, or second, or third reading, as the short provision in the Second Amendment of the Bill of Rights. No doubt this stumbling occurs because, despite the brevity of this amendment, as one reads, there is an apparent non sequitur — or disconnection of a sort — in midsentence. The amendment opens with a recitation about a need for "[a] well regulated Militia."[1] But having stipulated to the need for "[a] well regulated Militia," the amendment then declares that the right secured by the amendment — the described right that is to be free of "infringement" — is not (or not

*William Van Alstyne is the William R. and Thomas L. Perkins Professor of Law, Duke University School of Law. Reprinted from the *Duke Law Journal* (vol. 43, 1994) courtesy of the author and publisher.

An apparent disconnection

just) the right of a state, or of the United States, to provide a well regulated militia. Rather, it is "the right of the people to keep and bear Arms."

A well regulated Militia, being necessary to the security of a free State, the right of the people to keep and bear Arms, shall not be infringed.[2]

But made clear with an unforced reading

The postulation of a "right of the people to keep and bear Arms" would make sense standing alone, however, even if it necessarily left some questions still to be settled.[3] It would make sense in just the same unforced way we understand even upon a first reading of the neighboring clause in the Bill of Rights, which uses the exact same phrase in describing something as "the right of the people" that "shall not be violated" (or "infringed"). Just as the Second Amendment declares that "the right of the people to keep and bear Arms[] shall not be infringed," so, too, the Fourth Amendment declares:

The right of the people to be secure in their persons, houses, papers, and effects, against unreasonable searches and seizures, shall not be violated. . . .[4]

Here, in the familiar setting of the Fourth Amendment, we are not at all confused in our take on the meaning of the amendment; it secures to each of us personally (as well as to all of us collectively) a certain right — even if we are also uncertain of its scope.[5] Nor are we confused in turning to other clauses. For example, the Sixth Amendment provides:

> In all criminal prosecutions, the accused shall enjoy the right to a speedy and public trial. . . .[6]

And so, too, the Seventh Amendment provides:

> In Suits at common law, where the value in controversy shall exceed twenty dollars, the right of trial by jury shall be preserved. . . .[7]

That each of these rights — that all of these rights — are examples of personal rights protected by the Bill of Rights seems perfectly clear. And, were it not for the opening clause in the Second Amendment, though there would still be much to thrash out, it is altogether likely the Second Amendment would be taken in the same way.

To be sure, as we have already once noted, were the Second Amendment taken in just this way, the scope of the right that *is* protected (namely, the right to keep and bear arms) would still remain to be defined.[8] But by itself, that sort of definitional determination would be of no unusual difficulty. For so much is true with respect to every right secured from government infringement, whether it be each person's freedom of speech (that freedom is not unbounded, either) or any other right specifically protected from infringement elsewhere in the Bill of Rights.[9] And in addressing this type of (merely general) problem, neither has the Supreme Court nor have other courts found it intrac-

The scope of the Amendment still needs to be defined

table and certainly none of these other clauses have
been disparaged, much less have they been ignored. To the contrary, with respect to each, a
strong, supportive case law has developed in the
courts, albeit case law that has developed gradually, over quite a long time.

**Useful
case law
is missing
in action**

In startling contrast, during this same time,
however, the Second Amendment has generated
almost no useful body of law. Indeed, it is substantially accurate to say that the useful case law of the
Second Amendment, even in 1994, is mostly just
missing in action. In its place, what we have is
roughly of the same scanty and utterly underdeveloped nature[10] as was characteristic of the equally
scanty and equally underdeveloped case law (such
as it then was) of the First Amendment in 1904, as
of which date there was still to issue from the
Supreme Court a single decision establishing the
First Amendment as an amendment of any genuine importance at all.[11] In short, what was true of
the First Amendment as of 1904 remains true of
the Second Amendment even now.

The reason for this failure of useful modern case
law, moreover, is not that there has been no occasion to develop such law. So much is true only of
the Third Amendment.[12] In contrast, it is no more
true of the Second Amendment than of the First
Amendment or the Fourth Amendment that we
have lacked for appropriate occasions to join issue
on these questions. The tendency in the twentieth
century (though not earlier) of the federal govern-

ment has been ever increasingly to tax, ever more
greatly to regulate, and ever more substantially to
prohibit various kinds of personal gun ownership
and use.[13] This tendency, that is, is at least as
commonplace as it was once equally the heavy
tendency to tax, to regulate, and too often also to
prohibit, various kinds of speech. The main reason
there is such a vacuum of useful Second Amendment understanding, rather, is the arrested jurisprudence of the subject as such, a condition due
substantially to the Supreme Court's own inertia
— the same inertia that similarly afflicted the First
Amendment virtually until the third decade of this
twentieth century when Holmes and Brandeis finally were moved personally to take the First
Amendment seriously[14] (as previously it scarcely
ever was).

With respect to the larger number of state and
local regulations (many of these go far beyond the
federal regulations), moreover, the case law of the
Second Amendment is even more arrested; and
this for the reason that the Supreme Court has
simply declined to reconsider its otherwise dis-
carded nineteenth-century decisions — decisions
holding that the Fourteenth Amendment enacted
little protection of anything, and none (i.e., *no*
protection) drawn from the Bill of Rights.[15]

A case of
arrested
develop-
ment

To trust to this arrested treatment of the Second
Amendment — and of the Fourteenth Amendment — in 1994, in short, is as though one were
inclined so to trust to the arrested treatment of the

Perhaps the NRA is not wrong in its general Second Amendment stance

First Amendment in 1904. The difficulty in such a starting place is perfectly plain. No convincing jurisprudence is itself really possible under such circumstances. In the case of the First Amendment, we know quite well that such a jurisprudence effectively became possible only rather late, in the 1920s (but, one may add, better late than never). In the case of the Second Amendment, in an elementary sense, that jurisprudence is even now not possible until something more in the case law of the Second Amendment begins finally to fall into place. That "something more," I think, requires one to consider what one might be more willing to think about in the following way — that *perhaps the NRA is not wrong, after all, in its general Second Amendment stance* — a stance we turn here briefly to review.

I

The stance of those inclined to take the Second Amendment seriously reverts to the place we ourselves thought to be somewhat worthwhile to consult — namely, the express provisions of the Second Amendment — and it offers a series of suggestions fitting the respective clauses the amendment contains. Here is how these several propositions run:

A well-regulated militia is the citizenry

1. The reference to a "well regulated *Militia*" is in the first as well as the last instance a reference to the ordinary citizenry. It is not at all a reference to regular armed soldiers as members of some

standing army.[16] And quite obviously, neither is it a reference merely to the state or to the local police.

2. The very assumption of the clause, moreover, is that ordinary citizens (rather than merely soldiers, or merely the police) *may* themselves possess arms, for it is from these ordinary citizens who as citizens have a right to keep and bear arms (as the second clause provides) that such well regulated militia as a state may provide for, is itself to be drawn.

Ordinary citizens may possess arms

3. Indeed, it is more than merely an "assumption," however, precisely because "the right of the people to keep and bear Arms" is itself stipulated in the second clause. It is *this* right that is expressly identified as *"the* right" that is not to be *("shall not be")* infringed. That right is made the express guarantee of the clause.[17] There is thus no room left for a claim that, despite this language, the amendment actually means to reserve to Congress some power to contradict its very terms (e.g., that "the Congress may, if it thinks it proper, forbid the people to keep and bear arms to such extent Congress sees fit to do").[18]

"The right" is the express guarantee of the Amendment

4. Nor is there any basis so to read the Second Amendment as though it said anything like the following: "Congress may, if it thinks it proper, forbid the people to keep and bear arms if, not withstanding that these restrictions it may thus enact are inconsistent with the right of the people to keep and bear arms, they are not inconsistent with the right of each state to maintain some kind

of militia as it may deem necessary to its security as a free state."[19]

Rather, the Second Amendment adheres to the guarantee of the right of the people to keep and bear arms as the predicate for the other provision to which it speaks, i.e., the provision respecting a militia, as distinct from a standing army separately subject to congressional regulation and control. Specifically, it looks to an ultimate reliance on the common citizen who has a right to keep and bear arms rather than only to some standing army, or only to some other politically separated, defined, and detached armed cadre, as an essential source of security of a free state.[20] In relating these propositions within one amendment, moreover, it does not disparage, much less does it subordinate, "the right of the people to keep and bear arms." To the contrary, it expressly *embraces* that right and indeed it erects the very scaffolding of a free state upon *that* guarantee. *It derives its definition of a well-regulated militia in just this way for a "free State":* The militia to be well regulated is a militia to be drawn from just such people (i.e., people with a right to keep and bear arms) rather than from some other source (i.e., from people without rights to keep and bear arms).

It embraces rather than disparages the right to keep and bear arms

II

There is, to be sure, in the Second Amendment, an express reference to the security of a *"free* State."[21] It is not a reference to *the* security of THE

STATE.[22] There are doubtless certain national constitutions that put a privileged emphasis on the security of "the state," but such as they are, they are all *unlike* our Constitution and the provisions they have respecting their security do not appear in a similarly phrased Bill of Rights. Accordingly, such constitutions make no reference to any right of the people to keep and bear arms, apart from state service.[23] And why do they not do so? Because, in contrast with the premises of constitutional government in this country, they reflect the belief that recognition of any such right "in the people" might well pose a threat to the security of "the state." In the view of these different constitutions, it is commonplace to find that no one within the state other than its own authorized personnel has any right to keep and bear arms[24] — a view emphatically rejected, rather than embraced, however, by the Second Amendment to the Constitution of the United States.

This rather fundamental difference among kinds of government was noted by James Madison in *The Federalist Papers,* even prior to the subsequent assurance expressly furnished by the Second Amendment in new and concrete terms. Thus, in *The Federalist* No. 46, Madison contrasted the "advantage . . . the Americans possess" (under the proposed constitution) with the circumstances in "several kingdoms of Europe . . . [where] the governments are afraid to trust the people with arms."[25] Here, in contrast, as Madison noted, they

The difference was pointed out by Madison in The Federalist, No. 46

were, and no provision was entertained to em-
power Congress to abridge or to violate that trust,
any more than, as Alexander Hamilton noted,
there was any power proposed to enable government to abridge the freedom of the press.[26]

**The quick
resolve of
Congress
to add the
Second
Amend-
ment
is not dif-
ficult to
under-
stand**

To be sure, in the course of the ratification
debates, doubts were expressed respecting the ade-
quacy of this kind of assurance (i.e., the assurance
that no power was affirmatively proposed for Congress to provide any colorable claim of authority to
take away or to abridge these rights of freedom of
the press and of the right of the people to keep and
bear arms).[27] And the quick resolve to add the
Second Amendment, so to confirm that right more
expressly, as not subject to infringement by Congress, is not difficult to understand.

The original constitutional provisions regarding
the militia[28] placed major new powers in Congress
beyond those previously conferred by the Articles
of Confederation. These new powers not only included a wholly new power to provide for a regular
standing, national army even in peacetime,[29] but
also powers for "calling forth the Militia,"[30] for
"*organizing, arming, and disciplining,* the Militia,"[31] and for "governing such Part of them as may
be employed in the Service of the United States."[32]
Indeed, all that was *expressly* reserved from Congress's reach was "the Appointment of the officers"
of this citizen militia, for even "the Authority of
training the Militia," though reserved in the first
instance from Congress, was itself subordinate to
Congress in the important sense that such training

was to be "according to the discipline prescribed *by Congress.*"[33]

These provisions were at once highly controversial, respecting their scope and possible implications of congressional power. In attempting to counter anti-ratification objections to the proposed constitution — objections that these lodgments of powers would concentrate excessive power in Congress in derogation of the rights of the people — Hamilton and Madison argued essentially three points:[34] (a) the appointment of militia officers was exclusively committed to state hands;[35] (b) the localized civilian-citizen nature of the militia would secure its loyalty to the rights of the people;[36] and (c) the people otherwise possessed a right to keep and bear arms — which right Congress was given no power whatever to regulate or to forbid.[37] And, as to the argument that the plan was defective insofar as it left the protection of the rights of the people insecure because no *express* prohibition on Congress was *separately* provided in respect to those rights (rather, the powerlessness of Congress to infringe them was solely a deduction from the doctrine of enumerated powers alone), Hamilton insisted that to specify anything further — to provide an *express* listing of particular prohibitions on Congress — was not only unnecessary but itself would be deeply problematic, because the implication of such a list would be that anything not named in the list might somehow be thought therefore in fact to be subject to regulation or prohibition by Congress though no enumerated power to affect

The three arguments of Hamilton and Madison

any such subject was provided by the Constitution itself.[38] In brief, Hamilton maintained that to do anything in the nature of adding a Bill of Rights would cast doubt upon the doctrine of enumerated powers itself.

Madison produces the Bill of Rights

These several explanations were deemed insufficient, however, and to meet the objections of those in the state ratifying conventions unwilling to leave the protection of certain rights to mere inference from the doctrine of enumerated powers, objections raised in the course of several state ratification debates, the Bill of Rights was promptly produced by Madison, in the first Congress to assemble under the new Constitution, in 1789. Accordingly, as with "the freedom of the press," the protection of "the right of the people to keep and bear arms" was thus made *doubly* secure in the Bill of Rights.[39] Thomas Cooley quite accurately recapitulated the controlling circumstances in the leading nineteenth century treatise on constitutional law:

> The [Second] [A]mendment, like most other provisions in the Constitution, has a history. It was adopted with some modification and enlargement from the English Bill of Rights of 1688, where it stood as a protest against arbitrary action of the overturned dynasty in disarming the people, and as a pledge of the new rulers that this tyrannical action should cease. . . .
>
> The Right is General. . . . The meaning of the provision undoubtedly is, that the people, from whom the militia must be taken, shall have the

right to keep and bear arms; and they need no permission or regulation of law for the purpose.[40]

Cooley's reference to English history, moreover, in illuminating the Second Amendment right (as personal to the citizen as such), is useful as well. For in this, he merely followed William Blackstone, from Blackstone's general treatise from 1765.

In chapter 1, appropriately captioned "Of The Rights of Persons," Blackstone divided what he called natural personal rights into two kinds: "primary" and "auxiliary."[41] The distinction was between those natural rights primary to each person intrinsically and those inseparable from their protection (thus themselves indispensable, "auxiliary" personal rights). Of the first kind, generically, are "the free enjoyment of personal security, of personal liberty, and of private property."[42] Of the latter are rights possessed "to vindicate" one's primary rights; and among these latter, Blackstone listed such things as access to "courts of law," and, so, too, "the right of petition[]," and *the right of having and using arms for self-preservation and defence.*"[43]

In contrast with all of this, the quite different view — the view of "the secure state" we were earlier considering — of countries *different* from the United States — assumes no right of the people to keep and bear arms. Rather, these differently constituted states put their own first stress on having a well regulated army (and also, of course, an

Blackstone defines two kinds of personal rights

internal state police). To be sure, such states also may provide for some kind of militia, but insofar as they may (and several do),[44] one can be quite certain that it will *not* be a militia drawn from the people with a "right to keep and bear Arms." For in these kinds of states, there is assuredly no such right. To the contrary, such a state is altogether likely to forbid the people to keep and bear arms unless and until they are conscripted into the militia, after which — to whatever extent they are deemed suitably "trustworthy" by the state — they might then (and only then) have arms fit for some assigned task.

The Second Amendment rejects the vision of the security state

But, again, the point to be made here is that the Second Amendment represented not an adoption, but a rejection, of this vision — a vision of the security state. It did not concede to any such state. Rather, it speaks to sources of security within a free state, within which (to quote the amendment itself still again) *"the right of the people to keep and bear Arms[] shall not be infringed."* The precautionary text of the amendment refutes the notion that the "well regulated Militia" the amendment contemplates is somehow a militia drawn from a people "who have no right to keep and bear arms." Rather, the opposite is what the amendment enacts.[45]

III

The Second Amendment of course does not assume that the right of the people to keep and bear arms will not be abused. Nor is the amendment insensible to the *many* forms which such abuses may take (e.g., as in robbing banks, in settling personal disputes, or in threatening varieties of force to secure one's will). But the Second Amendment's answer to the avoidance of abuse is to support such laws as are directed to those who threaten or demonstrate such abuse and to no one else. Accordingly, those who do neither — who neither commit crimes nor threaten such crimes — are entitled to be left alone.

To put the matter most simply, the governing principle here, in the Second Amendment, is not different from the same principle governing the First Amendment's provisions on freedom of speech and the freedom of the press. A person may be held to account for an abuse of that freedom (for example, by being held liable for using it to publish false claims with respect to the nutritional value of the food offered for public sale and consumption). Yet, no one today contends that just because the publication of such false statements is a danger one might in some measure reduce if, say, *licenses* also could be required as a condition of owning a newspaper or even a mimeograph machine, that therefore licensing can be made a requirement of owning either a newspaper or a mimeograph machine.[46]

The law-abiding citizen no more needs a license to keep and bear arms than he does to operate a printing press

The Second Amendment, like the First Amendment, is thus not mysterious. Nor is it equivocal. Least of all is it opaque. Rather, one may say, today it is simply unwelcome in any community that wants no one (save perhaps the police?) to keep or bear arms at all. But assuming it to be so, i.e., assuming this is how some now want matters to be, it is for them to seek a repeal of this amendment (and so the repeal of its guarantee), in order to have their way. Or so the Constitution itself assuredly appears to require, if that is the way things are to be.

IV

The Bill of Rights was designed to prevent Congress from preempting state powers

In the first instance, enacted as it was as part of the original Bill of Rights of 1791, the Second Amendment merely was addressed to Congress and not to the states. The mistrust and uncertainty of how *Congress* might presume to construe its new powers — powers newly enumerated in Article I of the Constitution — resulted in the Bill of Rights inclusive of the Second Amendment, proposed in the very first session of the new Congress in 1789. As it was then apprehended that although Congress was never given any power to preempt state constitutional provisions respecting freedom of speech or of the press, Congress might nonetheless presume to regulate those subjects to its own liking under pretext of some other authority if not barred from doing so by amendment, the Second Amendment — and the other amendments composing the original Bill of Rights — reflected the same mistrust and were adopted for the same reason as well. But, to be sure, neither the First nor the Second Amendment,[47] nor any of the other amendments in the Bill of Rights were addressed as limits on the states.[48]

In 1866, however, this original constitutional toleration of state differences with respect to their internal treatment of these rights came to an end, in the aftermath of the Civil War. The immunities of citizens with respect to rights previously secured only from abridging acts of Congress were recast in the Fourteenth Amendment as immunities secured also from any similar act by any state.[49] It was precisely in this manner that the citizen's right to keep and bear arms, formerly protected only from acts of Congress, came to be equally protected from abridging acts of the states as well.

The Four-teenth Amend-ment was enacted to restrain states from abridging personal rights that were federally protected

So, in reporting the Fourteenth Amendment to the Senate on behalf of the Joint Committee on Reconstruction in 1866, Senator Jacob Meritt Howard of Michigan began by detailing the "first section" of that amendment, i.e., the section that "relates to the privileges and immunities of citizens."[50] He explained that the first clause of the amendment (the "first section"), once approved and ratified, would "restrain the power of the States"[51] even as Congress was already restrained (by the Bill of Rights) from abridging

> the personal rights guarantied and secured by the first eight amendments of the Constitution; such as the freedom of speech and of the press; the right of the people peaceably to assemble and petition the Government for a redress of grievances, a right appertaining to each and all the people; *the right*

Included among those rights protected was the right to keep and bear arms

to keep and to bear arms; the right to be exempted from the quartering of soldiers in a house without the consent of the owner; the right to be exempt from unreasonable searches and seizures [; etc., through the Eighth Amendment].[52]

In the end, Senator Howard concluded his remarks as follows: *"The great object of the first section of this amendment is, therefore, to restrain the power of the States and compel them at all times to respect these great fundamental guarantees."*[53] There was no dissent from this description of the clause.

Following ratification of the Fourteenth Amendment, therefore, some state constitutions might presume to provide even *more* protection of these same rights than the Fourteenth Amendment (and some continue even now to do so),[54] but none could thereafter presume to provide any less — whether the object of regulation was freedom of speech and of the press or of the personal right to arms. And it is quite clear that in the ratification debates of the Fourteenth Amendment, no distinction whatever was drawn between the "privileges and immunities" Congress was understood already to be bound to respect (pursuant to the Bill of Rights) and those now uniformly also to bind the states. Each was given the same constitutional immunity from abridging acts of state government as each was already recognized to possess from abridgment by Congress. What was previously forbidden only to Congress to do was, by the passage of the Fourteenth Amendment, made equally forbidden to any state. Moreover, the point was acknowledged to be particularly important in settling the Second Amendment right as a citizen's personal right, i.e., personal to each citizen as such.[55]

V

Again, however, one does not derive from these observations that each citizen has an uncircumscribable personal constitutional right to acquire, to own, and to employ any and all such arms as one might desire so to do, or necessarily to carry them into any place one might wish. To the contrary, restrictions generally consistent merely with safe usage, for example, or restrictions even of a particular "Arms" kind, are not all per se precluded by the two constitutional amendments and provisions we have briefly reviewed. There is a "rule of reason" applicable to the First Amendment, for example, and its equivalent will also be pertinent here. It is not the case that one may say whatever one wants and however one wants, wherever one wants, and whenever one likes — location, time, and associated circumstances do make a difference, consistent even with a very strong view of the freedom of speech and press accurately reflected in conscientious decisions of the Supreme Court. The freedoms of speech and of the press, it has been correctly said, are not absolute.

But First and Second Amendment rights are not absolute

Neither is one's right to keep and bear arms absolute. It may fairly be questionable, for example, whether the type of arms one may have a "right to keep" consistent with the Second Amendment extend to a howitzer.[56] It may likewise be questionable whether the "arms" one *does* have a "right to keep" are necessarily arms one also may presume to "bear" wherever one wants, e.g., in courtrooms or in public schools. To be sure, each kind of example one might give will raise its own kind of question. And serious people are quite willing to confront serious problems in regulating "the right to keep and bear arms," as they are equally willing to confront serious problems in regulating "the freedom of speech and of the press."[57]

Serious people decline to trivialize any right expressly identified in the Bill of Rights

The difference between these serious people and others, however, was a large difference in the very beginning of this country and it remains as a large difference in the end. The difference is that such serious people begin with a constitutional understanding that declines to trivialize the Second Amendment or the Fourteenth Amendment, just as they likewise decline to trivialize any other right expressly identified elsewhere in the Bill of Rights. It is difficult to see why they are less than entirely right in this unremarkable view. That it has taken the NRA to speak for them, with respect to the Second Amendment, moreover, is merely interesting — perhaps far more as a comment on others, however, than on the NRA.

For the point to be made with respect to Congress and the Second Amendment[58] is that the essential claim (certainly not every claim — but the essential claim) advanced by the NRA with respect to the Second Amendment is extremely strong. Indeed, one may fairly declare, it is at least as well anchored in the Constitution in its own way as were the essential claims with respect to the First Amendment's protection of freedom of speech as first advanced on the Supreme Court by Holmes and Brandeis, seventy years ago.[59] And until the Supreme Court manages to express the central premise of the Second Amendment more fully and far more appropriately than it has done thus far, the constructive role of the NRA today, like the role of the ACLU in the 1920s with respect to the First Amendment (as it then was), ought itself not lightly to be dismissed.[60] Indeed, it is largely by the "unreasonable" persistence of just such organizations in this country that the Bill of Rights has endured.

The essential claim advanced by the NRA is extremely strong

THE
EMBARRASSING
SECOND AMENDMENT

Sanford Levinson *

O ne of the best known pieces of American popular art in this century is the *New Yorker* cover by Saul Steinberg presenting a map of the United States as seen by a New Yorker. As most readers can no doubt recall, Manhattan dominates the map; everything west of the Hudson is more or less collapsed together and minimally displayed to the viewer. Steinberg's great cover depends for its force on the reality of what social psychologists call "cognitive maps." If one asks inhabitants ostensibly of the same cities to draw maps of that city, one will quickly discover that the images carried around in people's minds will vary by race, social class, and the like. What is true of maps of places — that they differ according to the perspectives of the mapmakers — is certainly true of all conceptual maps.

> The conceptual images we draw in our minds result from each of our unique perspectives on life

To continue the map analogy, consider in this context the Bill of Rights: Is there an agreed upon

*Sanford Levinson is the W. St. John Garwood and W. St. John Garwood, Jr., Centennial Professor of Law, University of Texas Law School. Reprinted from the *Yale Law Journal* (vol. 99, 1989) courtesy of the author and publisher.

"projection" of the concept? Is there even a canonical text of the Bill of Rights? Does it include the first eight, nine, or ten Amendments to the Constitution?[1] Imagine two individuals who are asked to draw a "map" of the Bill of Rights. One is a (stereo-) typical member of the American Civil Liberties Union (of which I am a card-carrying member); the other is an equally (stereo-) typical member of the "New Right." The first, I suggest, would feature the First Amendment[2] as Main Street, dominating the map, though more, one suspects, in its role as protector of speech and prohibitor of established religion than as guardian of the rights of religious believers. The other principal avenues would be the criminal procedure aspects of the Constitution drawn from the Fourth,[3] Fifth,[4] Sixth,[5] and Eighth[6] Amendments. Also depicted prominently would be the Ninth Amendment,[7] although perhaps as in the process of construction. I am confident that the ACLU map would exclude any display of the just compensation clause of the Fifth Amendment[8] or of the Tenth Amendment.[9]

Therefore we all draw different maps of the Bill of Rights

The second map, drawn by the New Rightist, would highlight the free exercise clause of the First Amendment,[10] the just compensation clause of the Fifth Amendment,[11] and the Tenth Amendment.[12] Perhaps the most notable difference between the two maps, though, would be in regard to the Second Amendment: "A well regulated Militia being necessary to the security of a free State, the right of the people to keep and bear Arms shall not be infringed." What would be at most only a blind alley for the ACLU mapmaker would, I am confident, be a major boulevard in the map drawn by the New Right adherent. It is this last anomaly that I want to explore in this essay.

I

THE POLITICS OF INTERPRETING
THE SECOND AMENDMENT

To put it mildly, the Second Amendment is not at the forefront of constitutional discussion, at least as registered in what the academy regards as the venues for such discussion — law reviews,[13] casebooks,[14] and other scholarly legal publications. As Professor LaRue has recently written, "the second amendment is not taken seriously by most scholars."[15]

The Second Amendment has never been at the forefront of legal discussion

Both Laurence Tribe[16] and the Illinois team of Nowak, Rotunda, and Young[17] at least acknowledge the existence of the Second Amendment in their respective treatises on constitutional law, perhaps because the treatise genre demands more encyclopedic coverage than does the casebook. Neither, however, pays it the compliment of extended analysis. Both marginalize the Amendment by relegating it to footnotes; it becomes what a deconstructionist might call a "supplement" to the ostensibly "real" Constitution that is privileged by discussion in the text.[18] Professor Tribe's footnote appears as part of a general discussion of congressional power. He asserts that the history of the

Some legal scholars relegate it only to their footnotes

Amendment "indicate[s] that the central concern of [its] framers was to prevent such federal interferences with the state militia as would permit the establishment of a standing national army and the consequent destruction of local autonomy."[19] He does note, however, that "the debates surrounding congressional approval of the second amendment do contain references to individual self-protection as well as to states' rights," but he argues that the presence of the preamble to the Amendment, as well as the qualifying phrase " 'well regulated' makes an invocation of the amendment as a restriction on state or local gun control measures extremely problematic."[20] Nowak, Rotunda, and Young mention the Amendment in the context of the incorporation controversy, though they discuss its meaning at slightly greater length.[21] They state that "[t]he Supreme Court has not determined, at least not with any clarity, whether the amendment protects only a right of state governments against federal interference with state militia and police forces . . . or a right of individuals against the federal and state government[s]."[22]

Yet they agree that the Supreme Court has never clearly defined what right the Amendment protects

Clearly the Second Amendment is not the only ignored patch of text in our constitutional conversations. One will find extraordinarily little discussion about another one of the initial Bill of Rights, the Third Amendment: "No Soldier shall, in time of peace be quartered in any house, without the consent of the Owner, nor in time of war, but in a manner to be prescribed by law." Nor does one hear much about letters of marque and reprisal[23] or the granting of titles of nobility.[24] There are, however, some differences that are worth noting.

The Third Amendment, to take the easiest case, is ignored because it is in fact of no current importance whatsoever (although it did, for obvious reasons, have importance at the time of the founding). It has never, for a single instant, been viewed by any body of modern lawyers or groups of laity as highly relevant to their legal or political concerns. For this reason, there is almost no case law on the Amendment.[25] I suspect that few among even the highly sophisticated readers of this Journal can summon up the Amendment without the aid of the text.

The Second Amendment, though, is radically different from these other pieces of constitutional text just mentioned, which all share the attribute of being basically irrelevant to any ongoing political struggles. To grasp the difference, one might simply begin by noting that it is not at all unusual for the Second Amendment to show up in letters to the editors of newspapers and magazines.[26] That judges and academic lawyers, including the ones who write casebooks, ignore it is most certainly not evidence for the proposition that no one cares about it. The National Rifle Association, to name the most obvious example, cares deeply about the Amendment, and an apparently serious Senator of the United States averred that the right to keep and bear arms is the "right most valued by free men."[27] Campaigns for Congress in both political parties, and even presidential campaigns, may turn

But millions of Americans care deeply about it

on the apparent commitment of the candidates to a particular view of the Second Amendment. This reality of the political process reflects the fact that millions of Americans, even if (or perhaps *especially* if) they are not academics, can quote the Amendment and would disdain any presentation of the Bill of Rights that did not give it a place of pride.

Yet a finding that it protects the individual right to keep and bear arms may profoundly embarrass the liberal elite

I cannot help but suspect that the best explanation for the absence of the Second Amendment from the legal consciousness of the elite bar, including that component found in the legal academy,[28] is derived from a mixture of sheer opposition to the idea of private ownership of guns and the perhaps subconscious fear that altogether plausible, perhaps even "winning," interpretations of the Second Amendment would present real hurdles to those of us supporting prohibitory regulation. Thus the title of this essay — "The Embarrassing Second Amendment" — for I want to suggest that the Amendment may be profoundly embarrassing to many who both support such regulation and view themselves as committed to zealous adherence to the Bill of Rights (such as most members of the ACLU). Indeed, one sometimes discovers members of the NRA who are equally committed members of the ACLU, differing with the latter only on the issue of the Second Amendment but otherwise genuinely sharing the libertarian viewpoint of the ACLU.

It is not my style to offer "correct" or "incorrect" interpretations of the Constitution.[29] My major interest is in delineating the rhetorical structures of American constitutional argument and elaborating what is sometimes called the "politics of interpretation," that is, the factors that explain why one or another approach will appeal to certain analysts at certain times, while other analysts, or times, will favor quite different approaches. Thus my general tendency to regard as wholly untenable any approach to the Constitution that describes itself as obviously correct and condemns its opposition as simply wrong holds for the Second Amendment as well. In some contexts, this would lead me to label as tendentious the certainty of NRA advocates that the Amendment means precisely what they assert it does. In this particular context — i.e., the pages of a journal whose audience is much more likely to be drawn from an elite, liberal portion of the public — I will instead be suggesting that the skepticism should run in the other direction. That is, we might consider the possibility that "our" views of the Amendment, perhaps best reflected in Professor Tribe's offhand treatment of it, might themselves be equally deserving of the "tendentious" label.

If the NRA errs in its partisan support of an individual rights interpretation, so too may the liberal elite err in opposing that view

II

THE RHETORICAL STRUCTURES OF THE RIGHT TO BEAR ARMS

My colleague Philip Bobbitt has, in his book *Constitutional Fate*,[30] spelled out six approaches — or "modalities," as he terms them — of constitutional argument. These approaches, he argues, comprise what might be termed our legal grammar. They are the rhetorical structures within which "law-talk" as a recognizable form of conversation is carried on. The six are as follows:

1. textual argument — appeals to the unadorned language of the text;[31]

2. historical argument — appeals to the historical background of the provision being considered, whether the history considered be general, such as background but clearly crucial events (such as the American Revolution), or specific appeals to the so-called intentions of the framers;[32]

3. structural argument — analyses inferred from the particular structures established by the Constitution, including the tripartite division of the national government; the separate existence of both state and nation as political entities; and the structured role of citizens within the political order;[33]

4. doctrinal argument — emphasis on the implications of prior cases decided by the Supreme Court;[34]

5. prudential argument — emphasis on the consequences of adopting a proffered decision in any given case;[35] and, finally,

6. ethical argument — reliance on the overall "ethos" of limited government as centrally constituting American political culture.[36]

I want to frame my consideration of the Second Amendment within the first five of Bobbitt's cate-

Six approaches to constitutional argument

gories; they are all richly present in consideration of what the Amendment might mean. The sixth, which emphasizes the ethos of limited government, does not play a significant role in the debate of the Second Amendment.[37]

TEXT

I begin with the appeal to text. Recall the Second Amendment: "A well regulated Militia, being necessary to the security of a free State, the right of the people to keep and bear Arms, shall not be infringed." No one has ever described the Constitution as a marvel of clarity, and the Second Amendment is perhaps one of the worst drafted of all its provisions. What is special about the Amendment is the inclusion of an opening clause — a preamble, if you will — that seems to set out its purpose. No similar clause is a part of any other Amendment,[38] though that does not, of course, mean that we do not ascribe purposes to them. It would be impossible to make sense of the Constitution if we did not engage in the ascription of purpose. Indeed, the major debates about the First Amendment arise precisely when one tries to discern a purpose, given that "literalism" is a hopelessly failing approach to interpreting it. We usually do not even recognize punishment of fraud — a classic speech act — as a free speech problem because we so sensibly assume that the purpose of the

The textual argument

First Amendment could not have been, for example, to protect the circulation of patently deceptive information to potential investors in commercial enterprises. The sharp differences that distinguish those who would limit the reach of the First Amendment to "political" speech from those who would extend it much further, encompassing non-deceptive commercial speech, are all derived from different readings of the purpose that underlies the raw text.[39]

Some legal analysts assert that the opening clause restricts the right of the individual to keep and bear arms

A standard move of those legal analysts who wish to limit the Second Amendment's force is to focus on its "preamble" as setting out a restrictive purpose. Recall Laurence Tribe's assertion that that purpose was to allow the states to keep their militias and to protect them against the possibility that the new national government will use its power to establish a powerful standing army and eliminate the state militias. This purposive reading quickly disposes of any notion that there is an "individual" right to keep and bear arms. The right, if such it be, is only a state's right. The consequence of this reading is obvious: the national government has the power to regulate — to the point of prohibition — private ownership of guns, since that has, by stipulation, nothing to do with preserving state militias. This is, indeed, the position of the ACLU, which reads the Amendment as protecting only the right of "maintaining an effective state militia. . . . [T]he individual's right to bear arms applies only to the preservation or efficiency of a well-regulated [state] militia. Except for lawful police and military purposes, the possession of weapons by individuals is not constitutionally protected."[40]

This is not a wholly implausible reading, but one might ask why the Framers did not simply say something like "Congress shall have no power to prohibit state-organized and directed militias." Perhaps they in fact meant to do something else. Moreover, we might ask if ordinary readers of late 18th century legal prose would have interpreted it as meaning something else. The text at best provides only a starting point for a conversation. In this specific instance, it does not come close to resolving the questions posed by federal regulation of arms. Even if we accept the preamble as significant, we must still try to figure out what might be suggested by guaranteeing to "the people the right to keep and bear arms"; moreover, as we shall see presently, even the preamble presents unexpected difficulties in interpretation.

But perhaps the Framers meant to do something else

HISTORY

One might argue (and some have) that the substantive right is one pertaining to a collective body — "the people" — rather than to individuals. Professor Cress, for example, argues that state constitutions regularly used the words "man" or "person" in regard to "individual rights such as freedom of conscience," whereas the use in those constitutions of the term "the people" in regard to a right to bear

The historical argument

arms is intended to refer to the "sovereign citizenry" collectively organized.[41] Such an argument founders, however, upon examination of the text of the federal Bill of Rights itself and the usage there of the term "the people" in the First, Fourth, Ninth, and Tenth Amendments.

Consider that the Fourth Amendment protects "[t]he right of the people to be secure in their persons," or that the First Amendment refers to the "right of the people peaceably to assemble, and to petition the Government for a redress of grievances." It is difficult to know how one might plausibly read the Fourth Amendment as other than a protection of individual rights, and it would approach the frivolous to read the assembly and petition clause as referring only to the right of state legislatures to meet and pass a remonstrance directed to Congress or the President against some governmental act. The Tenth Amendment is trickier, though it does explicitly differentiate between "states" and "the people" in terms of retained rights.[42] Concededly, it would be possible to read the Tenth Amendment as suggesting only an ultimate right of revolution by the collective people should the "states" stray too far from their designated role of protecting the rights of the people. This reading follows directly from the social contract theory of the state. (But, of course, many of these rights are held by individuals.)

Although the record is suitably complicated, it seems tendentious to reject out of hand the argu-

The collective interpretation of the Second Amendment founders when one compares its language to that of the First, Fourth, and Tenth

ment that one purpose of the Amendment was to recognize an individual's right to engage in armed self-defense against criminal conduct.[43] Historian Robert E. Shalhope supports this view, arguing in his article "The Ideological Origins of the Second Amendment"[44] that the Amendment guarantees individuals the right "to possess arms for their own personal defense."[45] It would be especially unsurprising if this were the case, given the fact that the development of a professional police force (even within large American cities) was still at least a half century away at the end of the colonial period.[46] I shall return later in this essay to this individualist notion of the Amendment, particularly in regard to the argument that "changing circumstances," including the development of a professional police force, have deprived it of any continuing plausibility. But I want now to explore a second possible purpose of the Amendment, which as a sometime political theorist I find considerably more interesting.

Assume, as Professor Cress has argued, that the Second Amendment refers to a communitarian, rather than an individual, right.[47] We are still left the task of defining the relationship between the community and the state apparatus. It is this fascinating problem to which I now turn.

Defining the relationship between community and state

Consider once more the preamble and its reference to the importance of a well-regulated militia. Is the meaning of the term obvious? Perhaps we should make some effort to find out what the term "militia" meant to 18th century readers and writers, rather than assume that it refers only to Dan Quayle's Indiana National Guard and the like. By no means am I arguing that the discovery of that meaning is dispositive as to the general meaning of the Constitution for us today. But it seems foolhardy to be entirely uninterested in the historical philology behind the Second Amendment.

What does "militia" mean?

I, for one, have been persuaded that the term "militia" did not have the limited reference that Professor Cress and many modern legal analysts assign to it. There is strong evidence that "militia" refers to all of the people, or at least all of those treated as full citizens of the community. Consider, for example, the question asked by George Mason, one of the Virginians who refused to sign the Constitution because of its lack of a Bill of Rights: "Who are the Militia? They consist now of the whole people."[48] Similarly, the *Federal Farmer,* one of the most important Anti-Federalist opponents of the Constitution, referred to a "militia, when properly formed, [as] in fact the people themselves."[49] We have, of course, moved now from text to history. And this history is most interesting, especially when we look at the development of notions of popular sovereignty. It has become almost a cliché of contemporary American historiography to link the development of American political thought, including its constitutional aspects, to republican thought in England, the "country" critique of the powerful "court" centered in London.

One of this school's important writers, of course, was James Harrington, who not only was influential at the time but also has recently been given a certain pride of place by one of the most prominent of contemporary "neo-republicans," Professor Frank Michelman.[50] One historian describes Harrington as having made "the most significant contribution to English libertarian attitudes toward arms, the individual, and society."[51] He was a central figure in the development of the ideas of popular sovereignty and republicanism.[52] For Harrington, preservation of republican liberty requires independence, which rests primarily on possession of adequate property to make men free from coercion by employers or landlords. But widespread ownership of land is not sufficient. These independent yeomen should also bear arms. As Professor Morgan puts it, "[T]hese independent yeomen, armed and embodied in a militia, are also a popular government's best protection against its enemies, whether they be aggressive foreign monarchs or scheming demagogues within the nation itself."[53]

Harrington's fears of a standing army

A central fear of Harrington and of all future republicans was a standing army, composed of professional soldiers. Harrington and his fellow republicans viewed a standing army as a threat to freedom, to be avoided at almost all costs. Thus, says Morgan, "A militia is the only safe form of military power that a popular government can employ; and because it is composed of the armed yeomanry, it will prevail over the mercenary professionals who man the armies of neighboring monarchs."[54]

The possibility that an armed populace provides a "checking value" against tyranny

Scholars of the First Amendment have made us aware of the importance of John Trenchard and Thomas Gordon, whose *Cato's Letters* were central to the formation of the American notion of freedom of the press. That notion includes what Vincent Blasi would come to call the "checking value" of a free press, which stands as a sturdy exposer of governmental misdeeds.[55] Consider the possibility, though, that the ultimate "checking value" in a republican polity is the ability of an armed populace, presumptively motivated by a shared commitment to the common good, to resist governmental tyranny.[56] Indeed, one of Cato's letters refers to "the Exercise of despotick Power [as] the unrelenting War of an armed Tyrant upon his unarmed Subjects. . . ."[57]

Cress persuasively shows that no one defended universal possession of arms. New Hampshire had no objection to disarming those who "are or have been in actual rebellion," just as Samuel Adams stressed that only "peaceable citizens" should be protected in their right of "keeping their own arms."[58] All these points can be conceded, however, without conceding as well that Congress — or, for that matter, the States — had the power to disarm these "peaceable citizens."

Surely one of the foundations of American political thought of the period was the well-justified concern about political corruption and consequent governmental tyranny. Even the Federalists, fending off their opponents who accused them of foisting an oppressive new scheme upon the American people, were careful to acknowledge the risks of tyranny. James Madison, for example, speaks in *Federalist* Number Forty-Six of "the advantage of being armed, which the Americans possess over the people of almost every other nation."[59] The advantage in question was not merely the defense of American borders; a standing army might well accomplish that. Rather, an armed public was advantageous in protecting political liberty. It is therefore no surprise that the Federal Farmer, the nom de plume of an anti-federalist critic of the new Constitution and its absence of a Bill of Rights, could write that "to preserve liberty, it is essential that the whole body of the people always possess arms, and be taught alike, especially when young, how to use them. . . ."[60] On this matter, at least, there was no cleavage between the pro-ratification Madison and his opponent.

Madison's agreement with the Anti-federalists

In his influential *Commentaries on the Constitution,* Joseph Story, certainly no friend of Anti-Federalism, emphasized the "importance" of the Second Amendment.[61] He went on to describe the militia as "the natural defence of a free country" not only "against sudden foreign invasions" and "domestic insurrections," with which one might well expect a Federalist to be concerned, but also against "domestic usurpations of power by rulers."[62] "The right of the citizens to keep and bear

Justice Story's influential *Commentaries*

arms has justly been considered," Story wrote, "as the palladium of the liberties of a republic; since it offers a strong moral check against the usurpation and arbitrary power of rulers; and will generally, even if these are successful in the first instance, enable the people to resist and triumph over them."[63]

The opinions of Cooley and Schroeder   We also see this blending of individualist and collective accounts of the right to bear arms in remarks by Judge Thomas Cooley, one of the most influential 19th century constitutional commentators. Noting that the state might call into its official militia only "a small number" of the eligible citizenry, Cooley wrote that "if the right [to keep and bear arms] were limited to those enrolled, the purpose of this guaranty might be defeated altogether by the action or neglect to act of the government it was meant to hold in check."[64] Finally, it is worth noting the remarks of Theodore Schroeder, one of the most important developers of the theory of freedom of speech early in this century.[65] "[T]he obvious import [of the constitutional guarantee to carry arms]," he argues, "is to promote a state of preparedness for self-defense even against the invasions of government, because only governments have ever disarmed any considerable class of people as a means toward their enslavement."[66]

Such analyses provide the basis for Edward Abbey's revision of a common bumper sticker, "If guns are outlawed, only the government will have guns."[67] One of the things this slogan has helped me to understand is the political tilt contained within the Weberian definition of the state — i.e., the repository of a monopoly of the legitimate means of violence[68] — that is so commonly used by political scientists. It is a profoundly statist definition, the product of a specifically German tradition of the (strong) state rather than of a strikingly different American political tradition that is fundamentally mistrustful of state power and vigilant about maintaining ultimate power, including the power of arms, in the populace.

We thus see what I think is one of the most interesting points in regard to the new historiography of the Second Amendment — its linkage to conceptions of republican political order. Contemporary admirers of republican theory use it as a source both of critiques of more individualist liberal theory and of positive insight into the way we today might reorder our political lives.[69] One point of emphasis for neo-republicans is the value of participation in government, as contrasted to mere representation by a distant leadership, even if formally elected. But the implications of republicanism might push us in unexpected, even embarrassing, directions: just as ordinary citizens should participate actively in governmental decision-making through offering their own deliberative insights, rather than be confined to casting ballots once every two or four years for those very few individuals who will actually make decisions, so should ordinary citizens participate in the process of law

The Second Amendment is linked to the conception of political order

enforcement and defense of liberty rather than rely on professionalized peacekeepers, whether we call them standing armies or police.

STRUCTURE

The structural argument

We have also passed imperceptibly into a form of structural argument, for we see that one aspect of the structure of checks and balances within the purview of 18th century thought was the armed citizen. That is, those who would limit the meaning of the Second Amendment to the constitutional protection of state-controlled militias agree that such protection rests on the perception that militarily competent states were viewed as a potential protection against a tyrannical national government. Indeed, in 1801 several governors threatened to call out state militias if the Federalists in Congress refused to elect Thomas Jefferson president.[70] But this argument assumes that there are only two basic components in the vertical structure of the American polity — the national government and the states. It ignores the implication that might be drawn from the Second, Ninth, and Tenth Amendments: the citizenry itself can be viewed as an important third component of republican governance insofar as it stands ready to defend republican liberty against the depredations of the other two structures, however futile that might appear as a practical matter.

One implication of this republican rationale for the Second Amendment is that it calls into question the ability of a state to disarm its citizenry. That is, the strongest version of the republican argument would hold it to be a "privilege and immunity of United States citizenship" — of membership in a liberty-enhancing political order — to keep arms that could be taken up against tyranny wherever found, including, obviously, state government. Ironically, the principal citation supporting this argument is to Chief Justice Taney's egregious opinion in *Dred Scott*,[71] where he suggested that an uncontroversial attribute of citizenship, in addition to the right to migrate from one state to another, was the right to possess arms. The logic of Taney's argument at this point seems to be that, because it was inconceivable that the Framers could have genuinely imagined blacks having the right to possess arms, it follows that they could not have envisioned them as being citizens, since citizenship entailed that right. Taney's seeming recognition of a right to arms is much relied on by opponents of gun control.[72] Indeed, recall Madison's critique, in *Federalist* Numbers Ten and Fourteen, of republicanism's traditional emphasis on the desirability of small states as preservers of republican liberty. He transformed this debate by arguing that the states would be less likely to preserve liberty because they could so easily fall under the sway of a local dominant faction, whereas an extended republic would guard against this dan-

Justice Taney's opinion that an uncontroversial attribute of citizenship was the right to possess arms

ger. Anyone who accepts the Madisonian argument could scarcely be happy enhancing the powers of the states over their own citizens; indeed, this
has been one of the great themes of American
constitutional history, as the nationalization of
the Bill of Rights has been deemed necessary in
order to protect popular liberty against state dep-
redation.

DOCTRINE

**The
doctrinal
argument**
Inevitably one must at least mention, even though
there is not space to discuss fully, the so-called
incorporation controversy regarding the applica-
tion of the Bill of Rights to the states through the
Fourteenth Amendment. It should be no surprise
that the opponents of gun control appear to take a
"full incorporationist" view of that Amendment.[73]
They view the privileges and immunities clause,
which was eviscerated in the *Slaughterhouse
Cases*,[74] as designed to require the states to honor
the rights that had been held, by Justice Marshall
in *Barron v. Baltimore* in 1833,[75] to restrict only
the national government. In 1875 the Court stated,
in *United States v. Cruikshank*,[76] that the Second
Amendment, insofar as it grants any right at all,
"means no more than that it shall not be infringed
by Congress. This is one of the amendments that
has no other effect than to restrict the powers of the
national government . . ." Lest there be any remaining doubt on this point, the Court specifically

cited the *Cruikshank* language eleven years later in *Presser v. Illinois,*[77] in rejecting the claim that the Second Amendment served to invalidate an Illinois statute that prohibited "any body of men whatever, other than the regular organized volunteer militia of this State, and the troops of the United States . . . to drill or parade with arms in any city, or town, of this State, without the license of the Governor thereof. . . ."[78]

The first "incorporation decision," *Chicago, B. & Q. R. R. Co. v. Chicago,*[79] was not delivered until eleven years after *Presser;* one therefore cannot know if the judges in *Cruikshank* and *Presser* were willing to concede that *any* of the amendments comprising the Bill of Rights were anything more than limitations on congressional or other national power. The obvious question, given the modern legal reality of the incorporation of almost all of the rights protected by the First, Fourth, Fifth, Sixth, and Eighth Amendments, is what exactly justifies treating the Second Amendment as the great exception? Why, that is, should *Cruikshank* and *Presser* be regarded as binding precedent any more than any of the other "pre-incorporation" decisions refusing to apply given aspects of the Bill of Rights against the states?

What justifies excepting the Second Amendment from the protections of the Fourteenth?

If one agrees with Professor Tribe that the Amendment is simply a federalist protection of state rights, then presumably there is nothing to incorporate.[80] If, however, one accepts the Amendment as a serious substantive limitation on the

The Supreme Court has almost shamelessly refused to discuss the issue

ability of the national government to regulate the private possession of arms based on either the "individualist" or "neo-republican" theories sketched above, then why not follow the "incorporationist" logic applied to other amendments and limit the states as well in their powers to regulate (and especially to prohibit) such possession? The Supreme Court has almost shamelessly refused to discuss the issue,[81] but that need not stop the rest of us.

The only modern case is *United States v. Miller*

Returning, though, to the question of Congress' power to regulate the keeping and bearing of arms, one notes that there is, basically, only one modern case that discusses the issue, *United States v. Miller,*[82] decided in 1939. Jack Miller was charged with moving a sawed-off shotgun in interstate commerce in violation of the National Firearms Act of 1934. Among other things, Miller and a compatriot had not registered the firearm, as required by the Act. The court below had dismissed the charge, accepting Miller's argument that the Act violated the Second Amendment.

The Supreme Court reversed unanimously, with the arch-conservative Justice McReynolds writing the opinion.[83] Interestingly enough, he emphasized that there was no evidence showing that a sawed-off shotgun "at this time has some reasonable relationship to the preservation or efficiency of a well regulated militia."[84] And "[c]ertainly it is not within judicial notice that this weapon is any part of the ordinary military equipment or that its use could contribute to the common defense."[85] *Miller* might have had a tenable argument had he been able to show that he was keeping or bearing a weapon that clearly had a potential military use.[86]

Justice McReynolds went on to describe the purpose of the Second Amendment as "assur[ing] the continuation and render[ing] possible the effectiveness of [the Militia]."[87] He contrasted the Militia with troops of a standing army, which the Constitution indeed forbade the states to keep without the explicit consent of Congress. "The sentiment of the time strongly disfavored standing armies; the common view was that adequate defense of country and laws could be secured through the Militia — civilians primarily, soldiers on occasion."[88] McReynolds noted further that "the debates in the Convention, the history and legislation of Colonies and States, and the writings of approved commentators [all] [s]how plainly enough that the Militia comprised all males physically capable of acting in concert for the common defense."[89]

It is difficult to read *Miller* as rendering the Second Amendment meaningless as a control on Congress. Ironically, *Miller* can be read to support some of the most extreme anti-gun control arguments, e.g., that the individual citizen has a right to keep and bear bazookas, rocket launchers, and other armaments that are clearly relevant to modern warfare, including, of course, assault weapons. Arguments about the constitutional legitimacy of a

Ironically, *Miller* can be read as supporting the right to own such weapons as bazookas

prohibition by Congress of private ownership of handguns or, what is much more likely, assault rifles, might turn on the usefulness of such guns in military settings.

PRUDENTIALISM

The prudential argument: dealing with practical consequences

We have looked at four of Bobbitt's categories — text, history, structure, and case law doctrine — and have seen, at the very least, that the arguments on behalf of a "strong" Second Amendment are stronger than many of us might wish were the case. This, then, brings us to the fifth category, prudentialism, or an attentiveness to practical consequences, which is clearly of great importance in any debates about gun control. The standard argument in favor of strict control and, ultimately, prohibition of private ownership focuses on the extensive social costs of widespread distribution of firearms. Consider, for example, a recent speech given by former Justice Lewis Powell to the American Bar Association. He noted that over 40,000 murders were committed in the United States in 1986 and 1987, and that fully sixty percent of them were committed with firearms. England and Wales, however, saw only 662 homicides in 1986, less than eight percent of which were committed with firearms.[90] Justice Powell indicated that, "[w]ith respect to handguns," in contrast "to sporting rifles and shotguns[,] it is not easy to understand why the Second Amendment, or the notion of liberty, should be viewed as creating a right to own and carry a weapon that contributes so directly to the shocking number of murders in our society."[91]

It is hard to disagree with Justice Powell; it appears almost crazy to protect as a constitutional right something that so clearly results in extraordinary social costs with little, if any, compensating social advantage. Indeed, since Justice Powell's talk, the subject of assault rifles has become a staple of national discussion, and the opponents of regulation of such weapons have deservedly drawn the censure even of conservative leaders like William Bennett. It is almost impossible to imagine that the judiciary would strike down a determination by Congress that the possession of assault weapons should be denied to private citizens.

Even if one accepts the historical plausibility of the arguments advanced above, the overriding temptation is to say that time and circumstances have changed and that there is simply no reason to continue enforcing an outmoded, and indeed dangerous, understanding of private rights against public order. This criticism is clearest in regard to the so-called individualist argument, for one can argue that the rise of a professional police force to enforce the law has made irrelevant, and perhaps even counterproductive, the continuation of a strong notion of self-help as the remedy for crime.[92]

Some argue that the rise of professional police forces makes self-protection unnecessary

I am not unsympathetic to such arguments. It is no purpose of this essay to solicit membership for the National Rifle Association or to express any sympathy for what even Don Kates, a strong critic of the conventional dismissal of the Second Amendment, describes as "the gun lobby's obnoxious habit of assailing all forms of regulation on 2nd Amendment grounds."[93] And yet . . .

Circumstances may well have changed in regard to individual defense, although we ignore at our political peril the good-faith belief of many Americans that they cannot rely on the police for protection against a variety of criminals. Still, let us assume that the individualist reading of the Amendment has been vitiated by changing circumstances. Are we quite so confident that circumstances are equally different in regard to the republican rationale outlined earlier?

It is foolhardy to believe that the armed state will be benevolent

One would, of course, like to believe that the state, whether at the local or national level, presents no threat to important political values, including liberty. But our propensity to believe that this is the case may be little more than a sign of how truly different we are from our radical forebears. I do not want to argue that the state is necessarily tyrannical; I am not an anarchist. But it seems foolhardy to assume that the armed state will necessarily be benevolent. The American political tradition is, for good or ill, based in large measure on a healthy mistrust of the state. The development of widespread suffrage and greater majoritarianism in our polity is itself no sure protection, at least within republican theory. The republican theory is predicated on the stark contrast between mere democracy, where people are motivated by selfish personal interest, and a republic, where civic virtue, both in citizens and leadership, tames selfishness on behalf of the common good. In any event, it is hard for me to see how one can argue that circumstances have so changed as to make mass disarmament constitutionally unproblematic.[94]

Indeed, only in recent months have we seen the brutal suppression of the Chinese student demonstrations in Tiananmen Square. It should not surprise us that some NRA sympathizers have presented that situation as an object lesson to those who unthinkingly support the prohibition of private gun ownership. "[I]f all Chinese citizens kept arms, their rulers could hardly have dared to massacre the demonstrators. . . . The private keeping of hand-held personal firearms is within the constitutional design for a counter to government run amok. . . . As the Tiananmen Square tragedy showed so graphically, AK-47s fall into that category of weapons, and that is why they are protected by the Second Amendment."[95] It is simply silly to respond that small arms are irrelevant against nuclear-armed states: Witness contemporary Northern Ireland and the territories occupied by Israel, where the sophisticated weaponry of Great Britain and Israel have proved almost totally beside the point. The fact that these may not be pleasant examples does not affect the principal point, that a state facing a totally disarmed population is in a far better position, for good or for ill, to suppress popu-

It is simply silly to argue that small arms are irrelevant against nuclear-armed states

lar demonstrations and uprisings than one that must calculate the possibilities of its soldiers and officials being injured or killed.[96]

III
TAKING THE SECOND AMENDMENT SERIOUSLY

If we take our rights seriously we must honor them even at great social cost

There is one further problem of no small import: If one does accept the plausibility of any of the arguments on behalf of a strong reading of the Second Amendment, but, nevertheless, rejects them in the name of social prudence and the present-day consequences produced by finicky adherence to earlier understandings, why do we not apply such consequentialist criteria to each and every part of the Bill of Rights?[97] As Ronald Dworkin has argued, what it means to take rights seriously is that one will honor them even when there is significant social cost in doing so. If protecting freedom of speech, the rights of criminal defendants, or any other part of the Bill of Rights were always (or even most of the time) clearly costless to the society as a whole, it would truly be impossible to understand why they would be as controversial as they are. The very fact that there are often significant costs — criminals going free, oppressed groups having to hear viciously racist speech and so on — helps to account for the observed fact that those who view themselves as defenders of the Bill of Rights are generally antagonistic to prudential arguments. Most often, one finds them embracing versions of textual, historical, or doctrinal argument that dismiss as almost crass and vulgar any insistence that times might have changed and made too "expensive" the continued adherence to a given view. "Cost-benefit" analysis, rightly or wrongly, has come to be viewed as a "conservative" weapon to attack liberal rights.[98] Yet one finds that the tables are strikingly turned when the Second Amendment comes into play. Here it is "conservatives" who argue in effect that social costs are irrelevant and "liberals" who argue for a notion of the "living Constitution" and "changed circumstances" that would have the practical consequence of removing any real bite from the Second Amendment.

As Fred Donaldson of Austin, Texas, wrote, commenting on those who defended the Supreme Court's decision upholding flag-burning as compelled by a proper (and decidedly non-prudential) understanding of the First Amendment, "[I]t seems inconsistent for [defenders of the decision] to scream so loudly" at the prospect of limiting the protection given expression "while you smile complacently at the Second torn and bleeding. If the Second Amendment is not worth the paper it is written on, what price the First?"[99] The fact that Mr. Donaldson is an ordinary citizen rather than an eminent law professor does not make his question any less pointed or its answer less difficult.

For too long, most members of the legal academy have treated the Second Amendment as the equivalent of an embarrassing relative, whose men-

If the Second Amendment is not worth the paper it is written on, what price the First?

tion brings a quick change of subject to other, more respectable, family members. That will no longer do. It is time for the Second Amendment to enter full scale into the consciousness of the legal academy. Those of us who agree with Martha Minow's emphasis on the desirability of encouraging different "voices" in the legal conversation[100] should be especially aware of the importance of recognizing the attempts of Mr. Donaldson and his millions of colleagues to join the conversation. To be sure, it is unlikely that Professor Minow had those too often peremptorily dismissed as "gun nuts" in mind as possible providers of "insight and growth," but surely the call for sensitivity to different or excluded voices cannot extend only to those groups "we" already, perhaps "complacent[ly]," believe have a lot to tell "us."[101] I am not so naive as to believe that conversation will overcome the chasm that now separates the sensibility of, say, Senator Hatch and myself as to what constitutes the "right[s] most valued by free men [and women]."[102] It is important to remember that one will still need to join up sides and engage in vigorous political struggle. But it might at least help to make the political sides appear more human to one another. Perhaps "we" might be led to stop referring casually to "gun nuts" just as, maybe, members of the NRA could be brought to understand the real fear that the currently almost uncontrolled system of gun ownership sparks in the minds of many whom they casually dismiss as "bleeding-heart liberals." Is not,

Is it not time to take the Second Amendment seriously and engage in a vigorous political struggle?

after all, the possibility of serious, engaged discussion about political issues at the heart of what is most attractive in both liberal *and* republican versions of politics?

The possibility does exist

A NATION OF COWARDS

*Jeffrey R. Snyder**

O ur society has reached a pinnacle of self-expression and respect for individuality rare or unmatched in history. Our entire popular culture — from fashion magazines to the cinema — positively screams the matchless worth of the individual, and glories in eccentricity, nonconformity, independent judgment, and self-determination. This enthusiasm is reflected in the prevalent notion that helping someone entails increasing that person's "self-esteem"; that if a person properly values himself, he will naturally be a happy, productive, and, in some inexplicable fashion, responsible member of society.

And yet, while people are encouraged to revel in their individuality and incalculable self-worth, the media and the law enforcement establishment continually advise us that, when confronted with the threat of lethal violence, we should not resist, but simply give the attacker what he wants. If the crime under consideration is rape, there is some notable waffling on this point, and the discussion quickly moves to how the woman can change her behavior to minimize the risk of rape, and the various ridicu-

Media and law enforcement advise we should not resist violence

*Jeffrey R. Snyder is an attorney in private practice in Washington, D.C. Reprinted from *The Public Interest* (no. 113, 1993) courtesy of the author and publisher.

lous, non-lethal weapons she may acceptably carry, such as whistles, keys, mace or, that weapon which really sends shivers down a rapist's spine, the portable cellular phone.

Now how can this be? How can a person who values himself so highly calmly accept the indignity of a criminal assault? How can one who believes that the essence of his dignity lies in his self-determination passively accept the forcible deprivation of that self-determination? How can he, quietly, with great dignity and poise, simply hand over the goods?

Are we to believe that a criminal threat to our person is some sort of new social contract? The assumption, of course, is that there is no inconsistency. The advice not to resist a criminal assault and simply hand over the goods is founded on the notion that one's life is of incalculable value, and that no amount of property is worth it. Put aside, for a moment, the outrageousness of the suggestion that a criminal who proffers lethal violence should be treated as if he has instituted a new social contract: "I will not hurt or kill you if you give me what I want." For years, feminists have labored to educate people that rape is not about sex, but about domination, degradation, and control. Evidently, someone needs to inform the law enforcement establishment and the media that kidnapping, robbery, carjacking, and assault are not about property.

Crime is not only a complete disavowal of the social contract, but also a commandeering of the victim's person and liberty. If the individual's dignity lies in the fact that he is a moral agent engaging in actions of his own will, in free exchange with others, then crime always violates the victim's dignity. It is, in fact, an act of enslavement. Your wallet, your purse, or your car may not be worth your life, but your dignity is; and if it is not worth fighting for, it can hardly be said to exist.

THE GIFT OF LIFE

Although difficult for modern man to fathom, it was once widely believed that life was a gift from God, that to not defend that life when offered violence was to hold God's gift in contempt, to be a coward and to breach one's duty to one's community. A sermon given in Philadelphia in 1747 unequivocally equated the failure to defend oneself with suicide:

> He that suffers his life to be taken from him by one that hath no authority for that purpose, when he might preserve it by defense, incurs the Guilt of self murder since God hath enjoined him to seek the continuance of his life, and Nature itself teaches every creature to defend itself.

"Cowardice" and "self-respect" have largely disappeared from public discourse. In their place we are offered "self-esteem" as the bellwether of success and a proxy for dignity. "Self-respect" implies that one recognizes standards, and judges oneself worthy by the degree to which one lives up to them.

"Cowardice" and "self-respect" have largely disappeared from public discourse

"Self-esteem" simply means that one feels good about oneself. "Dignity" used to refer to the self-mastery and fortitude with which a person conducted himself in the face of life's vicissitudes and the boorish behavior of others. Now, judging by campus speech codes, dignity requires that we never encounter a discouraging word and that others be coerced into acting respectfully, evidently on the assumption that we are powerless to prevent our degradation if exposed to the demeaning behavior of others. These are signposts proclaiming the insubstantiality of our character, the hollowness of our souls.

Crime is rampant because we condone it, excuse it, permit it, submit to it

It is impossible to address the problem of rampant crime without talking about the moral responsibility of the intended victim. Crime is rampant because the law-abiding, each of us, condone it, excuse it, permit it, submit to it. We permit and encourage it because we do not fight back, immediately, then and there, where it happens. Crime is not rampant because we do not have enough prisons, because judges and prosecutors are too soft, because the police are hamstrung with absurd technicalities. The defect is there, in our character. We are a nation of cowards and shirkers.

DO YOU FEEL LUCKY?

In 1991, when then-Attorney General Richard Thornburgh released the FBI's annual crime statistics, he noted that it is now more likely that a person will be the victim of a violent crime than that he will be in an auto accident. Despite this, most people readily believe that the existence of the police relieves them of the responsibility to take full measures to protect themselves. The police, however, are not personal bodyguards. Rather, they act as a general deterrent to crime, both by their presence and by apprehending criminals after the fact. As numerous courts have held, they have no legal obligation to protect anyone in particular. You cannot sue them for failing to prevent you from being the victim of a crime.

The police have no legal obligation to protect any particular citizen

Insofar as the police deter by their presence, they are very, very good. Criminals take great pains not to commit a crime in front of them. Unfortunately, the corollary is that you can pretty much bet your life (and you are) that they won't be there at the moment you actually need them.

Should you ever be the victim of an assault, a robbery, or a rape, you will find it very difficult to call the police while the act is in progress, even if you are carrying a portable cellular phone. Nevertheless, you might be interested to know how long it takes them to show up. Department of Justice statistics for 1991 show that, for all crimes of violence, only 28 percent of calls are responded to within five minutes. The idea that protection is a service people can call to have delivered and expect to receive in a timely fashion is often mocked by gun owners, who love to recite the challenge, "Call for a cop, call for an ambulance, and call for a pizza. See who shows up first."

Many people deal with the problem of crime by convincing themselves that they live, work, and travel only in special "crime-free" zones. Invariably, they react with shock and hurt surprise when they discover that criminals do not play by the rules and do not respect these imaginary boundaries. If, however, you understand that crime can occur anywhere at any time, and if you understand that you can be maimed or mortally wounded in mere seconds, you may wish to consider whether you are willing to place the responsibility for safeguarding your life in the hands of others.

POWER AND RESPONSIBILITY

Can you rightfully ask another human being to risk his life to protect yours, when you will assume no responsibility yourself?

Is your life worth protecting? If so, whose responsibility is it to protect it? If you believe that it is the police's, not only are you wrong — since the courts universally rule that they have no legal obligation to do so — but you face some difficult moral quandaries. How can you rightfully ask another human being to risk his life to protect yours, when you will assume no responsibility yourself? Because that is his job and we pay him to do it? Because your life is of incalculable value, but his is only worth the $30,000 salary we pay him? If you believe it reprehensible to possess the means and will to use lethal force to repel a criminal assault, how can you call upon another to do so for you?

Do you believe that you are forbidden to protect yourself because the police are better qualified to protect you, because they know what they are doing but you're a rank amateur? Put aside that this is equivalent to believing that only concert pianists may play the piano and only professional athletes may play sports. What exactly are these special qualities possessed only by the police and beyond the rest of us mere mortals?

One who values his life and takes seriously his responsibilities to his family and community will possess and cultivate the means of fighting back, and will retaliate when threatened with death or grievous injury to himself or a loved one. He will never be content to rely solely on others for his safety, or to think he has done all that is possible by being aware of his surroundings and taking measures of avoidance. Let's not mince words: He will be armed, will be trained in the use of his weapon, and will defend himself when faced with lethal violence.

Fortunately, there is a weapon for preserving life and liberty that can be wielded effectively by almost anyone — the handgun. Small and light enough to be carried habitually, lethal, but unlike the knife or sword, not demanding great skill or strength, it truly is the "great equalizer." Requiring only hand-eye coordination and a modicum of

The weapon for preserving life and liberty

ability to remain cool under pressure, it can be used effectively by the old and the weak against the young and the strong, by the one against the many.

The handgun is the only weapon that would give a lone female jogger a chance of prevailing against a gang of thugs intent on rape, a teacher a chance of protecting children at recess from a madman intent on massacring them, a family of tourists waiting at a mid-town subway station the means to protect themselves from a gang of teens armed with razors and knives.

The great American gun war

But since we live in a society that by and large outlaws the carrying of arms, we are brought into the fray of the Great American Gun War. Gun control is one of the most prominent battlegrounds in our current culture wars. Yet it is unique in the half-heartedness with which our conservative leaders and pundits — our "conservative elite" — do battle, and have conceded the moral high ground to liberal gun control proponents. It is not a topic often written about, or written about with any great fervor, by William F. Buckley or Patrick Buchanan. As drug czar, William Bennett advised President Bush to ban "assault weapons." George Will is on record as recommending the repeal of the Second Amendment, and Jack Kemp is on record as favoring a ban on the possession of semiautomatic "assault weapons." The battle for gun rights is one fought predominantly by the common man. The beliefs of both our liberal and conservative elites are in fact abetting the criminal rampage through our society.

SELLING CRIME PREVENTION

By any rational measure, nearly all gun control proposals are hokum. The Brady Bill, for example, would not have prevented John Hinckley from obtaining a gun to shoot President Reagan; Hinckley purchased his weapon five months before the attack, and his medical records could not have served as a basis to deny his purchase of a gun, since medical records are not public documents filed with the police. Similarly, California's waiting period and background check did not stop Patrick Purdy from purchasing the "assault rifle" and handguns he used to massacre children during recess in a Stockton schoolyard; the felony conviction that would have provided the basis for stopping the sales did not exist, because Mr. Purdy's previous weapons violations were plea-bargained down from felonies to misdemeanors.

By any rational measure nearly all gun control laws are hokum

In the mid-sixties there was a public service advertising campaign targeted at car owners about the prevention of car theft. The purpose of the ad was to urge car owners not to leave their keys in their cars. The message was, "Don't help a good boy go bad." The implication was that, by leaving his keys in his car, the normal, law-abiding car owner was contributing to the delinquency of minors who, if they just weren't tempted beyond their limits, would be "good." Now, in those days people still had a fair sense of just who was responsible for whose behavior. The ad succeeded in enraging a goodly portion of the populace, and was soon dropped.

Nearly all of the gun control measures offered by Handgun Control, Inc. (HCI) and its ilk embody the same philosophy. They are founded on the belief that America's law-abiding gun owners are the source of the problem. With their unholy desire for firearms, they are creating a society awash in a sea of guns, thereby helping good boys go bad, and helping bad boys be badder. This laying of moral blame for violent crime at the feet of the law-abiding, and the implicit absolution of violent criminals for their misdeeds, naturally infuriates honest gun owners.

It is ludicrous to expect gun control laws to significantly curb crime

The files of HCI and other gun control organizations are filled with proposals to limit the availability of semiautomatic and other firearms to law-abiding citizens, and barren of proposals for apprehending and punishing violent criminals. It is ludicrous to expect that the proposals of HCI, or any gun control laws, will significantly curb crime. According to Department of Justice and Bureau of Alcohol, Tobacco and Firearms (ATF) statistics, fully 90 percent of violent crimes are committed without a handgun, and 93 percent of the guns obtained by violent criminals are not obtained through the lawful purchase and sale transactions that are the object of most gun control legislation. Furthermore, the number of violent criminals is minute in comparison to the number of firearms in America — estimated by the ATF at about 200 million, approximately one-third of which are handguns. With so abundant a supply, there will always be enough guns available for those who wish to use them for nefarious ends, no matter how complete the legal prohibitions against them, or how draconian the punishment for their acquisition or use. No, the gun control proposals of HCI and other organizations are not seriously intended as crime control. Something else is at work here.

THE TYRANNY OF THE ELITE

Gun control is a moral crusade against a benighted, barbaric citizenry. This is demonstrated not only by the ineffectualness of gun control in preventing crime, and by the fact that it focuses on restricting the behavior of the law-abiding rather than apprehending and punishing the guilty, but also by the execration that gun control proponents heap on gun owners and their evil instrumentality, the NRA. Gun owners are routinely portrayed as uneducated, paranoid rednecks fascinated by and prone to violence, i.e., exactly the type of person who opposes the liberal agenda and whose moral and social "re-education" is the object of liberal social policies. Typical of such bigotry is New York Gov. Mario Cuomo's famous characterization of gun

Gun owners are routinely portrayed as uneducated paranoid rednecks

owners as "hunters who drink beer, don't vote, and lie to their wives about where they were all weekend." Similar vituperation is rained upon the NRA, characterized by Sen. Edward Kennedy as the "pusher's best friend," lampooned in political cartoons as standing for the right of children to carry firearms to school and, in general, portrayed as standing for an individual's God-given right to blow people away at will.

But the stereotype is false

The stereotype is, of course, false. As criminologist and constitutional lawyer Don B. Kates, Jr., and former HCI contributor Dr. Patricia Harris have pointed out, "[s]tudies consistently show that, on the average, gun owners are better educated and have more prestigious jobs than non-owners. . . . Later studies show that gun owners are *less* likely than non-owners to approve of police brutality, violence against dissenters, etc."

Conservatives must understand that the antipathy many liberals have for gun owners arises in good measure from their statist utopianism. This habit of mind has nowhere been better explored than in *The Republic*. There, Plato argues that the perfectly just society is one in which an unarmed people exhibit virtue by minding their own business in the performance of their assigned functions, while the government of philosopher-kings, above the law and protected by armed guardians unquestioning in their loyalty to the state, engineers, implements, and fine-tunes the creation of that society, aided and abetted by myths that both hide and justify their totalitarian manipulation.

THE UNARMED LIFE

When columnist Carl Rowan preaches gun control and uses a gun to defend his home, when Maryland Gov. William Donald Schaefer seeks legislation year after year to ban semiautomatic "assault weapons" whose only purpose, we are told, is to kill people, while he is at the same time escorted by state police armed with large-capacity 9mm semi-automatic pistols, it is not simple hypocrisy. It is the workings of that habit of mind possessed by all superior beings who have taken upon themselves the terrible burden of civilizing the masses and who understand, like our Congress, that laws are for other people.

The philosopher-kings protect themselves with guns but believe that gun control laws are needed for all others

The liberal elite know that they are philosopher-kings. They know that the people simply cannot be trusted; that they are incapable of just and fair self-government; that left to their own devices, their society will be racist, sexist, homophobic, and inequitable — and the liberal elite know how to fix things. They are going to help us live the good and just life, even if they have to lie to us and force us to do it. And they detest those who stand in their way.

The private ownership of firearms is a rebuke to this utopian zeal. To own firearms is to affirm that freedom and liberty are not gifts from the state. It is to reserve final judgment about whether the state is encroaching on freedom and liberty, to stand ready to defend that freedom with more than mere words, and to stand outside the state's totalitarian reach.

THE FLORIDA EXPERIENCE

The Florida concealed-carry law

The elitist distrust of the people underlying the gun control movement is illustrated beautifully in HCI's campaign against a new concealed-carry law in Florida. Prior to 1987, the Florida law permitting the issuance of concealed-carry permits was administered at the county level. The law was vague, and, as a result, was subject to conflicting interpretation and political manipulation. Permits were issued principally to security personnel and the privileged few with political connections. Permits were valid only within the county of issuance.

In 1987, however, Florida enacted a uniform concealed-carry law which mandates that county authorities issue a permit to anyone who satisfies certain objective criteria. The law requires that a permit be issued to any applicant who is a resident, at least twenty-one years of age, has no criminal record, no record of alcohol or drug abuse, no history of mental illness, and provides evidence of having satisfactorily completed a firearms safety course offered by the NRA or other competent instructor. The applicant must provide a set of fingerprints, after which the authorities make a background check. The permit must be issued or denied within ninety days, is valid throughout the state, and must be renewed every three years, which provides authorities a regular means of reevaluating whether the permit holder still qualifies.

Passage of this legislation was vehemently opposed by HCI and the media. The law, they said, would lead to citizens shooting each other over everyday disputes involving fender benders, impolite behavior, and other slights to their dignity. Terms like "Florida, the Gunshine State" and "Dodge City East" were coined to suggest that the state, and those seeking passage of the law, were encouraging individuals to act as judge, jury, and executioner in a "Death Wish" society.

No HCI campaign more clearly demonstrates the elitist beliefs underlying the campaign to eradicate gun ownership. Given the qualifications required of permit holders, HCI and the media can only believe that common, law-abiding citizens are seething cauldrons of homicidal rage, ready to kill to avenge any slight to their dignity, eager to seek out and summarily execute the lawless. Only lack of immediate access to a gun restrains them and prevents the blood from flowing in the streets. They are so mentally and morally deficient that they would mistake a permit to carry a weapon in self-defense as a state-sanctioned license to kill at will.

HCI apparently believes that a gun-carry permit for self-defense is a state-sanctioned license to kill

Did the dire predictions come true? Despite the fact that Miami and Dade County have severe problems with the drug trade, the homicide rate fell in Florida following enactment of this law, as it did in Oregon following enactment of similar legislation

From 1987 to 1993, of 160,823 permits issued, only 16 have been revoked for criminal use of a firearm

there. There are, in addition, several documented cases of new permit holders successfully using their weapons to defend themselves. Information from the Florida Department of State shows that, from the beginning of the program in 1987 through June 1993, 160,823 permits have been issued, and only 530, or about 0.33 percent of the applicants, have been denied a permit for failure to satisfy the criteria, indicating that the law is benefitting those whom it was intended to benefit — the law-abiding. Only 16 permits, *less than 1/100th of 1 percent,* have been revoked due to the post-issuance commission of a crime involving a firearm.

The Florida legislation has been used as a model for legislation adopted by Oregon, Idaho, Montana, and Mississippi. There are, in addition, seven other states (Maine, North and South Dakota, Utah, Washington, West Virginia, and, with the exception of cities with a population in excess of 1 million, Pennsylvania) which provide that concealed-carry permits must be issued to law-abiding citizens who satisfy various objective criteria. Finally, no permit is required at all in Vermont. Altogether, then, there are thirteen states in which law-abiding citizens who wish to carry arms to defend themselves may do so. While no one appears to have compiled the statistics from all of these jurisdictions, there is certainly an ample data base for those seeking the truth about the trustworthiness of law-abiding citizens who carry firearms.

Other evidence also suggests that armed citizens are very responsible in using guns to defend themselves. Florida State University criminologist Gary Kleck, using surveys and other data, has determined that armed citizens defend their lives or property with firearms against criminals approximately 1 million times a year. In 98 percent of these instances, the citizen merely brandishes the weapon or fires a warning shot. Only in 2 percent of the cases do citizens actually shoot their assailants. In defending themselves with their firearms, armed citizens kill 2,000 to 3,000 criminals each year, three times the number killed by the police. A nationwide study by Kates, the constitutional lawyer and criminologist, found that only 2 percent of civilian shootings involved an innocent person mistakenly identified as a criminal. The "error rate" for the police, however, was 11 percent, over five times as high.

Armed citizens defend their lives or property 1,000,000 times per year

It is simply not possible to square the numbers above and the experience of Florida with the notions that honest, law-abiding gun owners are borderline psychopaths itching for an excuse to shoot someone, vigilantes eager to seek out and summarily execute the lawless, or incompetent fools incapable of determining when it is proper to use lethal force in defense of their lives. Nor upon reflection should these results seem surprising. Rape, robbery, and attempted murder are not typically actions rife with ambiguity or subtlety, requiring special powers of observation and great book-learning to discern. When a man pulls a knife on a woman and says, "You're coming with me," her judgment that a crime is being committed is not likely to be in error. There is little chance that she is going to shoot the wrong person. It is the police, because they are rarely at the scene of the crime when it occurs, who are more likely to find themselves in circumstances where guilt and innocence are not so clear-cut, and in which the probability for mistakes is higher.

ARMS AND LIBERTY

The posses-sion of arms is vital for resisting tyranny

Classical republican philosophy has long recognized the critical relationship between personal liberty and the possession of arms by a people ready and willing to use them. Political theorists as dissimilar as Niccolò Machiavelli, Sir Thomas More, James Harrington, Algernon Sidney, John Locke, and Jean-Jacques Rousseau all shared the view that the possession of arms is vital for resisting tyranny, and that to be disarmed by one's government is tantamount to being enslaved by it. The possession of arms by the people is the ultimate warrant that government governs only with the consent of the governed. As Kates has shown, the Second Amendment is as much a product of this political philosophy as it is of the American experience in the Revolutionary War. Yet our conservative elite has abandoned this aspect of republican theory. Although our conservative pundits recognize and embrace gun owners as allies in other arenas, their battle for gun rights is desultory. The problem here is not a statist utopianism, although goodness knows that liberals are not alone in the confidence they have in the state's ability to solve society's problems. Rather, the problem seems to lie in certain cultural traits shared by our conservative and liberal elites. **The problem may lie in certain of our cultural traits**

One such trait is an abounding faith in the power of the word. The failure of our conservative elite to defend the Second Amendment stems in great measure from an overestimation of the power of the rights set forth in the First Amendment, and a general undervaluation of action. Implicit in calls for the repeal of the Second Amendment is the assumption that our First Amendment rights are sufficient to preserve our liberty. The belief is that liberty can be preserved as long as men freely speak their minds; that there is no tyranny or abuse that can survive being exposed in the press; and that the truth need only be disclosed for the culprits to be shamed. The people will act, and the truth shall set us, and keep us, free. **The First Amendment is not sufficient to protect us**

History is not kind to this belief, tending rather to support the view of Hobbes, Machiavelli, and other republican theorists that only people willing and able to defend themselves can preserve their liberties. While it may be tempting and comforting to believe that the existence of mass electronic communication has forever altered the balance of power between the state and its subjects, the belief has certainly not been tested by time, and what little history there is in the age of mass communication is not especially encouraging. The camera, radio, and press are mere tools and, like guns, can be used for good or ill. Hitler, after all, was a masterful orator, used radio to very good effect, and is well known to have pioneered and exploited the propaganda opportunities afforded by film. And then, of course, there were the Brownshirts, who knew very well how to quell dissent among intellectuals.

Like guns, the camera, radio, and press are mere tools that can be used for good or ill

POLITE SOCIETY

In addition to being enamored of the power of words, our conservative elite shares with liberals the notion that an armed society is just not civilized or progressive, that massive gun ownership is a blot on our civilization. This association of personal disarmament with civilized behavior is one of the great unexamined beliefs of our time.

Should you read English literature from the sixteenth through nineteenth centuries, you will discover numerous references to the fact that a gentleman, especially when out at night or traveling, armed himself with a sword or a pistol against the chance of encountering a highwayman or other such predator. This does not appear to have shocked the ladies accompanying him. True, for the most part there were no police in those days, but we have already addressed the notion that the presence of the police absolves people of the responsibility to look after their safety, and in any event the existence of the police cannot be said to have reduced crime to negligible levels.

It is by no means obvious why it is "civilized" to permit oneself to fall easy prey to criminal violence, and to permit criminals to continue unobstructed in their evil ways. While it may be that a society in which crime is so rare that no one ever needs to carry a weapon is "civilized," a society that stigmatizes the carrying of weapons by the law-abiding — because it distrusts its citizens more than it fears rapists, robbers, and murderers — certainly cannot claim this distinction. Perhaps the notion that defending oneself with lethal force is not "civilized" arises from the view that violence is always wrong, or the view that each human being is of such intrinsic worth that it is wrong to kill anyone under any circumstances. The necessary implication of these propositions, however, is that life is not worth **Is life** defending. Far from being "civilized," the beliefs **not worth** that counterviolence and killing are always wrong **defending?** are an invitation to the spread of barbarism. Such beliefs announce loudly and clearly that those who do not respect the lives and property of others will rule over those who do.

In truth, one who believes it wrong to arm himself against criminal violence shows contempt of God's gift of life (or, in modern parlance, does not properly value himself), does not live up to his responsibilities to his family and community, and proclaims himself mentally and morally deficient, because he does not trust himself to behave responsibly. In truth, a state that deprives its law-abiding citizens of the means to effectively defend themselves is not civilized but barbarous, becoming an accomplice of murderers, rapists, and thugs and revealing its totalitarian nature by its tacit admission that the disorganized, random havoc created by criminals is far less a threat than are men and women who believe themselves free and independent, and act accordingly.

We do not live in an armed society; we live in a society in which criminals are armed

While gun control proponents and other advocates of a kinder, gentler society incessantly decry our "armed society," in truth we do not live in an armed society. We live in a society in which violent criminals and agents of the state habitually carry weapons, and in which many law-abiding citizens own firearms but do not go about armed. Department of Justice statistics indicate that 87 percent of all violent crimes occur *outside* the home. Essentially, although tens of millions own firearms, we are an unarmed society.

TAKE BACK THE NIGHT

Clearly the police and the courts are not providing a significant brake on criminal activity. While liberals call for more poverty, education, and drug treatment programs, conservatives take a more direct tack. George Will advocates a massive increase in the number of police and a shift toward "community-based policing." Meanwhile, the NRA and many conservative leaders call for laws that would require violent criminals serve at least 85 percent of their sentences and would place repeat offenders permanently behind bars.

Our society suffers greatly from the beliefs that only official action is legitimate and that the state is the source of our earthly salvation. Both liberal and conservative prescriptions for violent crime suffer from the "not in my job description" school of thought regarding the responsibilities of the law-abiding citizen, and from an overestimation of the ability of the state to provide society's moral moorings. As long as law-abiding citizens assume no personal responsibility for combatting crime, liberal and conservative programs will fail to contain it.

Society overestimates the ability of the state to provide moral moorings

Judging by the numerous articles about concealed-carry in gun magazines, the growing number of products advertised for such purpose, and the increase in the number of concealed-carry applications in states with mandatory-issuance laws, more and more people, including growing numbers of women, are carrying firearms for self-

defense. Since there are still many states in which
the issuance of permits is discretionary and in
which law enforcement officials routinely deny applications, many people have been put to the hard
choice between protecting their lives or respecting
the law. Some of these people have learned the
hard way, by being the victim of a crime, or by
seeing a friend or loved one raped, robbed, or
murdered, that violent crime can happen to anyone, anywhere at any time, and that crime is not
about sex or property but life, liberty, and dignity.

The hard choice of protecting your life or respecting the law

The laws proscribing concealed-carry of firearms
by honest, law-abiding citizens breed nothing but
disrespect for the law. As the Founding Fathers
knew well, a government that does not trust its
honest, law-abiding, taxpaying citizens with the
means of self-defense is not itself worthy of trust.
Laws disarming honest citizens proclaim that the
government is the master, not the servant, of the
people. A federal law along the lines of the Florida
statute — overriding all contradictory state and local laws and acknowledging that the carrying of
firearms by law-abiding citizens is a privilege and
immunity of citizenship — is needed to correct the
outrageous conduct of state and local officials operating under discretionary licensing systems.

What we do not need is more gun control

What we certainly do not need is more gun
control. Those who call for the repeal of the Second
Amendment so that we can really begin controlling
firearms betray a serious misunderstanding of the

Bill of Rights. The Bill of Rights does not *grant* rights to the people, such that its repeal would legitimately confer upon government the powers otherwise proscribed. The Bill of Rights is the list of the fundamental, inalienable rights, endowed in man by his Creator, that define what it means to be a free and independent people, the rights which must exist to ensure that government governs only with the consent of the people.

At one time this was even understood by the Supreme Court. In *United States v. Cruikshank* (1876), the first case in which the Court had an opportunity to interpret the Second Amendment, it stated that the right confirmed by the Second Amendment "is not a right granted by the constitution. Neither is it in any manner dependent upon that instrument for its existence." The repeal of the Second Amendment would no more render the outlawing of firearms legitimate than the repeal of the due process clause of the Fifth Amendment would authorize the government to imprison and kill people at will. A government that abrogates any of the Bill of Rights, with or without majoritarian approval, forever acts illegitimately, becomes tyrannical, and loses the moral right to govern.

This is the uncompromising understanding reflected in the warning that America's gun owners will not go gently into that good, utopian night: "You can have my gun when you pry it from my cold, dead hands." While liberals take this state-

"You can have my gun when you pry it from my cold, dead hands"

The republic depends upon devotion to our fundamental rights

ment as evidence of the retrograde, violent nature of gun owners, we gun owners hope that liberals hold equally strong sentiments about their printing presses, word processors, and television cameras. The republic depends upon fervent devotion to all our fundamental rights.

BIOGRAPHICAL
PROFILES OF
QUOTED AUTHORITIES

Adams, John (1735–1826). First vice president and second president of the United States; delegate to the First and Second Continental Congresses; co-author with Thomas Jefferson of the Declaration of Independence.

Adams, Samuel (1722–1803). American patriot and a leading figure of the American Revolution. Adams was active and instrumental in every aspect of the pre-Revolutionary struggle against Great Britain in Massachusetts. He wrote numerous political pamphlets championing rebellion, promoted the formation of the Boston chapter of the Sons of Liberty, headed the demonstrations that led to the Boston Massacre, and directed the Boston Tea Party. He became a delegate to the First and Second Continental Congresses and was a signer of the Declaration of Independence. He ended his career as governor of Massachusetts.

Amar, Akhil Reed. Southmayd Professor of Law, Yale Law School, and a leading American scholar in the fields of constitutional law, criminal procedure, American legal history, and federal jurisdiction.

Aristotle (384–322 BC). Greek philosopher and scientist and one of the major figures in the development of Western civilization. Aristotle made important contributions to man's early understanding of logic, ethics, politics, psychology, biology, zoology, astronomy, and physics. Even today his writings, particularly in the field of philosophy, exert a strong influence upon modern thought and language.

Barclay, William (1546–1608). Scottish jurist and monarchist, and professor of civil law at Angers, France. Barclay's major writing was *De Regno et Regali Potestate,* etc. (1600), a defense of the divine rights of kings.

Barlow, Joel (1754–1812). American writer and diplomat who served as a chaplain in Washington's Continental army and later died during Napoleon's retreat from Moscow. Barlow is principally remembered for his treatise *Advice to the Privileged Orders in the Several States of Europe, Resulting from the Necessity and Propriety of a General Revolution in the Principle of Government* (1792).

Beccaria, Cesare Bonesana, Marchese di (1738–94). Italian jurist, criminologist, and economist. Beccaria's chief work is *On Crimes and Punishments* (1764), which stimulated and provided a guide to penal reform in Europe and the United States. Beccaria argued against the severity and abuses of criminal law, especially capital punishment and torture, and for the value of education as a means of deterring crime.

Blackstone, Sir William (1723–80). British jurist and legal scholar. His *Commentaries on the Laws of England* (4 vols., 1765–9) was for more than a century the foundation of legal education in Great Britain and the United States. As such, his *Commentaries* was one of the major influences upon the thinking of the Founding Fathers, most of whom were lawyers trained in the English common-law tradition. Blackstone endorsed the view that a free society must retain for its citizens the right to keep and bear arms both for self-defense and to restrain the violence of oppressive governments. His unequivocal arguments in support of that right were widely quoted during the constitutional debates in the Colonies and even today are commonly cited in Second Amendment debates.

Blizard, William (1743–1835). The Recorder of London and chief legal adviser to the city. His legal opinion, as set forth in his book *Desultory Reflections on Police: With an Essay on the Means of Preventing Crimes and Amending Criminals* (issued in 1780, published in 1785), was one of the clearest statements of the time regarding the individual and collective right of Englishmen to possess arms.

Buckley, James L. Former Republican senator from New York; presently circuit judge, United States Court of Appeals, District of Columbia Circuit.

Burgh, James (1714–75). English Whig political writer whose major work, *Political Disquisitions: Or, an Enquiry into Public Errors, Defects and Abuses* (1774), attributed England's difficulties with its American colonies to the existence in the Colonies of an English standing army. Among the American subscribers to Burgh's writings were George Washington, Thomas Jefferson, John Adams, and John Hancock.

Caplan, David I. American attorney in private practice, author of numerous law review articles, and a leading expert and commentator on Second Amendment issues.

Cardozo, Benjamin Nathan (1870–1938). An associate justice of the United States Supreme Court, to which he was appointed in 1932 to succeed Oliver Wendell Holmes. Cardozo is recognized as one of the finest legal minds this country has ever produced. He was the author of several noteworthy books, among them *The Nature of the Judicial Process* (1921) and *The Growth of the Law* (1924), as well as numerous clearly written and influential legal opinions.

Christian, Edward (1755?–1823). Professor of law, Cambridge University, and editor of the Christian edition of Blackstone's *Commentaries on the Laws of England* (1793–5), which enjoyed great popularity in the United States as well as in England.

Cicero, Marcus Tullius (106–43 BC). Roman statesman, orator, and writer. An important historical figure for his service in the later Roman Republic, Cicero remains influential today through his body of writings, particularly the four treatises *On the Republic, On the Laws, On Duty,* and *On the Nature of the Gods.*

Coke, Sir Edward (1552–1634). English jurist. Coke was one of the principal drafters of the Petition of Right, a statement of the principles of liberty that was to become an integral part of the English constitution. He was the author of the great legal classic *Institutes of the Laws of England* (4 vols., 1628–44).

Cooley, Thomas McIntyre (1824–98). Chief justice of the Michigan Supreme Court, first chairman of the Interstate Commerce Commission, and author of the leading nineteenth-century works on constitutional law.

Coxe, Tench (1755–1824). Political economist, colonial legislator, and attorney general of the Province of Pennsylvania. Initially a royalist, Coxe joined the British army under General Howe in 1777. After the defeat of the British, Coxe was arrested but then paroled, at which time he became a Whig and a staunch Federalist, as evidenced by one of his earliest writings, *An Examination of the Constitution of the United States*. A friend of Madison and Jefferson, he was appointed by Jefferson to the post of Purveyor of Public Supplies. Coxe's chief contribution to public service was in the area of economics, where he was influential in formulating national policy regarding agriculture, imports, exports, and free trade among the states.

Dalton, Michael (?–1648). English jurist and author of two notable legal texts of the seventeenth century, *The Countrey Justice* (1618) and *Officium Vicecomitum* (1623).

DeLolme, Jean L. (1740?–1807) Swiss historian who immigrated to England, where he wrote *The Constitution of England* (1775). The book was so influential that DeLolme became known as "the English Montesquieu."

Dershowitz, Alan. Professor of law at Harvard Law School, distinguished defense attorney, and author.

Fletcher, Andrew (1655–1716). Scottish statesman and patriot, author of *A Discourse of Government with Relations to Militias* (1698).

Fletcher, George. Professor of law at Columbia University and one of America's foremost criminal law theorists.

Fortescue, Sir John (1394?–1476?). English jurist, chief justice of the King's Bench, and author of *De Laudibus Legum Angliae* (1470).

Gallatin, (Abraham Alfonse) Albert (1761–1849). American statesman and secretary of the treasury under President Thomas Jefferson from 1801 to 1814. A native Swiss, Gallatin immigrated to Pennsylvania, which he represented in Congress both in the House of Representatives and in the United States Senate. A staunch Anti-federalist, he was a vigorous proponent of free trade with other nations. He also served as the U.S. minister to France from 1816 to 1823 and as minister to Great Britain from 1831 to 1839.

Gandhi, Mohandas Karamchand (Mahatma) (1869–1948). Indian nationalist who led the nonviolent movement that freed his country from British colonial rule.

Gerry, Elbridge (1744–1814). Vice president of the United States in the administration of President James Madison. Gerry was a compatriot of Samuel Adams and a leader of the opposition to British rule in his home state of Massachusetts. He was a member of the Continental Congress and a signer of the Declaration of Independence.

Gibbon, Edward (1737–94). English historian and author of *The History of the Decline and Fall of the Roman Empire* (1776–88).

Gordon, Thomas (d. 1750). English political writer, schoolteacher, and co-author with John Trenchard of *Cato's Letters* (1721–2), a series of essays that were highly regarded by John Adams and Thomas Jefferson. It has been estimated that more than half the private libraries in the American Colonies contained bound volumes of *Cato's Letters*.

Grose, Francis (1731–91). English historian, author of *Military Antiquities Respecting a History of the British Army* (1812).

Grotius, Hugo (1583–1645). Dutch jurist and statesman whose legal writings laid the foundation for modern international law. His major work was *On the Law of War and Peace* (1625).

Halbrook, Stephen P. American attorney in private practice, counsel in many landmark Second Amendment cases, author of numerous law review articles and books on the Second Amendment, including *That Every Man Be Armed: The Evolution of a Constitutional Right* (1984), and a leading expert and commentator on Second Amendment issues.

Hamilton, Alexander (1757–1804). American statesman, aide-de-camp to George Washington as well as commander of a regiment of light infantry during the battle of Yorktown, first secretary of the treasury in George Washington's first administration, a co-author of *The Federalist* (1787–8), and a leading figure of the American Revolution.

Hardy, David T. American attorney in private practice, author of numerous law review articles on the Second Amendment, author of the book, *Origins and Development of the Second Amendment* (1986), and a leading expert and commentator on Second Amendment issues.

Harrington, James (1611–77). English political philosopher. In his principal work, *Commonwealth of Oceana,* Harrington restated Aristotle's theory of constitutional stability and revolution. He advocated the necessity of a written constitution and many other ideas that foreshadowed doctrines of the American and French Revolutions. A major influence on Harrington's thought was Machiavelli, and in turn, Harrington's doctrines exerted a particularly strong influence upon Thomas Jefferson.

Hatch, Orrin G. United States senator from Utah (Republican) and chairman of the Senate Committee of the Judiciary. Hatch is noted for his keen legal mind and his influential advocacy of a scholarly approach to constitutional issues. He is also the author of several highly regarded law review articles on such constitutional issues as equal rights, criminal law, First Amendment rights, and constitutional conflicts.

Hawkins, Sir William (1673–1746). English jurist and author of a celebrated legal tract of his time, *Treatise on the Pleas of the Crown* (1716).

Henry, Patrick (1736–99). American statesman and orator, one of the most influential figures in the American Revolution. Henry is remembered today chiefly for two of his most famous utterances: "If this be treason, make the most of it!" and "I know not what course others may take, but as for me, give me liberty or give me death!" A prominent Virginia lawyer, Henry was a member of its House of Burgesses, its revolutionary convention, and the First and Second Continental Congresses. He also served two terms as governor of the state. He was a strong advocate of the adoption of the Bill of Rights as the first ten amendments to the Constitution.

Heston, Charlton. Distinguished American stage, screen, and television actor.

Hitler, Adolf (1889–1945). German political leader and dictator who converted Germany into a fully militarized society and launched World War II in 1939. He caused the slaughter of millions of Jews and other people whom he considered racially inferior.

Hobbes, Thomas (1588–1679). English philosopher and political theorist. Along with Galileo, Gassendi, and Descartes, Hobbes was one of the advanced thinkers of the early seventeenth century. He is best known today for his philosophical treatise on the nature of sovereignty, *Leviathan; or, The Matter, Form and Power of a Commonwealth Ecclesiastical and Civil* (1651). Even though he was a monarchist, Hobbes supported the view that only people willing and able to defend themselves can preserve their liberties.

Horace (65–8 BC). Roman poet and satirist.

Humphrey, Hubert H. (1911–78) Thirty-eighth vice president of the United States and a leader of the liberal wing of the Democratic Party.

Jefferson, Thomas (1743–1826). Political philosopher, statesman, a key leader of the American Revolution, co-author with John Adams of the Declaration of Independence, governor of Virginia, secretary of state in George Washington's first administration, and third president of the United States.

Johnson, Nicholas J. Associate professor of law, Fordham University School of Law, and a leading scholar in American constitutional law.

Johnston, Zachariah (1742–1800). American statesman, captain of militia in the Revolutionary War, and a close friend of James Madison. As a delegate to the Virginia Convention of 1788, Johnston made the closing speech for ratification of the U.S. Constitution by that body.

Kates, Don B. American attorney in private practice, author of numerous law review articles, and a leading expert and commentator on Second Amendment issues.

Lee, Richard Henry (1732–94). A leader of the American Revolution. Lee was a member of the Virginia House of Burgesses, where he joined Thomas Jefferson and Patrick Henry in defending the rights of the Colonies against Great Britain. He was a delegate to the Continental Congress from 1774 to 1779, during which time he presented a resolution that formed the basis of the Declaration of Independence. An Anti-federalist, Lee believed that the proposed Constitution infringed states' rights. He was also instrumental in securing the adoption of the Tenth Amendment, which explicitly states: "The powers not delegated to the United States by the Constitution, nor prohibited by it to the States, are reserved to the States respectively, or to the people."

L'Estrange, Sir Roger (1616–1704). Tory journalist and pamphleteer.

Levinson, Sanford. W. St. John Garwood and W. St. John Garwood, Jr., Centennial Professor of Law, University of Texas Law School, and a leading scholar in American constitutional law.

Livy (Titus Livius) (59 BC–AD 17). Roman historian. His massive *History of Rome* (142 vols.) was widely read and admired in ancient times as well as during the Middle Ages and Renaissance.

Locke, John (1632–1704). English philosopher and founder of the school of empiricism. Locke resided most of his life in continental Europe but returned to England following the Glorious Revolution of 1688 and the restoration of the Protestantism movement. Two works he published in 1689 have had a profound influence on modern philosophy: *Essay Concerning Human Understanding,* in which Locke set forth his theory that all persons are good, independent, and equal; and *Two Treatises of Government*, in which Locke argued that sovereignty did not reside in the state but in the people and that, although the state is supreme, it is bound by "natural law." Many of Locke's concepts relating to these natural rights and the duty of government to protect those rights — the value of majority rule, religious freedom, and the separation of church and state — were later embodied in the U.S. Constitution.

Macaulay, Thomas Babington (1800–1859). British historian, statesman, and leading member of the Whig Party. Macaulay is best known for his *History of England* (5 vols., 1848–61), a great literary work of the nineteenth century.

Machiavelli, Niccolò (1469–1527). Italian statesman, political philosopher, author, and historian. His three most famous works are *On the Art of War* (1521), which contrasts the value of conscripted over mercenary troops, *Discourses on the First Ten Books of Titus Livius* (1531), a commentary on *History of Rome* by Roman historian Livy, and *The Prince* (1532), which advocates the use of political power without regard for traditional ethical values. Although today his name has become synonymous with the use of cunning and duplicity in power politics, many of his original philosophical concepts are still highly regarded for their freshness and originality, particularly those concerning the desirability that in a republic its citizens be armed.

Madison, James (1751–1836). One of the founders of the Jeffersonian Republican Party in the 1790s, secretary of state under Thomas Jefferson (1801–9), and fourth president of the United States (1809–17). Madison's influence on the formation of the government of the United States cannot be overestimated. He is known as the "father of the Constitution" because of his draft of the Virginia Plan, which became the foundation of the structure of the new federal government, the key role he played in the Constitutional Convention, and his co-authorship (with Alexander Hamilton and John Jay) of the celebrated *The Federalist* (1787–8). Leading advocate of the Federalist position in the constitutional debates, Madison supported a strong executive with veto power, a judiciary with the power to override state laws, and the formation of a strong central government, which would be better able to defend and preserve liberty than would smaller state jurisdictions unable to form absolute national majorities. Madison authored the Bill of Rights.

Malcolm, Joyce Lee. Professor of history, Bentley College, a leading scholar in English constitutional history, and author of *To Keep and Bear Arms: The Origins of an Anglo-American Right* (1994).

Mason, George (1725–92). American statesman. Born into the planter aristocracy of Virginia, Mason became a member of the Virginia House of Burgesses and a delegate to his state's constitutional convention in July 1775. He drafted Virginia's celebrated Declaration of Rights and a large portion of its constitution. As a delegate to the federal Constitutional Convention in 1789, he helped to draft the U.S. Constitution but refused to become a signer because of his opposition to the weaknesses he perceived in the document, chiefly its failure to limit slavery and to include a bill of rights. However, the Bill of Rights that was later incorporated into the Constitution was modeled after the Virginia Declaration of Rights that Mason had drafted.

Molesworth, Robert (1656–1725). English politician, a prominent leader of the Whig Party, and a close associate of John Locke and Algernon Sidney. Molesworth is best known today for the preface he wrote to the English translation of Francis Hotman's *Franco-Gallia, or an Account of the Ancient Free State of France and Most Other Parts of Europe Before the Loss of Their Liberties* (1711).

Montesquieu, Charles Louis de Secondat, Baron de la Brède et de (1689–1755). French jurist and political philosopher. His most influential writing, *The Spirit of Laws* (1748), compares the republican, despotic, and monarchal forms of government. Many of his concepts helped form the philosophical basis of the U.S. Constitution.

More, Sir Thomas (1478–1535). English statesman, writer, member of the Privy Council, Speaker of the House of Commons, and later lord chancellor of England, the first layman to occupy that post. More is remembered for his opposition to King Henry VIII's defiance of papal authority, for which More was condemned for the crime of treason and executed in 1535. He was canonized by the Roman Catholic Church in 1935. More's best-known writing is *Utopia* (1516), a satire about the fictitious island of Utopia, where the interests of the individual are subordinated to those of society and where all people must work, land is owned in common, and universal education and religious toleration are practiced.

Moyle, Walter (1672–1721). Whig politician and co-author with John Trenchard of the essay, *An Argument Shewing, That a Standing Army Is Inconsistent with a Free Govern-*

ment, and Absolutely Destructive to the Constitution of the English Monarchy (1697).

Neville, Henry (1620–94). English political writer. His major work, *Plato Redivivus, or a Dialogue Concerning Government* (1681), was much admired by Thomas Hobbes.

Ovid (43 BC–AD 17?). Roman poet of mythological narratives. His most celebrated work is *Metamorphoses*.

Paine, Thomas (1737–1809). Anglo-American political philosopher who enjoyed active and influential political careers in England, France, and the United States. After the publication of his *Rights of Man* (1791–2), a powerful condemnation of Edward Burke's *Reflections Upon the French Revolution,* Paine was indicted by the British government for treason. An active participant in French politics following the Revolution, while a deputy to the National Convention he was imprisoned by Robespierre for advocating the exile, rather than the execution, of Louis XVI. In the United States, he was an associate of most of the major figures in the American Revolution, including Benjamin Franklin, George Washington, and Thomas Jefferson. He is best known in this country for two writings: *The American Crisis* (1776–83), a series of pamphlets, the first of which opens with the famous lines: "Now are the times that try men's souls"; and for the pamphlet *Common Sense* (1776), in which Paine argued that common sense surely led to the conclusion that the American Colonies should become independent of Great Britain. This little pamphlet, which sold over 500,000 copies (an extraordinary figure for that time), was one of the most influential political documents in American history.

Paterson, James (1823–94). English jurist and historian, author of *Commentaries on the Liberty of the Subject and the Laws of England Relating to the Security of the Person* (1877).

Pitt, William (1759–1806). British prime minister from 1783 to 1801 and from 1804 to 1806.

Polsby, Daniel D. Kirkland & Ellis Professor of Law, Northwestern University, and a leading scholar in American constitutional law.

Raleigh, Sir Walter (1554–1618). Explorer, writer, and a leading intellectual in the court of Queen Elizabeth I.

Rawle, William (1759–1836). Philadelphia lawyer, associate of Benjamin Franklin, and United States attorney for Pennsylvania during the administration of President George Washington. Rawle's principal writing was *A View of the Constitution of the United States* (1825), which was adopted as a textbook by a number of institutions throughout the country, including the United States Military Academy.

Rehnquist, William H. Sixteenth chief justice of the United States Supreme Court.

Rousseau, Jean-Jacques (1712–78). French philosopher, political theorist, botanist, and a key figure during the Age of Enlightenment. Of Rousseau's many contributions to human learning, none have been more important than his contributions to political thought. His famous political treatise, *The Social Contract* (1762), a ringing endorsement of civil liberty and the defense of popular will against the divine right of kings, was one of the major influences behind the French Revolution.

Sharpe, Granville (1735–1813). English scholar and philanthropist who helped bring about the abolition of slavery in England. Sharpe corresponded frequently with John Adams, John Jay, and Benjamin Franklin. He became an advocate of American independence.

Sidney, Algernon (1622–83). English statesman, writer, and a leader of the Whig opposition to King Charles II. Sidney's writings, particularly his *Discourses Concerning Government* (published posthumously in 1763), were well known to the Founding Fathers and were likely an influence on their advocacy of the legality of resisting tyranny.

Smith, Adam (1723–90). Scottish philosopher and economist and author of the celebrated treatise on economics, *An Inquiry into the Nature and Causes of the Wealth of Nations* (1776).

Snyder, Jeffrey R. American attorney in private practice, author, and moral philosopher.

Story, Joseph (1779–1845). One of the most distinguished jurists in American history. Story served as associate justice on the United States Supreme Court from 1811 until his death, including many years alongside Chief Justice John Marshall. He was also a professor of law at Harvard University and was instrumental in establishing the reputation of the Harvard Law School. He is best known today for his *Commentaries on the Constitution of the United States* (1833).

Taft, William Howard (1857–1930). Twenty-seventh president of the United States and later chief justice of the United States Supreme Court.

Tocqueville, Alexis Charles Henri Maurice Clérel de (1805–59). French statesman and author of the classic work *Democracy in America* (1835–40). One of the most intelligent studies of American life ever published, the book is a thorough examination of our legislative, executive, and judicial systems, as well as our manners, customs, and morals during the post-Revolutionary period of the early eighteenth century. For generations thereafter, it exerted a profound influence on political thought both in Europe and in this country.

Trenchard, John (1662–1723). English lawyer, Whig political writer, and constitutional reformer. Trenchard co-authored with Walter Moyle the essay *An Argument Shewing, That a Standing Army Is Inconsistent with a Free Government, and Absolutely Destructive to the Constitution of the English Monarchy* (1697) and co-authored with Thomas Gordon *Cato's Letters* (1721–2), a series of essays that were highly regarded by John Adams and Thomas Jefferson. It has been estimated that more than half the private libraries in the American Colonies contained bound volumes of *Cato's Letters*.

Tuchman, Barbara W. (1912–89) American historian and Pulitzer Prize winner.

Tucker, Henry St. George (1780–1848). Virginia legislator, president of the supreme court of appeals of Virginia, professor of law at the University of Virginia, and author of *Commentaries on the Laws of Virginia* (1836–7).

Tucker, St. George (1752–1827). Virginia jurist, a colonel in the Revolutionary War, and editor of an edition of *Blackstone's Commentaries on the Law of England* (5 vols., 1803).

Van Alstyne, William. William R. and Thomas L. Perkins Professor of Law, Duke University School of Law, and a leading scholar in American constitutional law.

Warren, Earl (1891–1974). American jurist and political leader, chief justice of the United States Supreme Court from 1953 to 1969.

Washington, George (1732–99). Commander in chief of the Continental army during the American Revolution and first president of the United States.

Webster, Noah (1758–1843). American lexicographer who is best known for his *American Dictionary of the English Language*. Webster was also a newspaper publisher and an active participant in the American Revolution and the political discourse of his times. He was a keen advocate of the Federalist position in the constitutional debates and recommended the adoption of the proposed U.S. Constitution.

Young, David E. American author of *The Origin of the Second Amendment: A Documentary History of the Bill of Rights in Commentaries on Liberty, Free Government and an Armed Populace, 1787–1792* (2d ed., 1995).

NOTES

INTRODUCTION
(Pages 3–15)

1. *United States v. Verdugo-Urquidez*, 494 U.S. 259 (1990).

2. JOYCE LEE MALCOLM, TO KEEP AND BEAR ARMS: THE ORIGINS OF AN ANGLO-AMERICAN RIGHT 176–7 (1994).

I
EARLY EXPRESSIONS OF THE RIGHT IN ANCIENT TIMES
(Pages 17–25)

1. ALEXIS DE TOCQUEVILLE, 2 DEMOCRACY IN AMERICA 11 (1835–40).

2. STEPHEN P. HALBROOK, THAT EVERY MAN BE ARMED: THE EVOLUTION OF A CONSTITUTIONAL RIGHT 8 (1984).

3. Emperor Han, responding to a petition from the Imperial Chancellor Kung-Sun Hung to take arms from the people, 124 BC, from AMERICAN RIFLEMAN 14 (January 1959).

4. ARISTOTLE, POLITICS 71 (trans. T. Sinclair, 1962).

5. *Id.* at 78.

6. *Id.* at 79.

7. *Id.* at 82.

8. *Id.* at 136.

9. *Id.* at 272.

10. *Id.* at 274.

11. ARISTOTLE, PARTS OF ANIMALS 373 (trans. A. Peck, 1961).

12. CICERO, SELECTED POLITICAL SPEECHES 222 (trans. M. Grant, 1969).

13. *Id.* at 234.

14. 1 LIVY 148 n. 2 (trans. B. Foster, 1919).

15. *Id.* at 151.

16. HORACE, SATIRES AND EPISTLES, 24–5 (trans. J. Fuchs, 1977).

17. 2 OVID 152–3 (trans J. Mozley, 1969).

18. SIR EDWARD COKE, 3 INSTITUTES OF THE LAWS OF ENGLAND 162 (ed. Johnson and Warner, 1812).

II
EXPRESSIONS OF THE RIGHT IN SIXTEENTH- TO EIGHTEENTH-CENTURY CONTINENTAL EUROPE
(Pages 27–38)

1. STEPHEN P. HALBROOK, THAT EVERY MAN BE ARMED: THE EVOLUTION OF A CONSTITUTIONAL RIGHT 22 (1984).

2. NICCOLÒ MACHIAVELLI, DISCOURSES ON THE FIRST TEN BOOKS OF TITUS LIVIUS 492 (trans. L. Walker, 1965), in HALBROOK, THAT EVERY MAN BE ARMED 22.

3. HALBROOK, THAT EVERY MAN BE ARMED 22.

4. MACHIAVELLI, DISCOURSES 308, in HALBROOK, THAT EVERY MAN BE ARMED 21.

5. *Id*. at 309, HALBROOK at 21.

6. MACHIAVELLI, ON THE ART OF WAR 30 (trans. E. Farnsworth, 1965), in HALBROOK, THAT EVERY MAN BE ARMED 22.

Notes for pp. 30–35

7. MACHIAVELLI, THE PRINCE 73 (trans. L. Ricci, 1952), in HALBROOK, THAT EVERY MAN BE ARMED 24.

8. *Id*. at 81, HALBROOK at 24.

9. *Id*. at 105.

10. *Id*. at 72, HALBROOK at 24.

11. David T. Hardy, *The Second Amendment and the Historiography of the Bill of Rights*, 4 J.L. & POL. 11 (1987).

12. CESARE BECCARIA, ON CRIMES AND PUNISHMENTS 87–88 (trans. H. Paolucci, 1963), in HALBROOK, THAT EVERY MAN BE ARMED 35.

13. HALBROOK, THAT EVERY MAN BE ARMED 26.

14. HUGO GROTIUS, ON THE LAW OF WAR AND PEACE 32–33 (trans. W. Whewell, 1853), in HALBROOK, THAT EVERY MAN BE ARMED 26.

15. HALBROOK, THAT EVERY MAN BE ARMED 26–27.

16. MONTESQUIEU, THE SPIRIT OF LAWS 64 (trans. T. Nugent, 1899), in HALBROOK, THAT EVERY MAN BE ARMED 34.

Notes for pp. 36–37

17. *Id.* at 61, HALBROOK at 34.

18. *Id.* at 59, HALBROOK at 34.

19. *Id.* at 60, HALBROOK at 34.

20. *Id.* at 79–80, HALBROOK at 34.

21. JEAN-JACQUES ROUSSEAU, THE SOCIAL CONTRACT 320 (Everyman's Lib. ed., 1950).

III
THE DEVELOPMENT AND DECLARATION OF THE RIGHT IN ENGLAND
(Pages 39–68)

Notes for pp. 39–42

1. JOYCE LEE MALCOLM, TO KEEP AND BEAR ARMS: THE ORIGINS OF AN ANGLO-AMERICAN RIGHT (1994).

2. Laws of Alfred § 7, in 1 ENGLISH HISTORICAL DOCUMENTS c. 500–1042, 375 (ed. D. Douglas, 1968).

3. Laws of Cnut § 29; *Id.* at 422.

4. FRANCIS GROSE, MILITARY ANTIQUITIES RESPECTING A HISTORY OF THE BRITISH ARMY 1–2 (1812).

5. *Id.*

6. 13 Edward I, ch. 1 (1285).

7. Don B. Kates, *The Second Amendment and the Ideology of Self-Protection,* 9 CONST. COMMENTARY 94 (1992).

8. *Id.* at 94, citing A. V. B. NORMAN, THE MEDIEVAL SOLDIER 73 (1971).

9. *Id.* at 98–99.

10. 33 Hen. VIII, ch. 6 (1541).

11. 13 Car. II, ch. 6 (1661) and 13–14 Car. II, ch. 3 (1662).

12. 22–23 Car. II, ch. 25 (1671).

13. *Id.*

14. HOUSE OF COMMONS JOURNAL 29 (1688–89 GREGORIAN); 14 HOUSE OF LORDS JOURNAL 125 (1689).

15. W. & M., sess. 2, ch. 2 (1689).

16. 10 HOUSE OF COMMONS JOURNAL 17 (1689).

17. HOUSE OF COMMONS JOURNAL 29 (1688–89 GREGORIAN); 14 HOUSE OF LORDS JOURNAL 125 (1689).

18. *Rex [the King] v. Dewhurst,* 1 State Trials, New Series, 529, 601–2 (1820).

19. 1 W. & M., sess. 1, ch. 15 (1689); WILLIAM COBBETT, ED., 5 THE PARLIAMENTARY HISTORY OF ENGLAND FROM THE EARLIEST PERIOD TO THE YEAR 1803, 181–84 (1808–20).

20. *Id.*

21. SIR JOHN FORTESCUE, THE GOVERNANCE OF ENGLAND: THE DIFFERENCE BETWEEN AN ABSOLUTE

AND A LIMITED MONARCHY 114–15 (rev. ed. 1885; trans. David E. Young, 1995).

22. SIR THOMAS MORE, UTOPIA 71 (trans. and ed. Robert M. Adams, 1975).

23. MICHAEL DALTON, THE COUNTREY JUSTICE: CONTAINING THE PRACTICE OF THE JUSTICES OF THE PEACE OUT OF THEIR SESSIONS (1618).

24. *Payton v. New York*, 445 U.S. 573 at 594 (1980).

25. *Id.* at 596.

26. *Id.* at 594, n. 36.

Notes for pp. 50–54

27. SIR EDWARD COKE, 3 INSTITUTES OF THE LAWS OF ENGLAND 56 (2d ed. 1648).

28. 5 COKE REP. 91a at 91b, 77 ENGLISH REPRINTS 194 at 195 (King's Bench, 1604); quoted approvingly in *Payton v. New York*, 445 U.S. 573 at 596, n. 44.

29. COKE, 1 INSTITUTES OF THE LAWS OF ENGLAND 162a (ed. Johnson and Warner, 1812).

30. SIR WALTER RALEIGH, 3 THE WORKS OF SIR WALTER RALEIGH 22 (ed. T. Birch, 1829).

31. THOMAS HOBBES, LEVIATHAN 95 (1964).

32. *Id.* at 156.

33. JAMES HARRINGTON, POLITICAL WORKS 696 (ed. J. Pocock, 1977).

34. *Id.* at 443.

35. *Id.* at 442–43.

36. *Id.* at 454.

37. *Id.* at 430.

38. JOHN LOCKE, SECOND TREATISE OF CIVIL GOV-ERNMENT 153–54 (Chicago, 1955).

39. *Id.* at 174.

40. *Id.* at 173.

41. *Id.* at 195.

42. LOCKE, TWO TREATISES OF GOVERNMENT, SEC-OND TREATISE OF CIVIL GOVERNMENT 289 (rev. ed. P. Laslett, 1960).

43. *Id.* at 288.

44. *The Security of Englishmen's Lives,* in STATE TRACTS: BEING A FURTHER COLLECTION OF SEVERAL CHOICE TREATISES RELATING TO GOVERNMENT FROM THE YEAR 1600 TO 1689 (1692).

45. David T. Hardy, *Armed Citizens, Citizen Armies: Toward a Jurisprudence of the Second Amendment,* 9 HARV. J.L. & PUB. POL'Y. 587 (1986).

46. JOHN TRENCHARD AND WALTER MOYLE, AN ARGUMENT SHEWING, THAT A STANDING ARMY IS INCONSISTENT WITH A FREE GOVERNMENT, AND AB-SOLUTELY DESTRUCTIVE TO THE CONSTITUTION OF THE ENGLISH MONARCHY 114–15 (1697).

47. *Id.* at 7.

48. ALGERNON SIDNEY, DISCOURSES CONCERNING GOVERNMENT 266–67 (1763).

49. *Id.* at 434.

50. *Id.* at 157.

51. *Id.* at 165.

52. *Id.* at 270.

53. Robert Molesworth, foreword to FRANCIS HOT-MAN, FRANCO-GALLIA iv (trans. R. Molesworth, 1711).

54. Andrew Fletcher, *A Discourse of Government with Relations to Militias*, in THE POLITICAL WORKS OF ANDREW FLETCHER, ESQ. 9 (1737).

55. MALCOLM, TO KEEP AND BEAR ARMS 142 (1994), citing EDWIN S. CORWIN, THE "HIGHER LAW" BACKGROUND OF THE AMERICAN CONSTITUTION 85 (1st ed. 1928; Ithaca, 1974).

56. *Id*. at 142, citing Donald Lutz, *The Relative Influence of European Writers on Late Eighteenth-Century American Political Thought*, AM. POL. SCI. REV. 78, table 3, p. 194 (March 1984).

57. *Id*. at 142.

58. WILLIAM BLACKSTONE, 1 COMMENTARIES ON THE LAWS OF ENGLAND 136 (1st ed. 1765; repr. 1979).

59. *Id*. at 140.

60. *Id*. at 395.

61. JEAN L. DELOLME, THE CONSTITUTION OF ENGLAND 227 (1793).

62. JAMES BURGH, 2 POLITICAL DISQUISITIONS: OR, AN ENQUIRY INTO PUBLIC ERRORS, DEFECTS, AND ABUSES 390 (1775).

63. *Id*. at 475–76.

64. ADAM SMITH, 2 THE WEALTH OF NATIONS 309 (ed. Cannan, n.d.).

65. William Pitt, Speech to the House of Lords, November 1777.

Notes for pp. 58–63

66. GRANVILLE SHARPE, TRACTS, CONCERNING THE ANTIENT AND ONLY TRUE LEGAL MEANS OF NATIONAL DEFENCE, BY A FREE MILITIA 17–18 (1782).

67. WILLIAM BLIZARD, DESULTORY REFLECTIONS ON POLICE: WITH AN ESSAY ON THE MEANS OF PREVENTING CRIMES AND AMENDING CRIMINALS 59–61 (1785).

68. SIR WILLIAM HAWKINS, PLEAS OF THE CROWN, ch. 28, § 574 (7th ed. 1795).

69. *Id.*, § 267.

70. Thomas Babington Macauley, *Critical and Historical Essays, Contributed to the Edinburgh Review* 162 (1850).

71. JAMES PATERSON, 1 COMMENTARIES ON THE LIBERTY OF THE SUBJECT AND THE LAWS OF ENGLAND RELATING TO THE SECURITY OF THE PERSON 441 (1877).

IV
THE DEVELOPMENT
AND DECLARATION
OF THE RIGHT IN AMERICA

A

Drafting and Ratification of the Bill of Rights in the Colonial Period
(Pages 69–112)

1. *Ex parte Grossman,* 267 U.S. 87 (1925), at 108–109.

2. *Id.* at 107.

3. "Letter to William Johnson," June 12, 1823, THE COMPLETE JEFFERSON 322 (1957).

4. Letter from David I. Caplan to author, May 2, 1996. Dr. Caplan wishes to express his gratitude to Henry E. Schaffer, Ph.D., Professor of Genetics and Biomathematics, North Carolina State University, for supplying the reference to the cited passage from the Charter of the University of North Carolina.

5. DAVID E. YOUNG., ED., THE ORIGIN OF THE SECOND AMENDMENT: A DOCUMENTARY HISTORY OF THE BILL OF RIGHTS IN COMMENTARIES ON LIBERTY, FREE GOVERNMENT AND AN ARMED POPULACE, 1787–1792, xlv (2d ed. 1995).

Notes for pp. 71–84

6. Pamphlet, *An Additional Number of Letters from the Federal Farmer to the Republican,* Letter XVIII, May 1788 (repr. 1962) at 168–70.

7. THE FEDERALIST, NO. 29, 179–84, 1788 (American Classics Lib. ed., 1991).

8. Don B. Kates, *Handgun Prohibition and the Original Meaning of the Second Amendment,* 82 MICH. L. REV. 214–15 (1983), n. 90.

9. Letter from Don B. Kates to author, July 15, 1996.

10. YOUNG, ED., THE ORIGIN OF THE SECOND AMENDMENT xlii–xliii.

11. Glenn Harlan Reynolds and Don B. Kates, *The Second Amendment and States' Rights: Thought Experiment,* 36 WM. & MARY L. REV. 1747–48 (1995).

12. Letter from Don B. Kates to author, July 15, 1996.

13. Kates, *Handgun Prohibition and the Original Meaning of the Second Amendment,* 82 MICH. L. REV. 226 (1983).

14. YOUNG., ED., THE ORIGIN OF THE SECOND AMENDMENT xxiii–xxvi.

15. David T. Hardy, *The Second Amendment and the Historiography of the Bill of Rights,* 4 J.L. & POL. 52 (1987), n. 228.

16. Kates, *The Second Amendment and the Ideology of Self-Protection,* 9 CONST. COMMENTARY 103 (1992).

17. *Id.* at 99, citing BARBARA TUCHMAN, THE MARCH OF FOLLY 21 (1984).

18. *Id.* at 100, n. 46.

19. "Journal of Occurrences," NEW YORK JOURNAL, Dec. 29, 1768.

20. Kates, *The Second Amendment and the Ideology of Self-Protection,* 9 CONST. COMMENTARY 89 (1992), n. 9.

Notes for pp. 86–92

21. *Id.* at 93.

22. *Id.* at 102.

23. *Id.*

24. *Id* at 89.

25. *Id.* at 92.

26. Reprinted in YOUNG., ED., THE ORIGIN OF THE SECOND AMENDMENT 748.

27. *Id.* at 752.

28. *Id.* at 754.

29. *Id.* at 758.

30. *Id.* at 762.

31. *Id.* at 767.

32. *Id.* at 773.

33. *Id.* at 778.

34. MERRILL JENSEN, JOHN P. KAMINSKI, AND GASPARE J. SALDINO, ET AL., EDS., 3 THE DOCUMENTARY HISTORY OF THE RATIFICATION OF THE CONSTITUTION 439–40 (1976).

35. *Id.,* vol. 2 at 624.

36. BRADFORD K. PIERCE, CHARLES HALE, ET AL., EDS., DEBATES AND PROCEEDINGS IN THE CONVENTION OF THE COMMONWEALTH OF MASSACHUSETTS, HELD IN THE YEAR 1788, 86 (1856).

37. JONATHAN ELLIOTT, ED., 1 THE DEBATES IN THE SEVERAL STATE CONVENTIONS, ON THE ADOPTION OF THE FEDERAL CONSTITUTION, AS RECOMMENDED BY THE GENERAL CONVENTION IN PHILADELPHIA 325 (1836, repr. 1941).

38. *Id.,* vol. 3 at 660.

39. *Id.,* vol. 2 at 410.

40. *Id.,* vol. 1 at 327.

41. *Id.,* vol. 1 at 335.

42. 1 WRITINGS OF THOMAS PAINE 56 (Conway ed., 1894).

43. 8 PAPERS OF THOMAS JEFFERSON 407 (J. Boyd ed., 1953).

44. *Id.,* vol. 2 at 344.

45. "Letter to William Stephens Smith," Nov. 13, 1787, JENSEN, KAMINSKI, AND SALDINO, ET AL., EDS.,

Notes
for pp.
92–98

14 THE DOCUMENTARY HISTORY OF THE RATIFICA-
TION OF THE CONSTITUTION 465 (1976).

46. ELLIOTT, ED., 3 THE DEBATES IN THE SEVERAL
STATE CONVENTIONS 378 (1836, repr. 1941).

47. *Id.* at 168–169.

48. WRITINGS OF GEORGE WASHINGTON 388
(Fitzpatrick ed., 1931).

49. JOHN ADAMS, A DEFENCE OF THE CONSTITU-
TIONS OF GOVERNMENT OF THE UNITED STATES OF
AMERICA 475 (1787–88).

50. PIERCE, HALE, ET AL., EDS., DEBATES AND PRO-
CEEDINGS IN THE CONVENTION OF THE COMMON-
WEALTH OF MASSACHUSETTS, HELD IN THE YEAR
1788, 86 (1856).

51. ELLIOTT, ED., 5 THE DEBATES IN THE SEVERAL
STATE CONVENTIONS 464 (1836, repr. 1941).

52. THE FEDERALIST, NO. 46, 90–91, 1788 (American Classics Lib. ed., 1991).

53. 1 LETTERS AND WRITINGS OF JAMES MADISON
406 (1865).

54. Debates in the Virginia Constitutional Convention, June 6, 1788.

55. THE FEDERALIST, NO. 29, 181, 1788 (American
Classics Lib. ed., 1991).

56. ELLIOTT, ED., 3 THE DEBATES IN THE SEVERAL
STATE CONVENTIONS 380 (1836, repr. 1941).

57. *Id.*, vol. 3 at 425.

58. *Id.*, vol. 3 at 380.

**Notes
for pp.
98–103**

59. Richard Henry Lee, *Letters of a Federal Farmer* (1787–88) in PAMPHLETS ON THE CONSTITUTION OF THE UNITED STATES 305–6.

60. Joel Barlow, *Advice to the Privileged Orders in the Several States of Europe, Resulting from the Necessity and Propriety of a General Revolution in the Principle of Government* 46 (1792, repr. 1956).

61. BERNARD SCHWARTZ, ED., THE BILL OF RIGHTS: A DOCUMENTARY HISTORY 1107 (1971).

62. ELLIOTT, ED., 3 THE DEBATES IN THE SEVERAL STATE CONVENTIONS 645 (1836, repr. 1941).

63. JENSEN, KAMINSKI, AND SALDINO, ET AL., EDS., 3 THE DOCUMENTARY HISTORY OF THE RATIFICATION OF THE CONSTITUTION 431 (1976).

64. WILLIAM BLACKSTONE, 1 COMMENTARIES ON THE LAWS OF ENGLAND 330 (Tucker ed., 1803).

65. HENRY ST. GEORGE TUCKER, 1 COMMENTARIES ON THE LAWS OF VIRGINIA 43 (1831).

66. TUCKER, A FEW LECTURES ON NATURAL LAW 95 (1844).

67. Pamphlet, *An Examination into the Leading Principles of the Federal Constitution,* Oct. 10, 1787, in PAUL LEICESTER FORD, ED., PAMPHLETS ON THE CONSTITUTION OF THE UNITED STATES, PUBLISHED DURING ITS DISCUSSION BY THE PEOPLE, 1787–1788, 60 (1888, repr. 1968).

68. WILLIAM RAWLE, A VIEW OF THE CONSTITUTION OF THE UNITED STATES 125–6 (2d ed. 1829).

69. JOSEPH STORY, COMMENTARIES ON THE CONSTITUTION OF THE UNITED STATES 125 (1st ed. 1833).

70. THOMAS M. COOLEY, THE GENERAL PRINCI-
PLES OF CONSTITUTIONAL LAW 282–3 (2d ed. 1891).

71. HARDY, ORIGINS AND DEVELOPMENT OF THE
SECOND AMENDMENT 71–2 (1986). *See also* BERNARD
SCHWARZ, THE ROOTS OF THE BILL OF RIGHTS 1051
(1980).

**Notes
for pp.
107–112**

72. Nicholas J. Johnson, *Shots Across No Man's Land:
A Response to Handgun Control, Inc.'s, Richard Aborn,*
22 FORDHAM URB. L.J. 448 (1995).

73. William Van Alstyne, *The Second Amendment
and the Personal Right to Arms,* 43 DUKE L.J. 1237
(1994) (also contained in the Appendix to this book at
p. 165).

B

A Selection of Second Amendment
Commentary Appearing
in the Popular Press in Colonial Times

(Pages 113–127)

1. *See, e.g., The Zenger Trial* in KERMIT L. HALL ET
AL., AMERICAN LEGAL HISTORY, CASES AND MATERI-
ALS 27–9 (1991); *see also* Dan Gifford, *The Conceptual
Foundation of Anglo-American Jurisprudence in Religion
and Reason*, 62 TENN. L. REV. 763–5 (1995).

**Notes
for pp.
114–115**

2. THOMAS HAMILTON, MEN AND MANNERS IN
AMERICA (1833).

3. Roger L'Estrange, INTELLIGENCER, August 3, 1663.

Notes for p. 115

4. MITCHELL STEPHENS, A HISTORY OF NEWS (1788).

5. "Letter to Hezekiah Niles," February 13, 1818, 10 WORKS OF JOHN ADAMS (1850–56) at 282.

6. Cited by ROBERT W. DESMOND, THE INFORMATION PROCESS: WORLD NEWS REPORTING TO THE TWENTIETH CENTURY (1978).

C
The State of the Law
(Pages 129–143)

1. U.S. CONST., art. IV, § 2.

2. Michael J. Quinlan, *Is There a Neutral Justification for Refusing to Implement the Second Amendment or Is the Supreme Court Just "Gun Shy"?* 22 CAPITAL U. L. REV. 659–60 (1993).

Notes for pp. 129–135

3. CONG. GLOBE, 39th Cong., 1st Sess., 2765 (1866), in Stephen P. Halbrook, *The Jurisprudence of the Second and Fourteenth Amendments*, 4 GEO. MASON U. L. REV. 24 (1981).

4. *Id.* at 29.

5. *Id.* at 29.

6. William Van Alstyne, *The Second Amendment and the Personal Right to Arms*, 43 DUKE L.J. 1237–9

(1994) (also contained in the Appendix to this book at p. 165).

7. 60 U.S. (19 How.) 393 (1856).

8. 92 U.S. 542 (1876).

9. 116 U.S. 252 (1866).

10. 153 U.S. 535 (1894).

11. 165 U.S. 264 (1897)

12. 307 U.S. 174 (1939).

13. Id. at 178.

Notes for pp. 135–140

14. Nelson Lund, *The Second Amendment, Political Liberty, and the Right to Self-Preservation,* 39 ALA. L. REV. 109–10 (1987), internal quotation from *United States v. Miller,* 307 U.S. 179 (1939).

15. Van Alstyne, *The Second Amendment and the Personal Right to Arms,* 43 DUKE L.J. 1240 (1994) (Appendix to this book at p. 165).

16. David I. Caplan, *Restoring the Balance: The Second Amendment Revisited,* 5 FORDHAM URB. L.J. 46 (1976).

17. 26 U.S.C. §§ 5801–5872 (1934).

18. 18 U.S.C. §§ 921–928 (1938).

19. 18 U.S.C. § 922 (1968).

20. *See* Nicholas J. Johnson, *Beyond the Second Amendment: An Individual Right to Arms Considered Through the Ninth Amendment,* 24 RUTGERS L.J. 1 (1992).

21. U.S. Code Annot. 100 Unnumbered Statute at Large 449 (1986).

22. 18 U.S.C. § 922 (p) (1988).

Notes
for pp.
141–143
23. 18 U.S.C. § 922 (s & t) (1993).

24. 18 U.S.C. § 922 (v & w) (1994).

25. *United States v. Lopez*, 115 S. Ct. 1624 (1995).

26. 494 U.S. 259 (1990).

D
A Selection of
Contemporary Commentary
(Pages 145–155)

1. Akhil Reed Amar, *The Bill of Rights as a Constitution*, 100 YALE L.J. 1166 (1991).

2. Amar, *The Bill of Rights and the Fourteenth Amendment*, 101 YALE L.J. 1245 (1992), n. 228.

Notes
for pp.
146–147
3. CONG. REC. S6889 (daily edit., Apr. 28, 1975).

4. Quoted in Dan Gifford, *The Conceptual Foundations of Anglo-American Jurisprudence in Religion and Reason*, 62 TENN. L. REV. 759 (1995).

5. GEORGE FLETCHER, THE TRIAL OF BERNARD GOETZ 156 (1988), citing Don B. Kates, *Handgun Prohibition and the Original Meaning of the Second Amendment*, 82 MICH L. REV. 204 (1983).

6. 2 M. GANDHI, AN AUTOBIOGRAPHY OF THE STORY OF MY EXPERIMENTS WITH THE TRUTH (trans. M. Desai, 1927).

7. From an official commentary on the German Firearms Act of 1937, quoted in Don B. Kates, *Why a Civil Libertarian Opposes Gun Control*, 3 CIV. LIB. REV. 26 (1976).

8. STEPHEN P. HALBROOK, THAT EVERY MAN BE ARMED: THE EVOLUTION OF A CONSTITUTIONAL RIGHT 83 (1984).

9. From *Remarks for the 125th Annual National Rifle Association Members Banquet*, Apr. 20, 1996.

10. From *Edict of March 18, 1938*.

11. Quoted in David T. Hardy, *The Second Amendment as a Restraint on State and Federal Firearms Restrictions*, in KATES, ED., RESTRICTING HANDGUNS: THE LIBERAL SKEPTICS SPEAK OUT (1979). **Notes for pp. 148–153**

12. Nicholas J. Johnson, *Beyond the Second Amendment: An Individual Right to Arms Considered Through the Ninth Amendment*, 24 RUTGERS L.J. 1–81 (1992).

13. *Id.*

14. *Id.*

15. Sanford Levinson, *The Embarrassing Second Amendment*, 99 YALE L.J. 657 (1989) (also contained in the Appendix to this book at p. 187).

16. JOYCE LEE MALCOLM, TO KEEP AND BEAR ARMS: THE ORIGINS OF AN ANGLO-AMERICAN RIGHT 162 (1994).

17. From ATLANTIC MONTHLY, June 1994.

18. Quoted in Richard Munday, "The Monopoly of Power" (paper presented to the annual meeting of the American Society of Criminology, 1991).

19. Jeffrey R. Snyder, *A Nation of Cowards,* 113 PUB. INTEREST 40 (1993) (Appendix to this book at p. 221).

Notes for pp. 153–155

20. William Van Alstyne, *The Second Amendment and the Personal Right to Arms*, 43 DUKE L.J. 1255 (1994) (Appendix to this book at p. 165).

21. Earl Warren, *The Bill of Rights and the Military*, 37 N.Y.U. L. REV. 181 (1962).

A FINAL WORD
(Pages 157–161)

1. William Van Alstyne, *The Second Amendment and the Personal Right to Arms*, 43 DUKE L.J. 1239 (1994) (also contained in the Appendix to this book at p. 165).

2. *Id.* at 1240.

Notes for pp. 157–161

3. Letter from David I. Caplan to author, May 2, 1996.

4. 26 U.S.C. §§ 5801–5872 (1934).

5. Letter from David I. Caplan to author, May 2, 1996.

6. *Id.*

7. For an extensive discussion of current Second Amendment issues, see debate between Don B. Kates and Stephen P. Halbrook in 49 LAW & CONTEMP. PROBS. (1986)

8. SUBCOMMITTEE ON THE CONSTITUTION OF THE COMMITTEE ON THE JUDICIARY, 97th Cong., 2d. Sess., S. Doc. 2807 (1982) (from the foreword to a new edition by Orrin G. Hatch, Chairman, Senate Committee on the Judiciary, Apr. 2, 1995) at ii.

APPENDIX

The Second Amendment and the Personal Right to Arms
(Pages 165–185)

1. The subject is that of "A well regulated Militia" —
a militia the amendment declares to be "necessary to the
security of a free State." U.S. CONST. amend. II. But it
is hard to say on first reading whether the reference is to
a well-regulated *national* militia or, instead, to a well-
regulated *state* militia (i.e., a militia *in each state*). Perhaps, however, the reference is to both at once — a militia
in each state, originally constituted under each state's
authority, but subject to congressional authority to arm,
to organize, and to make provision to call into national
service, as a national militia. The possibility that this may
be so tends to send one looking for other provisions in the **Notes**
Constitution that may help to clear this matter away. And **for pp.**
a short search readily turns up several such provisions: **165–166**
Article I, section 8, clauses 15 and 16, and Article II,
section 2, clause 1. *See infra* note 16.

2. U.S. CONST. amend. II.

3. For example, one might well still be uncertain of the
breadth of the right to keep and bear arms (e.g., just what
kinds of "Arms"?).

4. U.S. CONST. amend. IV.

5. For example, does the protection of "houses" and
"effects" from unreasonable searches and seizures extend
to trash one may have put outside in a garbage can? May
it matter whether one has put the can itself outside one's
garage or farther out, beside the street? *See* California v.
Greenwood, 486 U.S. 35, 37 (1988).

6. U.S. CONST. amend. VI.

7. *Id.* amend. VII.

8. For example, with respect to the kind of "Arms" one may have. Perhaps these include all arms as may be useful (though not exclusively so) as an incident of service in a militia — and indeed, this would make sense of the introductory portion of the amendment as well. *See* United States v. Miller, 307 U.S. 174, 178 (1939).

Notes for p. 167

9. So, for example, though the Sixth Amendment provides a right to a *"speedy"* and *"public"* trial whenever one is accused of a (federal) crime, the amendment does not declare just *how* "speedy" the trial must be (i.e., exactly how soon following indictment the trial must be held) nor *how* "public" either (e.g., must it be televised to the world, or is an open courtroom, albeit with very limited seating, quite enough?). And the Fourth Amendment does not say there can be *no* searches and seizures — rather, only no "unreasonable" searches and seizures. Yet there is a very substantial body of highly developed case law that has given this genuine meaning and effect.

Likewise, when the Sixth and Seventh Amendments speak of the right to trial by "jury," then (even as is true of the Second Amendment in its reference to "Arms"?), though each of these amendments is silent as to what a jury means (a "jury" of how many people? a "jury" selected in what manner and by whom?), the provision means to be — and tends to be — given some real, some substantial, and some constitutionally significant effect. The point is, of course, that though there are questions of this sort with respect to *every* right furnished by the Bill of Rights, the expectation remains high that the right thus furnished will neither be ignored — treated as though it were not a right at all — nor so cynically misdefined or "qualified" in its ultimate description as to be reduced to an empty shell. It is only in the case of the Second Amendment that this is approximately the current state of the law. Indeed, it is only with respect to the Second Amendment that the current state of the law is roughly the same as was the state of the law with respect to the First Amendment's guarantees of freedom of speech and of the press as recently as 1904. As a restraint on the federal government, the First Amendment was deemed to be a restriction merely on certain kinds of prior restraint and hardly at all on what could be forbidden under threat of criminal sanction. *See,* e.g., Patterson v. Colorado, 205 U.S. 454, 462 (1907). As to the states, the amendment was not known as necessarily furnishing any restraint at all. *See id.*

10. The most one can divine from the Supreme Court's scanty decisions ("scanty" is used advisedly — essentially there are only two) is that such right to keep and bear arms as may be secured by this amendment may extend to such "Arms" as would be serviceable within a militia but not otherwise (so a "sawed-off" shotgun may not qualify, though presumably — by *this* test — heavy duty automatic rifles assuredly would). *See* United States v. Miller, 307 U.S. 174, 178 (1939); *see also* Lewis v. United States, 445 U.S. 55, 65 n.8 (1980) (noting that legislative restrictions on the right of felons to possess firearms do not violate any constitutionally protected liberty); Robertson v. Baldwin, 165 U.S. 275, 282 (1897) (referring to "the right of the people to keep and bear Arms" as a personal right). These casual cases aside ("casual," because in *Miller,* for example, there was not even an appearance entered by the defendant-appellant in the Supreme Court), there are a few 19th-century decisions denying any relevance of the Second Amendment to the states; but these decisions, which have never been revisited by the Supreme Court, merely mimicked others of the same era in holding that *none* of the rights or freedoms enumerated in the Bill of Rights were made

Notes for pp. 167—168

applicable by the Fourteenth Amendment to the states. *See,* e.g., Presser v. Illinois, 116 U.S. 252, 265 (1886) (citing United States v. Cruikshank, 92 U.S. 542, 553 (1875)). The shaky foundation of these cases ("shaky" because the effect was to eviscerate the Fourteenth Amendment itself) has long since been recognized — and long since repudiated by the Court in general. Notwithstanding, the lower courts continue ritually to rely upon them, and the Supreme Court quite as regularly declines to find any suitable for review. *See,* e.g., Quilici v. Village of Morton Grove, 695 F.2d 261, 269–70 (7th Cir. 1982) (holding that municipal handgun restrictions were constitutional), *cert. denied,* 464 U.S. 863 (1983). And why does one suppose that this is so?

Notes for pp. 168–169

11. *See supra* note 9.

12. Troops have not generally been quartered in private homes "in time of peace . . . without the consent of the Owner," nor even "in time of war," U.S. CONST. amend. III, for a very long time, and no Third Amendment case has ever been decided by the Supreme Court. Evidently, a Third Amendment case has arisen only once in a lower federal court. See Engblom v. Carey, 677 F.2d 957 (2d Cir. 1982) (holding that the Third Amendment protects the legitimate privacy interests of striking correction officers in keeping their housing from being used for quartering National Guard troops).

13. For a comprehensive review of congressional action since 1934, see United States v. Lopez, 2 F.3d 1342, 1348–60 (5th Cir. 1993).

14. *See,* e.g., Whitney v. California, 274 U.S. 357, 372 (1927) (Brandeis and Holmes, JJ., concurring); Gitlow v. New York, 268 U.S. 652, 672 (1925) (Holmes and Brandeis, JJ., dissenting); United States *ex rel.* Milwaukee Social Democratic Publishing Co. v. Burleson, 255 U.S. 407, 417 (1921) (Holmes and Brandeis, JJ., dissent-

ing); Abrams v. United States, 250 U.S. 616, 624 (1919) (Holmes and Brandeis, JJ., dissenting). *See generally* SAMUEL J. KONEFSKY, THE LEGACY OF HOLMES AND BRANDEIS 181–256 (1956) (reviewing the Holmes-Brandeis legacy of the First Amendment).

15. *See* Slaughter-House Cases, 83 U.S. (16 Wall.) 36 (1873); GERALD GUNTHER, CONSTITUTIONAL LAW 408–10 (12th ed. 1991). The *Slaughter-House Cases* denied that the Privileges and Immunities Clause of the Fourteenth Amendment extended any protection from the Bill of Rights against the states. Within three decades, however, the Court began the piecemeal abandonment of that position (albeit by relying on the Due Process Clause instead). *See* Chicago, B. & Q. R.R. v. Chicago, 166 U.S. 226 (1897) (applying the Fifth Amendment prohibition against the taking of private property for public use without just compensation and holding it to be equally a restraint against the states). In 1925, the Court proceeded in like fashion with respect to the Free Speech Clause of the First Amendment, *see Gitlow,* 268 U.S. at 666, and subsequently with respect to most of the rights enumerated in the Bill of Rights (exclusive, however, of the right to keep and bear arms). As already noted, the Court has declined to reexamine its 19th century cases *(Presser* and *Cruikshank)* that merely relied on the *Slaughter-House Cases* for their rationale. *Cf.* discussion *infra* Part IV.

Notes for pp. 169–171

16. Article I vests power in Congress "[t]o raise and support Armies," i.e., to provide for a national standing army as such, *see* U.S. CONST. art. I, § 8, cl. 12. It is pursuant to two different clauses that Congress is given certain powers with respect to the militia, such as the power "for *calling forth the Militia* to execute the Laws of the Union, suppress Insurrections and repel Invasions," *id.* cl. 15 (emphasis added), and the power "[t]o provide for organizing, arming, and disciplining, *the Militia,* and for governing such Part of them as may be employed in

the Service of the United States, reserving to the States respectively, the Appointment of the Officers, and the Authority of *training the Militia* according to the discipline prescribed by Congress," *id.* cl. 16 (emphasis added). So, too, the description of the executive power carries over the distinction between the regular armed forces of the United States in a similar fashion. Accordingly, Article II, section 2 provides that "[t]he President shall be Commander in Chief of the Army and Navy of the United States, *and of the Militia* of the several States, when called into the actual Service of the United States." *Id.* art. II, § 2, cl. 1 (emphasis added).

Notes
for pp.
171–172

17. And it is from the people, whose right this is, that such militia as the state may (as a free state) compose and regulate, shall be drawn — just as the amendment expressly declares.

18. Compare the utter incongruity of this suggestion with the actual provisions the Second Amendment enacts.

19. Compare this incompatible language and thought with the actual provisions of the amendment. Were the Second Amendment a mere federalism ("States' rights") provision, as it is not, it would assuredly appear in a place appropriate to that purpose (i.e., not in the same list with the First through the Eighth Amendments, but nearby the Tenth Amendment), and it would doubtless reflect the same federalism style as the Tenth Amendment; for example, it might read: *"Congress shall make no law impairing the right of each state to maintain such well regulated militia as it may deem necessary to its security as a free state."* But it neither reads in any such fashion nor is it situated even to imply such a thought. Instead, it is cast in terms that track the provisions in the neighboring personal rights clauses of the Bill of Rights. Just as the Fourth Amendment provides that *"[t]he right of the people to be secure in their persons, houses, papers, and*

effects . . . shall not be violated," U.S. CONST. amend. IV (emphasis added), so, too, the Second Amendment matches that language and likewise provides that *"the right of the people to keep and bear Arms, shall not be infringed,"* id. amend. II (emphasis added); *see also* United States v. Verdugo-Urquidez, 494 U.S. 259, 265 (1990) ("The Second Amendment protects the 'right of the people to keep and bear Arms'. . . ."). In further response to the suggestion that the Second Amendment is a mere States' rights clause in analogy with the Tenth Amendment (by, e.g., Keith A. Ehrman & Dennis A. Henigan, *The Second Amendment in the Twentieth Century: Have You Seen Your Militia Lately?*, 15 U. DAYTON L. REV. 5, 57 (1989)), *see* STEPHEN P. HALBROOK, THAT EVERY MAN BE ARMED: THE EVOLUTION OF A CONSTITUTIONAL RIGHT (1984). As Halbrook notes, "In recent years it has been suggested that the Second Amendment protects the 'collective' right of states to maintain militias, while it does not protect the right of 'the people' to keep and bear arms. If anyone entertained this notion in the period during which the Constitution and Bill of Rights were debated and ratified, it remains one of the most closely guarded secrets of the eighteenth century, for *no known writing surviving from the period between 1787 and 1791 states such a thesis." Id.* at 83 (emphasis added).

Notes for pp. 172–173

20. *See supra* note 16 and accompanying text.

21. U.S. CONST. amend. II (emphasis added). In James Madison's original draft of the amendment, moreover, the reference is to "a free country" (and not merely to "a free State"). *See* BERNARD SCHWARTZ, THE BILL OF RIGHTS: A DOCUMENTARY HISTORY 1026 (1971).

22. Once again, see the amendment, and compare the difference in thought conveyed in these different wordings as they might appear, in contrast, in actual print.

23. *See, e.g.,* XIANFA (1982) [Constitution] art. 55, cl. 2 (P.R.C.), *translated in* THE CONSTITUTION OF THE PEOPLE'S REPUBLIC OF CHINA 41 (1983); *infra* note 44.

24. A position evidently preferred by many today in this country as well, with the apparent approval even of the ACLU. *See* AMERICAN CIVIL LIBERTIES UNION, POLICY GUIDE OF THE AMERICAN CIVIL LIBERTIES UNION 95 (1986) ("Except for lawful police and military purposes, the possession of weapons by individuals is not constitutionally protected."). It is quite beyond the scope of this brief Essay to attempt to account for the ACLU's stance — which may even now be undergoing some disagreement and internal review.

25. THE FEDERALIST NO. 46, at 299 (James Madison) (Clinton Rossiter ed., 1961).

26. *Id.* NO. 84 at 513–14 (Alexander Hamilton).

27. *See, e.g.,* Leonard W. Levy, *Bill of Rights (United States), in* 1 ENCYCLOPEDIA OF THE AMERICAN CONSTITUTION 113, 114–15 (Leonard W. Levy et al. eds., 1986).

28. *See supra* note 16.

29. U.S. CONST. art. I, § 8, cls. 12–13.

30. *Id.* cl. 15.

31. *Id.* cl. 16 (emphasis added).

32. *Id.*

33. *Id.* (emphasis added).

34. *See* THE FEDERALIST NOS. 28, 29, 84 (Alexander Hamilton); *id.* NO. 46 (James Madison) (Clinton Rossiter ed., 1961).

35. *Id.* No. 29 at 182, 186 (Alexander Hamilton) (emphasizing this point).

36. *See id.* at 185–87.

37. *See id.* No. 46 at 299–300 (James Madison).

38. *Id.* No. 84 at 512–14 (Alexander Hamilton).

39. *See* JOYCE L. MALCOLM, TO KEEP AND BEAR ARMS 164 (1994). William Rawle, George Washington's candidate for the nation's first attorney general, made the same point. *See* WILLIAM RAWLE, A VIEW OF THE CONSTITUTION OF THE UNITED STATES OF AMERICA 125–26 (2d ed. 1829).

40. THOMAS M. COOLEY, THE GENERAL PRINCI-PLES OF CONSTITUTIONAL LAW IN THE UNITED STATES OF AMERICA 270–71 (1880). To be sure, Cooley went on to note that the Second Amendment had, as a "further" purpose (not the chief purpose — which, as he says, was to confirm the citizen's personal right to keep and bear arms — but as a "further purpose"), the purpose to preclude any excuse of alleged need for a large standing army. *Id.; see also* PA. CONST. of 1776, art. VIII ("That the people have a right to bear arms for the defence of themselves, and the state; and as standing armies in the time of peace, are dangerous to liberty, they ought not to be kept up: and that the military should be kept under strict subordination to, and governed by the civil power.").

Notes for pp. 175–177

41. 1 WILLIAM BLACKSTONE, COMMENTARIES *129, *141.

42. *Id.* at *144.

43. *Id.* (emphasis added). Against this background, incidentally, the Supreme Court's decision in DeShaney v. Winnebago County Dep't of Social Servs., 489 U.S. 189 (1989), may be important to take into account in

understanding the underpinnings of the personal right to keep and bear arms in the Blackstone minimal sense of the right to keep arms for self-preservation itself. To the extent that there is no enforceable constitutional obligation imposed on government in fact to protect every person from force or violence — and also no liability for a per se failure to come to any threatened person's aid or assistance (as *DeShaney* declares altogether emphatically) — the idea that the same government could nonetheless threaten one with criminal penalties merely "for having and using arms for self-preservation and defense" becomes impossibly difficult to sustain consistent with any plausible residual view of auxiliary natural rights. *See also* Nicholas Johnson, *Beyond the Second Amendment: An Individual Right to Arms Viewed Through The Ninth Amendment*, 24 RUTGERS L.J. 1, 64–67 (1992) (collecting prior articles and references to the strong natural rights history of the personal right to possess essential means of self defense).

Notes for p. 177

An impressive number of authors, whose work Nicholas Johnson reports (and to which he adds in this article), have sought to locate the right to keep and bear arms in the Ninth Amendment. They note that the Ninth Amendment provides precautionarily that "[t]he enumeration in the Constitution, of certain rights, shall not be construed to deny or disparage others retained by the people." U.S. CONST. amend. IX. And they go forward to show that the right to bear arms was a right of just this sort, i.e., that "the right to keep and bear Arms" was itself so utterly taken for granted, and so thoroughly accepted, that it fits the Ninth Amendment's description very aptly. *See* Johnson, *supra,* at 34–37. Unsurprisingly, however, the sources relied upon to show that this was so, strong as they are (and they are quite strong), are essentially just the very same sources that inform the Second Amendment with respect to the predicate clause on the right of the people to keep and bear arms. That is, they are the same materials that also show that there was a wide-spread understanding of a common right to keep and bear arms, which is itself the express right the Second Amendment expressly protects. Recourse to the same materials to fashion a Ninth Amendment ("unenumerated") right is not only largely replicative of the Second Amendment inquiry, but also singularly inappropriate under the circumstances — the right to bear arms is not left to the vagaries of Ninth Amendment disputes at all.

44. Eg., XIANA [Constitution] art. 55, c1.2 (P.R.C.), *translated in* THE CONSTITUTION OF THE PEOPLE'S REPUBLIC OF CHINA 41 (1983) ("It is the honourable duty of citizens of the People's Republic of China to perform military service and join the militia in accordance with the law.").

45. *See* MALCOLM, *supra* note 39, at 135–64 (tracing the English antecedents and reviewing the full original history of the Second Amendment). Professor Malcolm concludes, exactly as Thomas Cooley did a century earlier, *see supra* note 40, that "[t]he Second Amendment was meant to accomplish two distinct goals, each perceived as crucial to the maintenance of liberty. First, it was meant to guarantee the individual's right to have arms for self-defence and self-preservation. Such an individual right was a legacy of the English Bill of Rights [broadened in scope in America from the English antecedent]. . . .

". . . The clause concerning the militia was not intended to limit ownership of arms to militia members, or return control of the militia to the states, but rather to express the preference for a militia over a standing army."

MALCOLM, *supra,* at 162–63. For other strongly confirming reviews, see, e.g., SUBCOMMITTEE ON THE CONSTITUTION OF THE COMM. ON THE JUDICIARY, THE RIGHT TO KEEP AND BEAR ARMS, 97th Cong., 2d Sess. (1982); HALBROOK, *supra* note 19, at 67–80; David I.

Notes for pp. 177–178

Caplan, *Restoring the Balance: The Second Amendment Revisited*, 5 FORDHAM URB. L.J. 31, 33–43 (1976); Stephen P. Halbrook, *The Right of the People or the Power of the State: Bearing Arms, Arming Militias, and the Second Amendment*, 26 VAL. U.L. REV. 131 (1991); David T. Hardy, *Armed Citizens, Citizen Armies: Toward a Jurisprudence of the Second Amendment*, 9 HARV. J.L. & PUB. POL'Y 559, 604–15 (1986); David T. Hardy, *The Second Amendment and the Historiography of the Bill of Rights*, 4 J.L. & POL. 1, 43–62 (1987); Don B. Kates, Jr., *Handgun Prohibition and the Original Meaning of the Second Amendment*, 82 MICH. L. REV. 204, 206, 211–45 (1983); Sanford Levinson, *The Embarrassing Second Amendment*, 99 YALE L.J. 637, 645–51 (1989); Robert E. Shalhope, *The Armed Citizen in the Early Republic*, 49 LAW & CONTEMP. PROBS., Winter 1986, at 125, 133–41. *But see* Ehrman & Henigan, *supra* note 19; Dennis A. Henigan, *Arms, Anarchy and the Second Amendment*, 26 VAL. U.L. REV. 107, 111 n.17 (1991) (listing additional articles by others).

Notes for pp. 178–180

46. Compare the claim of a power in government to require "licensing" the right to keep arms.

47. The Second Amendment was originally the fourth amendment of twelve approved by the requisite two-thirds of both houses of Congress in 1789 and at once submitted for ratification by the state legislatures. Because only six states approved either the first or second of these twelve amendments during the ensuing two years (1789–1791), however, neither of these was adopted (since, unlike the others, they failed to be confirmed by three-fourths of the states). So, what was originally proposed as the third amendment became the First Amendment and what was originally proposed as the fourth amendment became the Second Amendment in turn. (On May 22, 1992, however, the original proposed second amendment of 1789 was declared by Congress to have

acquired sufficient state resolutions of ratification as of May 7, 1992, as also itself to have become effective as well. The result is that what was originally submitted as the second amendment has become the Twenty-Seventh Amendment instead.) *See* William Van Alstyne, *What Do You Think About the Twenty-Seventh Amendment?*, 10 CONST. COMMENTARY 9 (1993).

48. *See* Barron v. Mayor of Baltimore, 32 U.S. (7 Pet.) 243, 249 (1833) ("These amendments demanded security against the apprehended encroachments of the general government — not against those of the local governments.").

49. *See* U.S. CONST. amend. XIV.

Notes for pp. 180–182

50. CONG. GLOBE, 39th Cong., 1st Sess. 2765 (1866) (statement of Sen. Jacob Meritt Howard). Senator Howard is speaking here — and in his ensuing remarks — in explanation of the "first section" of the Fourteenth Amendment that provides: "No State shall make or enforce any law which shall abridge the privileges or immunities of citizens of the United States. . . ."

51. *Id.* at 2766.

52. *Id.* at 2765 (emphasis added).

53. *Id.* at 2766 (emphasis added). For the most recent review of this matter, with useful references to the previous scholarship on the same subject, and reaching the same conclusion still again, see Richard L. Aynes, *On Misreading John Bingham and the Fourteenth Amendment*, 103 YALE L.J. 57 (1993).

54. *See* Robert Dowlut, *Federal and State Constitutional Guarantees to Arms*, 15 U. DAYTON L. REV. 59, 79 (1989) ("State courts have on at least 20 reported occasions found arms laws to be unconstitutional."); Robert Dowlut & Janet A. Knoop, *State Constitutions*

and the Right to Keep and Bear Arms, 7 OKLA. CITY
U.L. REV. 177 (1982) (reviewing state constitutional
clauses and the right to keep and bear arms).

55. The inclusion of this entitlement for personal protection is, in the Fourteenth Amendment, even more
clear than as provided (as a premise) in the Second
Amendment itself. It was, after all, the defenselessness of
Negroes (denied legal rights to keep and bear arms by
state law) from attack by night riders — even to protect their own lives, their own families, and their own
homes — that made it imperative that they, as citizens,
could no longer be kept defenseless by a regime of state
law denying them the common right to keep and bear
arms. Note the description of the right as a personal right
in the report by Senator Howard. *See supra* text accompanying note 52. For confirming references, see also the
examples provided in MICHAEL K. CURTIS, NO STATE
SHALL ABRIDGE 24, 43, 56, 72, 138–41, 164, 203
(1986); HALBROOK, *supra* note 19, at 107–3; Skayoko
Blodgett-Ford, *Do Battered Women Have a Right to
Bear Arms?*, 11 YALE L. & POL'Y REV. 509, 513–24
(1993); Robert J. Cottrol & Raymond T. Diamond, *The
Second Amendment: Toward an Afro-Americanist Reconsideration*, 80 GEO. L.J. 309 (1991); Kates, *supra*
note 45, at 254–57. For an overall responsible general
review, see also Levinson, *supra* note 45. For the most
recent critical review, however, see Raoul Berger, *Constitutional Interpretation and Activist Fantasies*, 82 KY.
L.J. 1 (1993–1994) (with additional references to previous books and articles).

56. In contrast, the suggestion that it does not extend
to handguns (in contrast to howitzers) is quite beyond the
pale (i.e., it is wholly inconsistent with any sensible understanding of a meaningful right to keep arms as a
personal right).

57. Such questions, moreover, are hardly on that account (merely as questions) necessarily hard or difficult to answer in reasonable ways, even fully conceding a strong view of the right to keep and bear arms (e.g., rules of tort or of statutory liability for careless storage endangering minors or others foreseeably put at unreasonable risk).

58. And equally with respect to the states, pursuant to the Fourteenth Amendment.

59. *See supra* notes 9–14 and accompanying text.

Notes for pp. 184–185

60. Unless, of course, one holds the view that it is really desirable after all that the Constitution should indeed be construed — the Second and Fourteenth Amendments to the contrary notwithstanding — to say that the right to keep and bear arms is the right to keep and bear arms as it is sometimes understood (i.e., as though it had the added words, "but only according to the sufferance of the state").

The Embarrassing Second Amendment
(Pages 187–219)

1. It is not irrelevant that the Bill of Rights submitted to the states in 1789 included not only what are now the first ten Amendments, but also two others. Indeed, what we call the First Amendment was only the third one of the list submitted to the states. The initial "first amendment" in fact concerned the future size of the House of Representatives, a topic of no small importance to the Anti-Federalists, who were appalled by the smallness of the House seemingly envisioned by the Philadelphia Framers. The second prohibited any pay raise voted by

Notes for p. 188

members of Congress to themselves from taking effect until an election "shall have intervened." *See* J. GOEBEL, 1 THE OLIVER WENDELL HOLMES DEVISE HISTORY OF THE SUPREME COURT OF THE UNITED STATES: ANTECEDENTS AND BEGINNINGS TO 1801, at 442 n.162 (1971). Had all of the initial twelve proposals been ratified, we would, it is possible, have a dramatically different cognitive map of the Bill of Rights. At the very least, one would neither hear defenses of the "preferred" status of freedom of speech framed in terms of the "firstness" of (what we know as) the First Amendment, nor the wholly invalid inference drawn from that "firstness" of some special intention of the Framers to safeguard the particular rights laid out there.

Notes for p. 188

2. "Congress shall make no law respecting an establishment of religion . . . or abridging the freedom of speech, or of the press; or of the right of the people peaceably to assemble, and to petition the Government for a redress of grievances." U.S. CONST. amend. I.

3. "The right of the people to be secured in their persons, houses, papers, and effects, against unreasonable searches and seizures, shall not be violated; and no Warrants shall issue but upon probable cause, supported by Oath or affirmation, and particularly describing the place to be searched, and the persons or things to be seized." U.S. CONST. amend. IV.

4. "No person shall be held to answer for a capital, or otherwise infamous crime, unless on a presentment of indictment of a Grand Jury, except in cases arising in the land or naval forces, or in the Militia, when in actual services in the time of War or public danger; nor shall any person be subject for the same offense to be twice put in jeopardy of life or limb; nor shall be compelled in any criminal case to be a witness against himself, nor be

deprived of life, liberty, or property, without due process of law. . . ." U.S. CONST. amend. V.

5. "In all criminal prosecutions, the accused shall enjoy the right to a speedy and public trial, by an impartial jury of the State and district wherein the crime shall have been committed, which district shall have been previously ascertained by law, and to be informed of the nature and cause of the accusation; to be confronted with the witnesses against him; to have compulsory process for obtaining witnesses in his favor, and to have the Assistance of Counsel for his defense." U.S. CONST. amend. VI.

6. "Excessive bail shall not be required, nor excessive fines imposed, nor cruel and unusual punishments inflicted." U.S. CONST. amend. VIII.

Notes
for pp.
188–189

7. "The enumeration in the Constitution, of certain rights, shall not be construed to deny or disparage others retained by the people." U.S. CONST. amend. IX.

8. "[N]or shall private property be taken for public use, without just compensation." U.S. CONST. amend. V.

9. "The powers not delegated to the United States by the Constitution, nor prohibited by it to the States, are reserved to the States respectively, or to the people." U.S. CONST. amend. X.

10. "Congress shall make no law . . . prohibiting the free exercise thereof [religion]. . . ." U.S. CONST. amend. I.

11. *See supra* note 8.

12. *See supra* note 9.

13. There are several law review articles discussing the Amendment. See, e.g., Lund, *infra* note 96, and the articles cited in Dowlut & Knoop, *State Constitutions and*

the *Right to Keep and Bear Arms*, 7 OKLA. CITY U.L. REV. 177, 178 n.3 (1982). See also the valuable symposium on Gun Control, edited by Don Kates, in 49 LAW & CONTEMP. PROBS. 1–267 (1986), including articles by Shalhope, *The Armed Citizen in the Early Republic*, at 125; Kates, *The Second Amendment: A Dialogue*, at 143; Halbrook, *What the Framers Intended: A Linguistic Analysis of the Right to "Bear Arms,"* at 151. The symposium also includes a valuable bibliography of published materials on gun control, including Second Amendment considerations, at 251–67. The most important single article is almost undoubtedly Kates, *Handgun Prohibition and the Original Meaning of the Second Amendment*, 82 MICH. L. REV. 204 (1983). Not the least significant aspect of Kates' article is that it is basically the only one to have appeared in an "elite" law review. However, like many of the authors of other Second Amendment pieces, Kates is a practicing lawyer rather than a legal academic. I think it is accurate to say that no one recognized by the legal academy as a "major" writer on constitutional law has designed to turn his or her talents to a full consideration of the Amendment. *But see* LaRue, *Constitutional Law and Constitutional History*, 36 BUFFALO L. REV. 373, 375–78 (1988) (briefly discussing Second Amendment). Akhil Reed Amar's reconsiderations of the foundations of the Constitution also promises to delve more deeply into the implications of the Amendment. *See* Amar, *Of Sovereignty and Federalism*, 96 YALE L.J. 1425, 1495–1500 (1987). Finally, there is one book that provides more in-depth treatment of the Second Amendment: S. HALBROOK, THAT EVERY MAN BE ARMED, THE EVOLUTION OF A CONSTITUTIONAL RIGHT (1984). George Fletcher, in his study of the Bernard Goetz case, also suggests that Second Amendment analysis is not frivolous, though he does not elaborate the point. G. FLETCHER, A CRIME OF SELF DEFENSE 156–58, 210–11 (1988). One might well find this overt

Notes for p. 189

reference to "elite" law reviews and "major" writers objectionable, but it is foolish to believe that these distinctions do not exist within the academy or, more importantly, that we cannot learn about the sociology of academic discourse through taking them into account. No one can plausibly believe that the debates that define particular periods of academic discourse are a simple reflection of "natural" interest in the topic. Nothing helps an issue so much as its being taken up as an obsession by a distinguished professor from, say, Harvard or Yale.

14. One will search the "leading" casebooks in vain for any mention of the Second Amendment. Other than its being included in the text of the Constitution that all of the casebooks reprint, a reader would have no reason to **Notes** believe that the Amendment exists or could possibly be **for pp.** of interest to the constitutional analyst. I must include, **189–190** alas, P. BREST & S. LEVINSON, PROCESSES OF CONSTITUTIONAL DECISIONMAKING (2d ed. 1983), within this critique, though I have every reason to believe that this will not be true of the forthcoming third edition.

15. LaRue, *supra* note 13, at 375.

16. L. TRIBE, AMERICAN CONSTITUTIONAL LAW (2d ed. 1988).

17. J. NOWAK, R. ROTUNDA & J. YOUNG, CONSTITUTIONAL LAW (3d ed. 1986).

18. For a brilliant and playful meditation on the way the legal world treats footnotes and other marginal phenomena, see Balkin, *The Footnote,* 83 NW. U.L. REV. 275, 276–81 (1989).

19. TRIBE, *supra* note 16, at 299 n.6.

20. *Id.; see also* J. ELY, DEMOCRACY AND DISTRUST 95 (1980) ("[T]he framers and ratifiers . . . opted against

leaving to the future the attribution of [other] purposes, choosing instead explicitly to legislate the goal in terms of which the provision was to be interpreted."). As shall be seen below, *see infra* text accompanying note 38, the preamble may be less plain in its meaning than Tribe's (and Ely's) confident argument suggests.

21. J. NOWAK, R. ROTUNDA & J. YOUNG *supra* note 17, at 316 n.4. They do go on to cite a spate of articles by scholars who have debated the issue.

22. *Id.* at 316 n.4.

23. U.S. CONST. art. I, §10.

Notes for pp. 190–191

24. U.S. CONST. art. I, § 9, cl. 8.

25. *See, e.g.*, LEGISLATIVE REFERENCE SERV., LIBRARY OF CONGRESS, THE CONSTITUTION OF THE UNITED STATES OF AMERICA: ANALYSIS AND INTERPRETATION 923 (1964), which quotes the Amendment and then a comment from MILLER, THE CONSTITUTION 646 (1893): "This amendment seems to have been thought necessary. It does not appear to have been the subject of judicial exposition; and it is so thoroughly with our ideas, that further comment is unnecessary." *Cf.* Engblom v. Carey, 724 F.2d 28 (2d Cir.1983), *aff'g* 572 F. Supp. 44 (S.D.N.Y. 1983). *Engblom* grew out of a "statewide strike of correction officers, when they were evicted from their facility-residences . . . and members of the National Guard were housed in their residences without their consent." The district court had initially granted summary judgement for the defendants in a suit brought by the officers claiming a deprivation of their right under the Third Amendment. The Second Circuit, however, reversed on the ground that it could not "say that as a matter of law appellants were not entitled to the protection of the Third Amendment," Engblom v. Carey, 677 F.2d 957, 964 (2d Cir.1982). The District Court on

remand held that, as the Third Amendment rights had not been clearly established at the time of the strike, the defendants were protected by a qualified immunity, and it is this opinion that was upheld by the Second Circuit. I am grateful to Mark Tushnet for bringing this case to my attention.

26. *See,* e.g., *The Firearms the Second Amendment Protects,* N.Y. TIMES, June 9, 1988, at A22, col. 2 (three letters); *Second Amendment and Gun Control,* L.A. TIMES, March 11, 1989, Part II, at 9 col. 1 (nine letters); *What 'Right to Bear Arms'?,* N.Y. TIMES, July 20, 1989, at A23, col. 1 (national ed.) (op. ed. essay by Daniel Abrams); *see also We Rebelled To Protect Our Gun Rights,* WASHINGTON TIMES, July 20,1989, at F2, col. 4.

Notes for pp. 191—194

27. *See* SUBCOMMITTEE ON THE CONSTITUTION OF THE COMM. ON THE JUDICIARY, THE RIGHT TO KEEP AND BEAR ARMS, 97th Cong., 2d Sess. viii (1982) (preface by Senator Orrin Hatch) [thereinafter THE RIGHT TO KEEP AND BEAR ARMS].

28. *See supra* notes 13–14.

29. *See* Levinson, *Constitutional Rhetoric and the Ninth Amendment,* 64 CHI-KENT L. REV. 131 (1988).

30. P. BOBBITT, CONSTITUTIONAL FATE (1982).

31. *Id.* at 25–38.

32. *Id.* at 9–24.

33. *Id.* at 74–92.

34. *Id.* at 39–58.

35. *Id.* at 59–73.

36. *Id.* at 93–119.

37. For the record, I should note that Bobbitt disagrees with this statement, making an eloquent appeal (in conversation) on behalf of the classic American value of self-reliance for the defense of oneself and, perhaps more importantly, one's family. I certainly do not doubt the possibility of constructing an "ethical" rationale for limiting the state's power to prohibit private gun ownership. Nonetheless, I would claim that no one unpersuaded by any of the arguments derived from the first five models would suddenly change his or her mind upon being presented with an "ethical" argument.

Notes
for pp.
195–199
38. *Cf.,* e.g., the patents and copyrights clause, which sets out the power of Congress "[t]o promote the progress of Science and useful Arts, by securing for limited Times to Authors and Inventors the exclusive Right to their respective Writings and Discoveries." U.S. CONST. art. I, § 8.

39. For examples of this, see F. SCHAUER, FREEDOM OF SPEECH: A PHILOSOPHICAL ENQUIRY (1982); Levinson, *First Amendment, Freedom of Speech, Freedom of Expression: Does it Matter What We Call It?* 80 Nw. U.L. REV. 767 (1985) (reviewing M. REDISH, FREEDOM OF EXPRESSION: A CRITICAL ANALYSIS (1984)).

40. ACLU Policy #47. I am grateful to Joan Mahoney, a member of the national board of the ACLU, for providing me with a text of the ACLU's current policy on gun control.

41. Cress, *An Armed Community: The Origins and Meaning of the Right to Bear Arms,* 71 J. AM. HIST. 22, 31 (1984).

42. *See* U.S. CONST. amend. X.

43. For a full articulation of the individualist view of the Second Amendment, see Kates, *Handgun Prohibi-*

tion and the Original Meaning of the Second Amendment, 82 MICH. L. REV. 204 (1983). One can also find an efficient presentation of this view in Lund *infra* note 96, at 117.

44. Shalhope, *The Ideological Origins of the Second Amendment,* 69 J. AM. HIST. 599 (1982).

45. *Id.* at 614.

46. See Daniel Boorstin's laconic comment that "the requirements for self-defense and food-gathering had put firearms in the hands of nearly everyone" in colonial America. D. BOORSTIN, THE AMERICANS — THE COLONIAL EXPERIENCE 353 (1958). The beginnings of a professional police force in Boston are traced in R. LANE, POLICING THE CITY: BOSTON 1822–1855 (1967). Lane argues that as of the earlier of his two dates, "all the major eastern cities . . . had several kinds of officials serving various police functions, all of them haphazardly inherited from the British and colonial past. These agents were gradually drawn into better defined and more coherent organizations." *Id.* at 1. However, as Oscar Handlin points out in his introduction to the book, "to bring into being a professional police force was to create precisely the kind of hireling body considered dangerous by conventional political theory." *Id.* at vii.

Notes for pp. 199–200

47. *See* Cress, *supra* note 41.

48. 3 J. ELLIOT, DEBATES IN THE GENERAL STATE CONVENTIONS 425 (3d ed. 1937) (statement of George Mason, June 14, 1788), reprinted in Kates, *supra* note 13, at 216 n.51.

49. LETTERS FROM THE FEDERAL FARMER TO THE REPUBLICAN 123 (W. Bennett ed. 1978) (ascribed to Richard Henry Lee), reprinted in Kates, *supra* note 13, at 216 n.51.

50. Michelman, *The Supreme Court 1985 Term —
Foreword: Traces of Self-Government,* 100 HARV. L.
REV. 4, 39 (1986) (Harrington is a "pivotal figure in the
history of the 'Atlantic' branch of republicanism that
would find its way to America").

51. Shalhope, *supra* note 44, at 602.

52. Edmund Morgan discusses Harrington in his recent book, INVENTING THE PEOPLE 85–87 (1988) (analyzing notion of popular sovereignty in American
thought).

53. *Id.* at 156.

54. *Id.* at 157. Morgan argues, incidentally, that the
armed yeomanry was neither effective as a fighting force
nor particularly protective of popular liberty, but that is
another matter. For our purposes, the ideological percep-
tions are surely more important than the "reality" accompanying them. *Id.* at 160–65.

55. Blasi, *The Checking Value in First Amendment
Theory,* 1977 AM. B. FOUND. RES. J. 521.

56. See Lund, *infra* note 96, at 111–116.

57. Shalhope, *supra* note 44, at 603 (quoting 1755
edition of *Cato's Letters*). Shalhope also quotes from
James Burgh, another English writer well known to
American revolutionaries: "The possession of arms is the
distinction between a freeman and a slave. He, who has
nothing, and who himself belongs to another, must be
defended by him, whose property he is, and needs no
arms. But he, who thinks he is his own master, and has
what he can call his own, ought to have arms to defend
himself, and what he possesses; else he lives precariously;
and at discretion." *Id.* at 604. To be sure, Burgh also
wrote that only men of property should in fact comprise
the militia: "A militia consisting of any others than the

men of *property* in a country, is no militia; but a mungrel army." Cress, *supra* note 41, at 27 (emphasis in original) (quoting J. BURGH, 2 POLITICAL DISQUISITIONS: OR, AN ENQUIRY INTO PUBLIC ERRORS, DEFECTS, AND ABUSES (1774–75)). Presumably, though, the widespread distribution of property would bring with it equally widespread access to arms and membership in the militia.

58. *See* Cress, *supra* note 41, at 34.

59. THE FEDERALIST NO. 46 at 299 (J. MADISON) (C. Rossiter ed. 1961).

60. LETTERS FROM THE FEDERAL FARMER TO THE REPUBLICAN 124 (W. Bennett ed. 1978).

61. 3 J. STORY, COMMENTARIES § 1890 (1833), quoted in 5 THE FOUNDERS' CONSTITUTION 214 (P. Kurland & R. Lerner eds. 1987). **Notes for pp. 202–204**

62. *Id.*

63. *Id.* Lawrence Cress, despite his forceful critique of Shalhope's individualists rendering of the Second Amendment, nonetheless himself notes that "[t]he danger posed by manipulating demagogues, *ambitious rulers,* and foreign invaders to free institutions required the vigilance of citizen-soldiers cognizant of the common good." Cress, *supra* note 41, at 41 (emphasis added).

64. T. COOLEY, THE GENERAL PRINCIPLES OF CONSTITUTIONAL LAW IN THE UNITED STATES OF AMERICA 298 (3d ed. 1898): "The right of the people to bear arms in their own defence, and to form and drill military organizations in defence of the State, may not be very important in this country, but it is significant as having been reserved by the people as a possible and necessary resort for the protection of self-government against usurpation, and against any attempt on the part of those who may for the time be in possession of State authority or

resources to set aside the constitution and substitute their own rule for that of the people. Should the contingency ever arise when it would be necessary for the people to make use of the arms in their hands for the protection of constitutional liberty, the proceeding, so far from being revolutionary, would be in strict accord with popular right and duty." Cooley advanced this same idea in *The Abnegation of Self-Government*, 12 PRINCETON REV. 213–14 (1883).

65. See Rabban, *The First Amendment in Its Forgotten Years*, 90 YALE L.J. 514, 560 (1981) ("[P]rodigious theoretical writings of Theodore Schroeder . . . were the most extensive and libertarian treatments of freedom of speech in the prewar period"); *see also* GRABER, TRANSFORMING FREE SPEECH (forthcoming 1990) (manuscript at 4–12; on file with author).

66. T. SCHROEDER, FREE SPEECH FOR RADICALS 104 (reprint ed. 1969).

67. Shalhope, *supra* note 44, at 45.

68. *See* M. WEBER, THE THEORY OF SOCIAL AND ECONOMIC ORGANIZATION 156 (T. Parsons ed. 1947), where he lists among "[t]he primary formal characteristics of the modern state" the fact that: "to-day, the use of force is regarded as legitimate only so far as it is either permitted by the state or prescribed by it. . . . The claim of the modern state to monopolize the use of force is as essential to it as its character of compulsory jurisdiction and of continuous organization."

69. *See, e.g., Symposium: The Republican Civil Tradition*, 97 YALE L. J. 1493–1723 (1988).

70. *See* D. MALONE, 4 JEFFERSON AND HIS TIMES: JEFFERSON THE PRESIDENT: FIRST TERM, 1801–1805, at 7–11 (1970) (republican leaders ready to use state

militias to resist should lame duck Congress attempt to violate clear dictates of Article II by designating someone other than Thomas Jefferson as President in 1801).

71. Scott v. Sandford, 60 U.S. (19 How.) 393, 417 (1857).

72. *See,* e.g., Featherstone, Gardiner & Dowlut, *The Second Amendment to the United States Constitution Guarantees an Individual Right to Keep and Bear Arms,* in THE RIGHT TO KEEP AND BEAR ARMS, *supra* note 27, at 100.

73. *See,* e.g., Halbrook, *The Fourteenth Amendment and the Right to Keep and Bear Arms: The Intent of the Framers,* in THE RIGHT TO KEEP AND BEAR ARMS, *supra* note 27, at 79. Not the least of the ironies observed in the debate about the Second Amendment is that NRA conservatives like Senator Hatch could scarcely have been happy with the wholesale attack leveled by former Attorney General Meese on the incorporation doctrine, for here is one area where some "conservatives" may in fact be more zealous adherents of that doctrine than are most liberals, who, at least where the Second Amendment is concerned, have a considerably more selective view of incorporation.

Notes for pp. 206–209

74. 83 U.S. 36 (1873).

75. 32 U.S. (7 Pet.) 243 (1833).

76. 92 U.S. 542, 553 (1875).

77. 116 U.S. 252, 267 (1886). For a fascinating discussion of *Presser, see* LaRue, *supra* note 13, at 386–90.

78. 116 U.S. at 253. There is good reason to believe this statute, passed by the Illinois legislature in 1879, was part of an effort to control (and, indeed, suppress) widespread labor unrest linked to the economic troubles of the

time. For the background of the Illinois statute, see P.
AVRICH, THE HAYMARKET TRAGEDY 45 (1984): "As
early as 1875, a small group of Chicago socialists, most of
them German immigrants, had formed an armed club to
protect the workers against police and military assaults,
as well as against physical intimidation at the polls. In the
eyes of its supporters . . . the need for such a group was
amply demonstrated by the behavior of the police and
[state-controlled] militia during the Great Strike of 1877,
a national protest by labor triggered by a ten percent cut
in wages by the Baltimore and Ohio Railroad, which
included the breaking up of workers' meetings, the arrest
of socialist leaders, [and] the use of club, pistol, and
bayonet against strikers and their supporters. . . . Workers
. . . were resolved never again to be shot and beaten
without resistance. Nor would they stand idly by while
their meeting places were invaded or their wives and
children assaulted. They were determined, as Albert
Parsons [a leader of the anarchist movement in Chicago]
expressed it, to defend both 'their persons and their
rights.' "

**Notes
for p. 209**

79. 166 U.S. 226 (1897) (protecting rights of property
owners by requiring compensation for takings of property).

80. My colleague Douglas Laycock has reminded me
that a similar argument was made by some conservatives
in regard to the establishment clause of the First Amendment. Thus, Justice Brennan noted that "[i]t has been
suggested, with some support in history, that absorption
of the First Amendment's ban against congressional legislation 'respecting an establishment of religion' is concep-
tually impossible because the Framers meant the
Establishment Clause also to foreclose any attempt by
Congress to *disestablish* the existing official state
churches." Abington School Dist. v. Schempp, 374 U.S.
203, 254 (1963) (Brennan, J., concurring) (emphasis

added). According to this reading, it would be illogical to apply the establishment clause against the states "because that clause is not one of the provisions of the Bill of Rights which in terms protects a 'freedom' of the individual," *id.* at 256, inasmuch as it is only a federalist protection of states against a national establishment (or disestablishment). "The fallacy in this contention," responds Brennan, "is that it underestimates the role of the Establishment Clause as a co-guarantor, with the Free Exercise Clause, of religious liberty." *Id.* Whatever the sometimes bitter debates about the precise meaning of "establishment," it is surely the case that Justice Brennan, even as he almost cheerfully concedes that at one point in our history the "states-right" reading of the establishment clause would have been thoroughly plausible, expresses what has become the generally accepted view as to the establishment clause being some kind of limitation on the state as well as on the national government. One may wonder whether the interpretive history of the establishment clause might have any lessons for the interpretation of the Second Amendment.

Notes for pp. 209–211

81. It refused, for example, to review the most important modern gun control case, Quilici v. Village of Morton Grove, 695 F. 2d 261 (7th Cir. 1982), *cert. denied,* 464 U.S. 863 (1983), where the Seventh Circuit Court of Appeals upheld a local ordinance in Morton Grove, Illinois, prohibiting the possession of handguns within its borders.

82. 307 U.S. 174 (1939).

83. Justice Douglas, however, did not participate in the case.

84. *Miller,* 307 U.S. at 178.

85. *Id.* at 178 (citation omitted).

86. Lund notes that "commentators have since demonstrated that sawed-off or short-barreled shotguns are commonly used as military weapons." Lund, *infra* note 96, at 109.

87. 307 U.S. at 178.

88. *Id.* at 179.

89. *Id.*

90. L. Powell, Capital Punishment, Remarks Delivered to the Criminal Justice Section, ABA 10 (Aug 7, 1988).

91. *Id.* at 11.

92. This point is presumably demonstrated by the increasing public opposition of police officials to private possession of handguns (not to mention assault rifles).

93. D. Kates, Minimalist Interpretation of the Second Amendment 2 (draft Sept. 29, 1986) (unpublished manuscript available from author).

94. *See* Lund, *supra* note 96, at 116.

95. Wimmershoff-Caplan, *The Founders and the AK-47*, WASHINGTON POST, July 6, 1989, at A18, col. 4, reprinted as *Price of Gun Deaths Small Compared to Price of Liberty*, AUSTIN-AMERICAN STATESMAN, July 11, 1989, at A11. Ms. Wimmershoff-Caplan is identified as a "lawyer in New York" who is "a member of the National Board of the National Rifle Association." *Id.* One of the first such arguments in regard to the events in Tiananmen Square was made by William A. Black in a letter, *Citizens Without Guns*, N.Y. TIMES, June 18, 1989, at D26, col. 6. Though describing himself as "find[ing] no glory in guns [and] a profound anti-hunter," he nonetheless "stand[s] with those who would protect

our right to keep and bear arms" and cited for support the fact that "none [of the Chinese soldiers] feared bullets: the citizens of China were long ago disarmed by the Communists." "Who knows," he asks, "what the leaders and the military and the police of our America will be up to at some point in the future? We need an armed citizenry to protect our liberty." As one might expect, such arguments draw heated responses. *See* Rudlin, *The Founders and the AK-47 (Cont'd),* WASHINGTON POST, July 20, 1989, at A22, col. 3. Jonathan Rudlin accused Ms. Wimmershoff-Caplan of engaging in Swiftian satire, as no one could "take such a brilliant burlesque seriously." Neal Knox, however, endorsed her essay in full, adding the Holocaust to the list of examples: "Could the Holocaust have occurred if Europe's Jews had owned thousands of then-modern military Mauser bolt action rifles?" *See also* WASHINGTON POST, July 12, 1989, at A22, for other letters.

Notes for pp. 215–216

96. *See* Lund, *The Second Amendment, Political Liberty, and the Right to Self-Preservation,* 39 ALA. L. REV 103 (1987) at 115: "The decision to use military force is not determined solely by whether the contemplated benefits can be successfully obtained through the use of available forces, but rather determined by the *ratio* of those benefits to the expected costs. It follows that any factor increasing the anticipated cost of a military operation makes the conduct of that operation incrementally more unlikely. This explained why a relatively poorly armed nation with a small population recently prevailed in a war against the United States, and it explains why governments bent on the oppression of their people almost always disarm the civilian population before undertaking more drastically oppressive measures." I should note that I wrote (and titled) this article before reading Lund's article, which begins, "The Second Amendment to the United States Constitution has become the most embarrassing provision of the Bill of Rights." I did hear Lund

deliver a talk on the Second Amendment at the University of Texas Law School during the winter of 1987, which may have penetrated my consciousness more than I realized while drafting this article.

97. *See* D. Kates, *supra* note 93, at 24–25 n.13, for a discussion of this point.

98. *See,* e.g., Justice Marshall's dissent, joined by Justice Brennan, in Skinner v. Railway Labor Executive Ass'n, 109 S. Ct. 1402 (1989), upholding the government's right to require drug tests of railroad employees following accidents. It begins with his chastising the majority for "ignor[ing] the text and doctrinal history of the Fourth Amendment, which require that highly intrusive searches of this type be based on probable cause, not on the evanescent cost-benefit calculations of agencies or judges," *id.* at 1423, and continues by arguing that "[t]he majority's concern with the railroad safety problems caused by drug and alcohol abuse is laudable; its cavalier disregard for the Constitution is not. There is no drug exception to the Constitution, any more than there is a communism exception or an exception for other real or imagined sources of domestic unrest." *Id.* at 1426.

Notes for pp. 216–218

99. Donaldson, Letter to the Editor, AUSTIN-AMERICAN STATESMAN, July 8, 1989, at A19, col. 4.

100. *See* Minow, *The Supreme Court 1986 Term — Foreword: Justice Engendered,* 101 HARV. L. REV. 10 74–90 (1987). "We need settings in which to engage in the clash of realities that breaks us out of settled and complacent meanings and creates opportunities for insight and growth." *Id.* at 95; *see also* Getman, *Voices,* 66 TEX. L. REV. 577 (1988).

101. And, perhaps more to the point, "you" who insufficiently listen to "us" and to "our" favored groups.

102. *See supra* note 27 and accompanying text.

TWENTIETH-CENTURY BIBLIOGRAPHY

C ompared to the large body of legal commentary that has been generated by interest in other amendments to the Constitution — particularly the First, Fourth, Fifth, and Fourteenth Amendments — the literature of the Second Amendment is relatively small. That doesn't mean you can get through it in a day or two. To locate, copy, and read everything that has been written on the Second Amendment — cases, law review articles, scholarly articles, books — is a major enterprise. Believe me, I did it. On a study schedule of at least an hour or two each day, it took me *over a year*. Of course, you'll only have to spend a fraction of that time to attain a comprehensive knowledge of the history and development of the Second Amendment. That's what this little primer is for.

As I pointed out earlier in the book, the Second Amendment suffered from neglect by the legal and political communities in this country until the early 1960s. This is the reason I have chosen to call this a twentieth-century bibliography, because after the colonial period of proposal and ratification of the Bill of Rights, Second Amendment scholarship and legal activity were relatively dormant for almost two hundred years. You'll recall the Supreme Court addressed issues relating to the right to keep and bear arms only five times in the nineteenth century and once in the twentieth century.

However, it has been suggested — and this seems entirely reasonable to me — that new interest in the right was fueled by a number of traumatic events that occurred in our country between 1957 and 1981. In that relatively short span of time the nation witnessed the assassinations of President John F. Kennedy, the Reverend Martin Luther King, and Senator Robert F. Kennedy; the attempted assassinations of Presidents Gerald Ford and Ronald Reagan; the Vietnam War; street riots; and rising violent crime rates. In one way or another, all of these events were associated with firearms, giving rise to heretofore unaddressed concerns about what place guns should properly occupy in a modern democratic society. Surely it is no accident that our most far-reaching federal gun control legislation, the Gun Control Act of 1968 (18 U.S.C. § 921 et seq.), was enacted during this period in our history.

For ease of reference, this bibliography is divided into two categories: 1) the literature of the Second Amendment's historical, legal, and philosophical development; and 2) the literature of modern control and regulation of firearms, including crime and violence. And, in each of those categories, the literature is subdivided into one list for law review and scholarly articles and another for books.

Bibliographic references to the literature of the right to keep and bear arms prior to the twentieth century, that is, in the ancient, European, English, and American colonial periods, are included in the separate notes section (pp. 267–318), so they will not be repeated here.

You will find that the large majority of selections in this bibliography endorse the proposition that the Second Amendment confirms and guarantees to each citizen an "individual" (as well as a "collective") right to keep and bear arms; as opposed to the solely "collective" interpretation that is favored by the advocates of gun control. However, I have included

articles and books setting forth the arguments of the gun control proponents so you can judge for yourself and reach your
own conclusions. But as I mentioned at the beginning of this
book, it didn't take me long to conclude that the arguments
made by the proponents of gun control to invalidate the
freedoms guaranteed by the Second Amendment are wholly
unsupported by our history or law.

Just suppose — I have this fantasy I hope you'll indulge me
in — just suppose that all of us with an interest in this issue —
those of us against and those of us for gun control — boarded
a time machine that took us back to Philadelphia in 1787 for
a Second Amendment debate. And suppose that during the
trip I elected myself captain of the right-to-keep-and-bear-
arms debating team (hey, it's my fantasy, isn't it?) and gave
myself the power to choose anyone I wanted to argue our side.
Well, no matter who was arguing the case for the gun control
team, I wouldn't care. I'd simply pick old Sam Adams and
Patrick Henry to handle the rough stuff and choose as my chief
debater — *Thomas Jefferson!* Wow! Whose side do *you* think
would win?

HISTORY, CONSTITUTIONAL LAW,
AND PHILOSOPHICAL ISSUES

Law Review and Scholarly Articles

Amar, Akhil Reed, *The Bill of Rights and the Fourteenth Amendment,* 101 YALE L.J. 1193 (1992).
———, *The Bill of Rights as a Constitution,* 100 YALE L.J. 1131
(1991).
———, *Of Sovereignty and Federalism,* 95 YALE L.J. 1425 (1987).

Beale, Jr., *Homicide in Self-Defense*, 43 COLUM. L. REV. 526 (1903).

———, *Retreat From a Murderous Assault*, 16 HARV. L. REV. (1903)

Beschle, Donald L., *Reconsidering the Second Amendment: Constitutional Protection for a Right of Security*, 9 HAMLINE L. REV. 69 (1986).

Black, Hugo, *The Bill of Rights*, 35 N.Y.U. L. REV. 865 (1960).

Blodgett-Ford, Sayoko, *Do Battered Women Have a Right to Arms*, 11 YALE L. & POL'Y. REV. 509 (1993).

Bordenet, Bernard J., *The Right to Possess Arms: The Intent of the Framers of the Second Amendment*, 21 U.W.L.A. REV. 1 (1990).

Brown, Wendy, *Guns, Cowboys, Philadelphia Mayors, and Civic Republicanism: On Sanford Levinson's* The Embarrassing Second Amendment, 99 YALE L.J. 661 (1989).

Cantrell, Charles L., *The Right to Bear Arms: A Reply*, 53 WIS. BAR BULL. 21 (1980).

Caplan, David I., *Handgun Control: Constitutional or Unconstitutional? — A Reply to Mayor Jackson*, 10 N.C. CENT. L.J. 53 (1978).

———, *Restoring the Balance: The Second Amendment Revisited*, 5 FORDHAM URB L.J. 31 (1976).

———, *The Right of the Individual to Bear Arms: A Recent Judicial Trend*, ISSUE 4 DET. C. L. REV. 789 (1982).

———, *Weapons Control Laws: Gateways to Victim Oppression and Genocide*, in DIANE SANK AND DAVID I. CAPLAN, EDS., TO BE A VICTIM: ENCOUNTERS WITH CRIME AND INJUSTICE (1991).

Cottrol, Robert J., and Raymond T. Diamond, *The Fifth Auxiliary Right*, 104 YALE L.J. 995 (1994).

———, *Never Intended to Be Applied to the White Population: Firearms Regulation and Racial Disparity, the Redeemed South's Legacy to a National Jurisprudence?* 70 CHI.-KENT L. REV. (1995)

———, *The Second Amendment: Toward an Afro-Americanist Reconsideration*, 80 GEO. L.J. 309 (1991).

Cress, Lawrence Delbert, *An Armed Community: The Origins and Meaning of the Right to Bear Arms*, 71 J. AM. HIST. 22 (1984).

Cress, Lawrence Delbert, and Robert E. Shalhope, *The Second Amendment and the Right to Bear Arms: An Exchange*, 71 J. AM. HIST. 587 (1984).

Crosskey, William W., and Charles Fairman, *"Legislative History," and the Constitutional Limitations on State Authority*, 22 U. CHI. L. REV. 1 (1954).

Dennis, William G., *A Right to Keep and Bear Arms? The State of the Debate*, WASH. STATE BAR NEWS 47 (July 1995).

Douglas, William O., *The Bill of Rights Is Not Enough*, 38 N.Y.U. L. REV. 207 (1963).

Dowlut, Robert, *Bearing Arms in State Bills of Rights, Judicial Interpretation, and Public Housing*, 5 ST. THOMAS L. REV. 203 (1992).

———, *The Current Relevancy of Keeping and Bearing Arms*, 15 U. BALTIMORE L. FORUM 32 (1984).

———, *Federal and State Constitutional Guarantees to Arms*, 15 U. DAYTON L. REV. 59 (1989).

———, *The Right to Arms: Does the Constitution or the Predilection of Judges Reign?* 36 OKLA. REV. 65 (1983).

Dowlut, Robert, and Janet A. Knoop, *State Constitutions and the Right to Keep and Bear Arms*, 7 OKLA. CITY U. L. REV. 177 (1982).

Dunlap, Col. Charles J., Jr., *USAF, Welcome to the Junta: The Erosion of Civilian Control of the U.S. Military*, 29 WAKE FOREST L. REV. 341 (1994).

Ehrman, Keith A., and Dennis A. Henigan, *The Second Amendment in the Twentieth Century: Have You Seen Your Militia Lately?* 15 U. DAYTON L. REV. 5 (1989).

Eliot, *The Right to Keep and Bear Arms*, 53 WIS. BAR BULL. 34 (1980).

Emery, Lucilius A., *The Constitutional Right to Keep and Bear Arms,* 28 HARV. L. REV. 473 (1915).

Fairman, Charles, *Does the Fourteenth Amendment Incorporate the Bill of Rights?* 2 STAN. L. REV. 5 (1949).

Federal Gun Control and the Second Amendment, 48 REC. N.Y.C.B.A. COMM. FED. LEGIS. REP. 993 (Dec. 1993).

Feller, Peter Buck, and Karl L. Gotting, *The Second Amendment: A Second Look,* 61 NW. U. L. REV. 46 (1966).

Fields, William S., and David T. Hardy, *The Militia and the Constitution: A Legal History,* 136 MIL. L. REV. 1 (1992).

Fletcher, *The Corresponding Duty to the Right of Bearing Arms,* 39 FLA. B. J. 167 (1965).

Forkosch, M., *Who Are the "People" in the Preamble to the Constitution?* 19 CASE W. RES. L. REV. 644 (1968).

Friedman, Leon, *Conscription and the Constitution,* 67 MICH. L. REV. 1493 (1969).

Friendly, Henry J., *The Bill of Rights as a Code of Criminal Procedure,* 53 CAL. L. REV. 929 (1965).

Funk, T. Markus, *Is the True Meaning of the Second Amendment Really Such a Riddle?* 39 HOWARD L.J. 411 (1995).

Gardiner, Richard E., *To Preserve Liberty — A Look at the Right to Keep and Bear Arms,* 10 N. KY. L. REV. 63 (1982).

Gottlieb, Alan M., *Gun Ownership: A Constitutional Right,* 10 N. KY. L. REV. 113 (1982).

Graham, *The Early Antislavery Background of the Fourteenth Amendment,* W.S. L. REV. 479 (1950).

Granter, *The Machiavellianism of George Mason,* 17 WM. & MARY Q. 239 (2d ser., 1937).

Haight, George I., *The Right to Keep and Bear Arms,* 2 BILL OF RTS. REV. 31 (1941).

Halbrook, Stephen P., *Bearing Arms, Arming Militias and the Second Amendment*, 26 VAL. U. L. REV. 131 (1991).

———, *Encroachments of the Crown on the Liberty of the Subject: Pre-Revolutionary Origins of the Second Amendment*, 15 U. DAYTON L. REV. 91 (1989).

———, *The Jurisprudence of the Second and Fourteenth Amendments*, 4 GEO. MASON U. L. REV. 1 (1981).

———, *Personal Security, Personal Liberty, and "The Constitutional Right to Bear Arms": Visions of the Fourteenth Amendment*, 5 CONST. L.J. 343 (1995).

———, *Rationing Firearms Purchases and the Right to Keep Arms: Reflections on the Bills of Rights of Virginia, West Virginia, and the United States*, 96 W. VA. L. REV. 1 (1993).

———, *The Right of the People or the Power of the State: Bearing Arms, Arming Militias, and the Second Amendment*, 26 VAL. U. L. REV. 131 (1991).

———, *The Right to Keep and Bear Arms in the First State Bills of Rights: Pennsylvania, North Carolina, Vermont, Massachusetts*, 10 VT. L. REV. 255 (1985).

———, *To Keep and Bear Their Private Arms: The Adoption of the Second Amendment, 1787–1791*, 10 N. KY. L. REV. 13 (1982).

———, *What the Framers Intended: A Linguistic Interpretation of the Second Amendment*, 49 LAW & CONTEMP. PROBS. 153 (1986).

Hardy, David T., *Armed Citizens, Citizen Armies: Toward a Jurisprudence of the Second Amendment*, 9 HARV. J.L. & PUB. POL'Y. 559 (1986).

———, *The Second Amendment and the Historiography of the Bill of Rights*, 4 J.L. & POL. 1 (1987).

Hardy, David T., and John Stompoly, *Of Arms and the Law*, 51 CHI.-KENT L. REV. 62 (1974).

Hays, Stuart R., *The Right to Bear Arms: A Study in Judicial Misinterpretation*, 2 WM. & MARY L. REV. 381 (1960).

Henigan, Dennis A., *Arms, Anarchy and the Second Amendment*, 26 VAL. U. L. REV. 107 (1991).

————, *The Right to Be Armed: A Constitutional Illusion*, 8 SAN FRAN. BARRISTER L.J. 11 (1989).

Herz, Andrew D., *Gun Crazy: Constitutional False Consciousness and Dereliction of Dialogic Responsibility*, 75 B.U. L. REV. 57 (1995).

Jackson, Maynard H., Jr., *Handgun Control: Constitutional and Critically Needed*, 8 N.C. CENT. L.J. 189 (1976).

Johnson, Nicholas J., *Beyond the Second Amendment: An Individual Right to Arms Considered Through the Ninth Amendment*, 24 RUTGERS L.J. 1 (1992).

Kates, Don B., *Handgun Prohibition and the Original Meaning of the Second Amendment*, 82 MICH. L. REV. 204 (1983).

————, *The Second Amendment: A Dialogue*, 49 LAW & CONTEMP. PROBS. 143 (1986).

————, *The Second Amendment and the Ideology of Self-Protection*, 9 CONST. COMMENTARY 87 (1992).

Kates, Don B., and Daniel D. Polsby, *Of Genocide and Disarmament*, 86 J. CRIM. L. & CRIMINOL. 247 (1995).

Kopel, David B., *It Isn't About Duck Hunting: The British Origins of the Right to Arms*, 93 MICH. L. REV. 1333 (1995).

Larish, Inge Anna, *Why Annie Can't Get a Gun: A Feminist Appraisal of the Second Amendment*, 1996 U. ILL. L.F. 467.

Leddy, Edward, *Right to Bear Arms in State Constitutions*, 1 J. FIREARMS & PUB. POL'Y. 4 (1988).

Levin, John, *The Right to Bear Arms: The Development of the American Experience*, 48 CHI.-KENT L. REV. 148 (1971).

Levine, Ronald B., and David B. Saxe, *The Second Amendment: The Right to Bear Arms*, 7 HOUS. L. REV. 1 (1969).

Levinson, Sanford, *Democratic Politics and Gun Control*, 4 RECONSTRUCTION 137 (1992).

————, *The Embarrassing Second Amendment*, 99 YALE L.J. 637 (1989).

Lund, Nelson, *The Second Amendment, Political Liberty, and the Right to Self-Preservation*, 39 ALA. L. REV. 103 (1987).

Lutz, Donald S., *The States and the U.S. Bill of Rights*, 16 S. ILL. U. L.J. 2551 (1992).

Malcolm, Joyce Lee, *The Right of the People to Keep and Bear Arms: The Common Law Tradition*, 10 HAST. CONST. L.Q. 285 (1983).

Marina, *Militia, Standing Armies, and the Second Amendment*, 2 LAW & LIBERTY 1 (1976).

McClure, James A., *Firearms and Federalism*, 7 IDAHO L. REV. 197 (1970).

McKenna, Daniel J., *The Right to Keep and Bear Arms*, 12 MARQ. L. REV. 138 (1928).

McNeely, James W., *The Right of Who to Bear What, When, and Where — West Virginia Firearms Law v. the Right-to-Bear-Arms Amendment*, 89 W. VA. L. REV. 1125 (1987).

Moncure, Thomas M., Jr., *The Second Amendment Ain't About Hunting*, 1991 HOW. L.J. 589.

————, *Who Is the Militia — The Virginia Ratification Convention and the Right to Bear Arms*, 19 LINCOLN L. REV. 1 (1990).

Mullett, C., *Classical Influences on the American Revolution*, 35 CLASSICAL J. 932 (1939–40).

Murphy, *The American Revolutionary Army and the Concept of Levee en Masse*, MIL. AFFAIRS (spring 1959).

Nelson, *The Eighteenth Century Background of John Marshall's Constitutional Jurisprudence*, 76 MICH. L. REV. 893 (1978).

Olds, Nicholas V., *The Second Amendment and the Right to Keep and Bear Arms*, 46 MICH. STATE BAR J. 22 (1967).

Perkins, *Self-Defense Re-examined*, 1 U.C.L.A. L. REV. 133 (1954).

Pocock, J., *Machiavelli, Harrington and English Political Ideologies in the Eighteenth Century*, 22 WM. & MARY Q. (3d ser.) 549 (1965).

Quinlan, Michael J., *Is There a Neutral Justification for Refusing to Implement the Second Amendment or Is the Supreme Court Just "Gun Shy"?* 22 CAPITAL U. L. REV. 641 (1993).

Reynolds, Glenn Harlan, *A Critical Guide to the Second Amendment*, 62 TENN. L. REV. 461 (1995).

———, *Firearms Purchases and the Right to Bear Arms*, 96 W. VA. L. REV. 1 (1993).

———, *The Right to Keep and Bear Arms Under the Tennessee Constitution: A Case Study in Civic Republican Thought*, 61 TENN. L. REV. 647 (1994).

Reynolds, Glenn Harlan, and Don B. Kates, *The Second Amendment and States' Rights: A Thought Experiment*, 36 WM. & MARY L. REV. 1737 (1995).

Riseley, Richard F., Jr., *The Right to Keep and Bear Arms: A Necessary Constitutional Guarantee or an Outmoded Provision of the Bill of Rights?* 31 ALB. L. REV. 74 (1967).

Rohner, Ralph J., *The Right to Bear Arms: A Phenomenon of Constitutional History*, 16 CATH. U. L. REV. 53 (1966).

Santee, *The Right to Keep and Bear Arms*, 28 DRAKE L. REV. 423 (1976–7).

Scarry, Elaine, *War and the Social Contract: Nuclear Policy, Distribution, and the Right to Bear Arms*, 139 U. PA. L. REV. 1257 (1991).

Shalhope, Robert E., *The Armed Citizen in the Early Republic*, 49 LAW & CONTEMP. PROBS. 125 (1986).

————, *The Ideological Origins of the Second Amendment*, 69 J. AM. HIST. 599 (1982).

————, *Republicanism and Early American Historiography*, 39 WM. & MARY Q. 334 (1982).

————, *Toward a Republican Synthesis: The Emergence of an Understanding of Republicanism in American Historiography*, 29 WM. & MARY Q. (3d ser.) 49 (1972).

Snyder, Jeffrey R., *A Nation of Cowards*, 113 PUB. INTEREST 40 (1993).

Spannaus, Warren, *State Firearms Regulation and the Second Amendment*, 6 HAMLINE L. REV. 383 (1983).

Sprecher, Robert A., *The Lost Amendment*, 51 A.B.A. J. 554 & 665 (1965).

Tahmassebi, Stefan B., *Gun Control and Racism*, 2 CIV. RTS. L.J. 67 (1991).

Van Alstyne, William, *The Second Amendment and the Personal Right to Arms*, 43 DUKE L.J. 1236 (1994).

Vandercoy, David E., *The History of the Second Amendment*, 28 VAL. U. L. REV. 1007 (1994).

Warren, Earl, *The Bill of Rights and the Military*, 37 N.Y.U. L. REV. 181 (1962).

Weatherup, Roy G., *Standing Armies and Armed Citizens: An Historical Analysis of the Second Amendment*, 2 HAST. CONST. L.Q. 961 (1975).

Whisker, James B., *Historical Development and Subsequent Erosion of the Right to Keep and Bear Arms*, 78 W. VA. L. REV. 171 (1975).

Wiener, *The Militia Clause of the Constitution*, 54 HARV. L. REV. 181 (1940).

Will, George F., *The Gun Amendment Befogs a Gunfire Crisis*, ITHACA J., Mar. 22, 1991, at 8A.

Williams, David C., *Civic Republicanism and the Citizen Militia: The Terrifying Second Amendment*, 101 YALE L.J. 551 (1991).

Books

AMBROSE, S., THE ARMED FORCES AND CIVIL DISORDER, THE MILITARY AND AMERICAN SOCIETY (1972).

BAILYN, BERNARD, THE IDEOLOGICAL ORIGINS OF THE AMERICAN REVOLUTION (1967).
BERGER, RAOUL, THE FOURTEENTH AMENDMENT AND THE BILL OF RIGHTS (1989).
———, GOVERNMENT BY JUDICIARY: THE TRANSFORMATION OF THE FOURTEENTH AMENDMENT (1977).
BOORSTEIN, D., THE AMERICANS — THE COLONIAL EXPERIENCE (1958).
BORDEN, MORTON, ED.,THE ANTIFEDERALIST PAPERS (1965).
BOYD, JULIAN P., AND CHARLES T. CULLEN, EDS., THE PAPERS OF THOMAS JEFFERSON (1950–82).
BRANT, IRVING, THE BILL OF RIGHTS: ITS ORIGIN AND MEANING (1965).

COLBOURN, H., THE LAMP OF EXPERIENCE: WHIG HISTORY AND THE INTELLECTUAL ORIGINS OF THE AMERICAN REVOLUTION (1965).
CORWIN, E., THE "HIGHER LAW" BACKGROUND OF AMERICAN CONSTITUTIONAL LAW (1955).
COTTROL, ROBERT J., ED., GUN CONTROL AND THE CONSTITUTION: SOURCES AND EXPLORATIONS ON THE SECOND AMENDMENT (1994).
COUNTRYMAN, EDWARD, A PEOPLE IN REVOLUTION (1981).
CRESS, LAWRENCE D., CITIZENS IN ARMS: THE ARMY AND THE MILITIA IN AMERICAN SOCIETY TO THE WAR OF 1812 (1982).

CURTIS, MICHAEL K., NO STATE SHALL ABRIDGE: THE FOUR-TEENTH AMENDMENT AND THE BILL OF RIGHTS (1986).

CUSHING, HARRY A., ED., THE WRITINGS OF SAMUEL ADAMS (1908).

DAVIDSON, BILL R., TO KEEP AND BEAR ARMS (1969).

DAVIS, DAVID D., FROM HOMICIDE TO SLAVERY (1986).

DUBOIS, W. E. B., BLACK RECONSTRUCTION IN AMERICA (1962).

DUMBAULD, E., THE BILL OF RIGHTS AND WHAT IT MEANS TODAY (1957).

FLACK, HORACE E., THE ADOPTION OF THE FOURTEENTH AMENDMENT (1908).

FREEDMAN, WARREN, THE PRIVILEGE TO KEEP AND BEAR ARMS: THE SECOND AMENDMENT AND ITS INTERPRETATION (1989).

HALBROOK, STEPHEN P., A RIGHT TO BEAR ARMS: STATE AND FEDERAL BILLS OF RIGHTS AND CONSTITUTIONAL GUARANTEES (1989).

———, THAT EVERY MAN BE ARMED: THE EVOLUTION OF A CONSTITUTIONAL RIGHT (1984).

HARDY, DAVID T., ORIGINS AND DEVELOPMENT OF THE SECOND AMENDMENT (1986).

HICKOK, EUGENE W., ED., THE BILL OF RIGHTS: ORIGINAL UNDERSTANDING AND CURRENT MEANING (1991).

HOLLISTER, C., ANGLO-SAXON MILITARY INSTITUTIONS (1962).

HUNTINGTON, SAMUEL P., THE SOLDIER AND THE STATE (1957).

JENSEN, M., J. KAMINSKI, AND G. SALADINO, EDS., THE DOCU-MENTARY HISTORY OF THE RATIFICATION OF THE CONSTITUTION (9 vols. to date, 1976–).

KENYON, CECELIA M., ED., THE ANTIFEDERALISTS (1966).

KIRK, R., THE ROOTS OF AMERICAN ORDER (1975).
KUKLA, ROBERT J., ED., THE BILL OF RIGHTS: A LIVELY HERITAGE (1987).

LEACH, DOUGLAS E., ROOTS OF CONFLICT: BRITISH ARMED FORCES AND COLONIAL AMERICANS, 1677–1763 (1986).

MAIER, P., FROM RESISTANCE TO REVOLUTION: COLONIAL RADICALS AND THE DEVELOPMENT OF AMERICAN OPPOSITION TO BRITAIN, 1765–1776 (1972).
MALCOLM, JOYCE LEE, DISARMED: THE LOSS OF THE RIGHT TO BEAR ARMS IN RESTORATION ENGLAND (1980).
———, TO KEEP AND BEAR ARMS: THE ORIGINS OF AN ANGLO-AMERICAN RIGHT (1994).
MONAGHAN, FRANK, HERITAGE OF FREEDOM (1947).

NORMAN, A. V. B., THE MEDIEVAL SOLDIER (1971).

PERRY AND COOPER, EDS., SOURCES OF OUR LIBERTIES (1959).
POCOCK, J., THE MACHIAVELLIAN MOMENT: FLORENTINE POLITICAL THOUGHT AND THE ATLANTIC REPUBLICAN TRADITION (1975).
POUND, R., THE DEVELOPMENT OF CONSTITUTIONAL LIBERTY (1957).

RABB, F., THE ENGLISH FACE OF MACHIAVELLI: A CHANGING INTERPRETATION 1500–1700 (1964).
REID, JOHN P., IN DEFIANCE OF THE LAW: THE STANDING-ARMY CONTROVERSY, THE TWO CONSTITUTIONS AND THE COMING OF THE AMERICAN REVOLUTION (1981).
RIKER, R., SOLDIERS OF THE STATE (1957).
ROSSITER, C., THE POLITICAL THOUGHT OF THE AMERICAN REVOLUTION (1963).

ROTUNDA, RONALD D., AND JOHN E. NOWAK, TREATISE ON CONSTITUTIONAL LAW: SUBSTANCE AND PROCEDURE (2d ed., 1992).

ROYSTER, C., A REVOLUTIONARY PEOPLE AT WAR: THE CONTINENTAL ARMY AND AMERICAN CHARACTER (1979).

RUTLAND, ROBERT A., THE BIRTH OF THE BILL OF RIGHTS (1983).

———, ED., THE PAPERS OF GEORGE MASON (1970).

RUTLAND, ROBERT A., AND CHARLES F. HOBSON, EDS., THE PAPERS OF JAMES MADISON (1977–9).

SCHWARTZ, BERNARD, THE BILL OF RIGHTS: A DOCUMENTARY HISTORY (1971).

SMITH, HENRY N., VIRGIN LAND: THE AMERICAN WEST AS SYMBOL AND MYTH (1950).

SMITH, J., AND T. BARNES, THE ENGLISH LEGAL SYSTEM: CARRY OVER TO THE COLONIES (1975).

STORING, HERBERT J., THE COMPLETE ANTI-FEDERALIST (1981).

SUBCOMMITTEE ON THE CONSTITUTION OF THE SENATE COMMITTEE ON THE JUDICIARY, THE RIGHT TO KEEP AND BEAR ARMS, 97th Cong., 2d sess., S. Doc. 2807 (1982).

TANSIL, L., AND C. CHARLES, EDS., DOCUMENTS ILLUSTRATIVE OF THE FORMATION OF THE UNION OF THE AMERICAN STATES, 69th Cong., 1st sess., H.R. Doc. 398 (1927).

TEN BROCK, J., EQUAL UNDER THE LAW (1965).

TONSO, W. R., GUNS AND SOCIETY: THE SOCIAL AND EXISTENTIAL ROOTS OF THE AMERICAN ATTACHMENT TO FIREARMS (1982).

TREVELYAN, G., THE ENGLISH REVOLUTION (1954).

TRIBE, LAURENCE, AMERICAN CONSTITUTIONAL LAW (2d ed., 1988).

TUCHMAN, BARBARA, THE MARCH OF FOLLY (1984).

VEIT, HELEN E., AND KENNETH R. BOWLING, EDS., CREATING THE BILL OF RIGHTS: THE DOCUMENTARY RECORD FROM THE FIRST FEDERAL CONGRESS (1991).

WHISKER, JAMES B., OUR VANISHING FREEDOM: THE RIGHT TO KEEP AND BEAR ARMS (1972).
WOOD, G., THE CREATION OF THE AMERICAN REPUBLIC (1969).

YOUNG, DAVID E., ED., THE ORIGIN OF THE SECOND AMENDMENT: A DOCUMENTARY HISTORY OF THE BILL OF RIGHTS, 1787–1792 (2d ed., 1995).

MODERN GUN CONTROL
LEGISLATION AND REGULATION,
VIOLENCE AND CRIME

Law Review and Scholarly Articles

Aborn, Richard M., *The Battle Over the Brady Bill and the Future of Gun Control Advocacy*, 22 FORDHAM URB. L.J. 417 (1995).

Abrams, Daniel, *Ending the Other Arms Race: An Argument for a Ban on Assault Weapons*, Note, 10 YALE L. & POL'Y. REV. 488 (1992).

Ashbrook, *Against Comprehensive Gun Control*, 71 CURRENT HIST. 23 (1976).

Batey, Robert, *Strict Construction of Firearms Offenses: The Supreme Court and the Gun Control Act of 1968*, 49 LAW & CONTEMP. PROBS. 163 (1986).

Beard, Michael K., and Kristin M. Rand, *The Handgun Battle*, 20 BILL OF RTS. J. 13 (1987).

Benenson, *A Controlled Look at Gun Controls*, 14 N.Y. F. L. 718 (1968).

Bordua, David J., *Firearms Ownership and Violent Crime: A Comparison of Illinois Counties*, in J. BYRNE AND R. SAMPSON, EDS., THE SOCIAL ECOLOGY OF CRIME (1986).

———, *Gun Control and Opinion Measurement*, 5 LAW & POL'Y. Q. 345 (1983).

Bordua, David J., and Alan J. Lizotte, *Patterns of Legal Firearms Ownership: A Situational and Cultural Analysis of Illinois Counties*, 2 LAW & POL'Y. Q. 147 (1979).

Bruce-Briggs, Barry, *The Great American Gun War*, 45 PUB. INTEREST 37 (1976).

Centerwall, Brandon, *Homicide and the Prevalence of Handguns: Canada and the United States, 1976 to 1980*, 134 AM. J. EPID. 1245 (1991).

Cook, Philip J., *The Effect of Gun Availability on Robbery and Robbery-Murder: A Cross Section Study of 50 Cities*, 3 POL. STUD. REV. ANN. 743 (1979).

———, *The Effect of Gun Availability on Violent Crime Patterns*, 455 ANNALS AM. ACAD. POL. & SOC. SCI. (1981)

———, *The Relationship Between Victim Resistance and Injury in Non-Commercial Robbery*, 15 J. LEGAL STUD. 405, 407 (1986).

Cramer, Clayton E., and David B. Kopel, *"Shall Issue": The New Wave of Concealed Handgun Permit Laws*, 62 TENN. L. REV. 679 (1995).

Cunningham, Kevin M., *When Gun Control Meets the Constitution* (symposium: Federal Gun Control and the Brady Act), 10 ST. JOHNS J. LEGAL COMMENTARY 59 (1994).

Fields, *Handgun Prohibition and Social Necessity*, 23 ST. LOUIS U. L.J. 35 (1979).

Fields, Samuel, *Guns, Crime and the Negligent Gun Owner*, 10 N. KY. L. REV. 141 (1982).

Funk, T. Markus, *Gun Control and Economic Discrimination: The Melting-Point Case-in-Point*, 85 J. CRIM. & CRIMINOL. 764 (1995).

Gardiner, Richard E., *Gun Control: Is It a Legal and Effective Means of Controlling Firearms in the United States?* Note, 21 WASHBURN L.J. 244 (1982).

Gastil, *Homicide and a Regional Culture of Violence*, 36 AM. SOCIOLOGICAL REV. 412 (1971).

Geisel, Roll, and Wettick, *The Effectiveness of State and Local Regulation of Handguns: A Statistical Analysis*, 1969 DUKE L.J. 647.

Gurr, *Historical Trends in Violent Crime: A Critical Review of Evidence*, 3 ANNUAL REV. CRIME JUSTICE (1981).

Halbrook, Stephen P., *Tort Liability for the Manufacture, Sale and Ownership of Handguns?* 6 HAMLINE L. REV. 351 (1983).

Hardy, David T., *Firearm Ownership and Regulation: Tackling an Old Problem with Renewed Vigor*, 20 WM. & MARY L. REV. 235 (1978).

———, *Legal Restriction of Firearm Ownership As an Answer to Violent Crime: What Was the Question?* 6 HAMLINE L. REV. 391 (1983).

Jacobs, James B., *Exceptions to a General Prohibition on Handgun Possession: Do They Swallow Up the Rule?* 49 LAW & CONTEMP. PROBS. 5 (1986).

———, *The Regulation of Personal Chemical Weapons: Some Anomalies in American Weapons Law*, 15 U. DAYTON L. REV. 141 (1989).

Jacobs, James B., and Kimberly A. Potter, *Keeping Guns Out of the "Wrong" Hands: The Brady Law and the Limits of Regulation*, 86 J. CRIM. L. & CRIMINOL. 93 (1995).

Johnson, Nicholas J., *Shots Across No Man's Land: A Response to Handgun Control, Inc.'s, Richard Aborn*, 22 FORDHAM URB. L.J. 441 (1995).

Kaplan, J., *Controlling Firearms*, 28 CLEV. ST. L. REV. 1 (1979).
———— *The Wisdom of Gun Prohibition*, 455 ANNALS 11 (1981).
Kates, Don B., *Bigotry, Symbolism and Ideology in the Battle Over Gun Control*, PUB. INTEREST L. REV. 31 (1992).
————, *On Reducing Violence or Liberty*, 3 CIV. LIBERTIES REV. 56.
————, *The Value of Civilian Handgun Possession as a Deterrent to Crime or a Defense Against Crime*, 18 AM. J. CRIM. L. 1 (1991).
————, *Why a Civil Libertarian Opposes Gun Control*, 3 CIV. LIB. REV. 24 (1976).
Kates, Don. B., Henry E. Schaffer, et al., *Guns and Public Health: Epidemic of Violence or Pandemic of Propaganda*, 62 TENN. L. REV. 513 (1995).
Kessler, Raymond G., *Enforcement Problems of Gun Control: A Victimless Crimes Analysis*, 16 CRIM. L. BULL. 131 (1980).
————, *Gun Control and Political Power*, 5 LAW & POL'Y. Q. 381 (1983).
King, *Firearms and Crime*, 8 CRIMINOLOGIST 50 (1973).
Kleck, Gary, *Crime Control Through the Private Use of Armed Force*, 35 SOC. PROBS. 1 (Feb. 1988).
————, *Guns and Violence: An Interpretive Review of the Field*, 1 SOC. PATH. 12 (1995).
————, *Policy Lessons from Recent Gun Control Research*, 49 LAW & CONTEMP. PROBS. 35 (1986).
Kleck and Bordua, *The Factual Foundation for Certain Key Assumptions of Gun Control*, 5 LAW & POL'Y. Q. 271 (1983).
Kleck and DeLone, *Victim Resistance and Offender Weapon Effects in Robbery*, 9 J. QUANT. CRIMIN. 55 (1993).

Kleck and Gertz, *Armed Resistance to Crime: The Prevalence and Nature of Self-Defense with a Gun*, 86 J. CRIM. L. & CRIMINOL. 150 (1995).

Kleck and Patterson, *The Impact of Gun Control and Gun Ownership Levels on City Violence Rates*, 9 J. QUANT. CRIMIN. 249 (1993).

Kluin, Kurt F., *Gun Control: Is It a Legal and Effective Means of Controlling Firearms in the United States?* 21 WASHBURN L.J. 244 (1982).

Krug, *The True Facts on Firearms Legislation — Three Statistical Studies*, 116 CONG. REC. S292 (daily edit., Jan. 21, 1970).

Levi, *Control of Handguns*, 8 OFFICER 15 (1975).

Lizotte, Alan J., *The Costs of Using Gun Control to Reduce Homicide*, 62 BULL. N.Y. ACAD. MED. 539 (1986).

Lizotte, Alan J., and David J. Bordua, *Firearm Ownership for Sport and Protection: Two Divergent Models*, 45 AM. SOC. REV. 229 (1980).

Lizotte, Alan J., and Toch, *Research and Policy: The Case of Gun Control*, in PETER SUTFELD AND PHILIP TETLOCK, EDS., PSYCHOLOGY AND SOCIAL POLICY (1992).

Loftin and McDowall, *One with a Gun Gets You Two*, 455 ANNALS AM. ACAD. POL. & SOC. SCI. (May 1981)

Mauser, Gary A., *A Comparison of Canadian and American Attitudes Toward Firearms*, 32 CAN. J. CRIM. 573 (1990).

———, *Gun Control in the United States*, 3 CRIM. L. FORUM 147 (1992).

Mauser, Gary A., and Holmes, *Evaluating the 1977 Canadian Firearms Control Legislation: An Econometric Approach*, 16 EVAL. RES. 603 (Dec. 1992).

Mauser, Gary A., and Kopel, *Sorry, Wrong Number: Why Media Polls on Gun Control Are So Often Unreliable*, 9 POL. COMM. 69 (1992).

Mauser, Gary A., and Margolis, *The Politics of Gun Control: Comparing Canadian and American Patterns*, 10 GOV. & POL'Y. 189 (1992).

McClain, *Firearms Ownership, Gun Control Attitudes and Neighborhood Environment*, 5 LAW & POL'Y. Q. 299 (1983).

McDowall, David, *Gun Availability and Robbery Rates: A Panel Study of Large U.S. Cities, 1974–78*, 8 LAW & POL'Y. Q. 135 (1986).

McGrath, Roger, *Violence and Lawlessness of the Western Frontier*, in T. GURR, ED., VIOLENCE IN AMERICA (1989).

Moore, Mark, *The Bird in Hand: A Feasible Strategy for Gun Control*, 2 J. POL'Y. AN. & MANAGEMENT 187 (1983).

Morgan, Eric C., *Assault Right Legislation: Unwise and Unconstitutional*, 17 AM. J. CRIM. L. 143 (1990).

Mosk, Stanley, *Gun Control Legislation: Valid and Necessary*, 14 N.Y. L. FORUM 694 (1968).

Murray, *Handguns, Gun Control Laws and Firearm Violence*, 23 SOC. PROBS. 81 (1975).

Ohsfeldt, Robert L., and Michael A. Morrisey, *Firearms, Firearms Injury and Gun Control: A Critical Survey of the Literature*, 13 ADV. HEAL. ECON. & HEAL. SVS. RES. 65 (1992).

Olmsted, Alan, *Morally Controversial Leisure: The Social World of Gun Collectors*, 11 SYMB. INTERACTION (1988).

Polsby, Daniel D., *The False Promise of Gun Control*, ATL. MON. (Mar. 1993)

———, *Firearms Costs, Firearms Benefits and the Limits of Knowledge*, 86 J. CRIM. L. & CRIMINOL. 207 (1995).

———, *Reflections on Violence, Guns and the Defensive Use of Deadly Force*, 49 LAW & CONTEMP. PROBS. 89 (1986).

Seitz, *Firearms, Homicides and Gun Control Effectiveness*, 6 LAW & SOC. REV. 595 (1972).

Shelton, Gregory S., *In Search of the Lost Amendment: Challenging Federal Firearms Regulation through the State's Right Interpretation of the Second Amendment*, F.S.U. L. REV. 1 (1995).

Stell, Lance K., *Guns, Politics and Reason*, 9 J. AM. CULTURE 71 (1986).

Suter, Edgar A., *Guns in the Medical Literature: A Failure of Peer Review*, 83 J. GA. MED. ASS'N. 133 (1994).

Tonso, W. R., *Social Science and Sagecraft in the Debate over Gun Control*, 5 LAW & POL'Y. Q. 325 (1983).

Weiss, *A Reply to Advocates of Gun Control Law*, 52 J. URB. L. 577 (1974).

Wiegleb, Jennifer A., *Strong-Arming the States to Conduct Background Checks for Handgun Purchases: An Analysis of State Autonomy, Political Accountability, and the Brady Handgun Violence Prevention Act*, 48 J. URB. & CONTEMP. L. 373 (1995).

Wolfgang, Marvin E., *A Tribute to a View I Have Opposed*, 86 J. CRIM. L. & CRIMINOL. 188 (1995).

Wright, James D., *Public Opinion and Gun*, 455 ANNALS AM. ACAD. POL. & SOC. SCI. 24 (May 1981).

———, *Second Thoughts About Gun Control*, 91 PUB. INTEREST (1988).

———, *Ten Essential Observations on Guns in America*, 32 SOC. 63 (1995).

Wright, James D., and Linda L. Marston, *The Ownership of the Means of Destruction: Weapons in the United States*, 23 SOC. PROBS. 93 (1975).

Zimring, *Firearm Control, Hard Choices*, 8 TRIAL 53 (1972).

———, *Firearms and Federal Law: The Gun Control Act of 1968*, 4 J. LEGAL STUD. 133 (1975).

———, *Games with Guns and Statistics*, 1968 WIS. L. REV. 1113.

————, *Is Gun Control Likely to Reduce Violent Killing?* 35 U. CHI. L. REV. 721 (1968).

Books

ALVIANT AND W. DRAKE, HANDGUN CONTROL: ISSUES AND ALTERNATIVES (1975).

BAKAL, CARL, NO RIGHT TO BEAR ARMS (1968).
BRILL, S., FIREARM ABUSE: A RESEARCH AND POLICY REPORT (1977).

COURTNEY, PHOEBE, GUN CONTROL MEANS PEOPLE CONTROL (1974).

GOTTLIEB, ALAN M., THE RIGHTS OF GUN OWNERS (1981).
GREENWOOD, C., FIREARMS CONTROL: A STUDY OF ARMED CRIME AND FIREARMS CONTROL IN ENGLAND AND WALES (1972).
————, THE GUN CULTURE AND ITS ENEMIES (1990).

HARDY, DAVID T., THE BATF'S WAR ON CIVIL LIBERTIES: THE ASSAULT ON GUN OWNERS (1979).
HOOK, DONALD D., GUN CONTROL: THE CONTINUING DEBATE (1993).

KATES, DON B., FIREARMS AND VIOLENCE: ISSUES OF PUBLIC POLICY (1984).
————, GUNS, MURDERS, AND THE CONSTITUTION: A REALISTIC ASSESSMENT OF GUN CONTROL (1990).
————, ED., RESTRICTING HANDGUNS: THE LIBERAL SKEPTICS SPEAK OUT (1979).
KENNETT, LEE, AND JAMES LA VERNE ANDERSON, THE GUN IN AMERICA: THE ORIGINS OF A NATIONAL DILEMMA (1975).

KLECK, GARY, POINT BLANK: GUNS & VIOLENCE IN AMERICA (1991).

KOPEL, DAVID B., ED., GUNS: WHO SHOULD HAVE THEM? (1995)

————, THE SAMURAI, THE MOUNTIE, AND THE COWBOY: SHOULD AMERICA ADOPT THE GUN CONTROLS OF OTHER DEMOCRACIES? (1992)

KUKLA, ROBERT J., GUN CONTROL (1973).

LAPIERRE, WAYNE R., GUNS, CRIME, AND FREEDOM (1994).

LIBRARY OF CONGRESS, GUN CONTROL LAWS IN FOREIGN COUNTRIES (1976).

MORRIS, N., AND G. HAWKINS, THE HONEST POLITICIAN'S GUIDE TO CRIME CONTROL (1970).

NATIONAL INSTITUTE OF JUSTICE, U.S. DEPARTMENT OF JUSTICE, WEAPONS, CRIME AND VIOLENCE IN AMERICA (1981).

NEWTON, G., AND F. ZIMRING, FIREARMS AND VIOLENCE IN AMERICAN LIFE (1969).

NISBET, L., ED., THE GUN CONTROL DEBATE (1990).

SCHULMAN, J. NEIL, STOPPING POWER: WHY 70 MILLION AMERICANS OWN GUNS (1994).

SERVEN, JAMES E., AND JAMES B. TREFETHEN, EDS., AMERICANS AND THEIR GUNS (1967).

SHERRILL, R., THE SATURDAY NIGHT SPECIAL (1973).

U.S. DEPARTMENT OF JUSTICE, SOURCEBOOK OF CRIMINAL JUSTICE STATISTICS — 1987 (1988).

WALKER, SAMUEL, SENSE AND NONSENSE ABOUT CRIME AND DRUGS: A POLICY GUIDE, ch. 10 and 13 (1994).

WHISKER, JAMES B., THE CITIZEN SOLDIER AND UNITED STATES MILITARY POLICY (1979).

WRIGHT, JAMES, AND P. ROSSI, ARMED AND CONSIDERED DANGEROUS: A SURVEY OF FELONS AND THEIR FIREARMS (1986).

WRIGHT, JAMES, P. ROSSI, AND K. DALY, WEAPONS, CRIME AND VIOLENCE IN AMERICA (1983).

Symposia

86 J. CRIM. L. & CRIMINOL. #1 (fall 1995).

49 LAW & CONTEMP. PROBS. #1 (1986).

62 TENN. L. REV. #3 (spring 1995).

ACKNOWLEDGMENTS

Grateful acknowledgment is made to the authors and publishers of the three articles that are reproduced in their entirety in this book: William Van Alstyne, "The Second Amendment and the Personal Right to Arms," *Duke Law Journal* (vol. 43, 1994); Sanford Levinson, "The Embarrassing Second Amendment," *Yale Law Journal* (vol. 99, 1989); and Jeffrey R. Snyder, "A Nation of Cowards," *The Public Interest* (no. 113, 1993).

Also, I wish to thank the authors and publishers for granting permission to reproduce excerpts from the following books: Stephen P. Halbrook, That Every Man Be Armed: The Evolution of a Constitutional Right (University of New Mexico Press, 1984); David T. Hardy, *Origins and Development of the Second Amendment* (Blacksmith, 1986); Don B. Kates, ed., *Restricting Handguns: The Liberal Skeptics Speak Out* (North River Press, 1979); Joyce Lee Malcolm, *To Keep and Bear Arms: The Origins of an Anglo-American Right* (Harvard University Press, 1994); and David E. Young, ed., *The Origin of the Second Amendment: A Documentary History of the Bill of Rights, 1787–1792* (Golden Oak, 2d ed., 1995). For anyone desiring additional study of the Second Amendment, I highly recommend these five books as indispensable references.

Also, my thanks to the authors and publishers for permission to reproduce excerpts from the following law review articles: Akhil Reed Amar, "The Bill of Rights as a Constitution," 100 *Yale Law Journal* 1131 (1991); David I. Caplan, "Handgun Control: Constitutional or Unconstitutional? — A Reply to Mayor Jackson," 10 *North Carolina Central Law Journal* 53

(1978); Stephen P. Halbrook, "The Jurisprudence of the Second and Fourteenth Amendments," 4 *George Mason University Law Review* 1 (1981); David T. Hardy, "Armed Citizens, Citizen Armies: Toward a Jurisprudence of the Second Amendment," 9 *Harvard Journal of Law & Public Policy* 559 (1986); David T. Hardy, "The Second Amendment and the Historiography of the Bill of Rights," 4 *Journal of Law & Politics* 1 (1987); Nicholas J. Johnson, "Beyond the Second Amendment: An Individual Right to Arms Considered Through the Ninth Amendment," 24 *Rutgers Law Journal* 1 (1992); Nicholas J. Johnson, "Shots Across No Man's Land: A Response to Handgun Control, Inc.'s, Richard Aborn," 22 *Fordham Urban Law Journal* 441 (1995); Don B. Kates, "Handgun Prohibition and the Original Meaning of the Second Amendment," 82 *Michigan Law Review* 204 (1983); Don B. Kates, "The Second Amendment and the Ideology of Self-Protection," 9 *Constitutional Commentary* 87 (1992); Nelson Lund, "The Second Amendment, Political Liberty, and the Right to Self-Preservation," 39 *Alabama Law Review* 103 (1987); and Michael J. Quinlan, "Is There a Neutral Justification for Refusing to Implement the Second Amendment or Is the Supreme Court Just 'Gun Shy'?" 22 *Capital University Law Review* 641 (1993).

For legal research, copyediting, and typographic and page design, I would like to recognize the superlative work of Katharine Wiencke, Amanda Adams, and Selma Ordewer.

The manuscript was read and commented on by two of our leading Second Amendment experts, David I. Caplan and Don B. Kates. Their notes, advice, and criticisms materially improved this primer, and I am deeply indebted to them. But I am solely responsible for any errors, omissions, or misinterpretations that remain.

INDEX

ABOUT THE AUTHOR

Les Adams is a lawyer, editor, and publisher. He is currently engaged in publishing The Firearms Classics Library for the National Rifle Association. His academic degrees include a B.A. in English from the University of North Carolina, an M.A. in English from Columbia University, a J.D. cum laude from the Cumberland Law School of Samford University (where he was editor in chief of the law review), and an L.L.D. from Iowa's William Penn College. The citation that accompanied the award of his honorary doctorate cited Adams as being "one of the world's leading authorities in the publishing of fine editions." He is a member of the Alabama Bar Association and a Life Member of the National Rifle Association.

ABOUT THE BOOK

This book was designed by Selma Ordewer and composed in Bookman Old Style. It was printed on acid-free paper specially made for this edition by the P. H. Glatfelter Company and printed and bound by Kingsport Book.